BASIC
English
Grammar

FIFTH EDITION
WORKBOOK

Betty S. Azar
Stacy A. Hagen
Geneva Tesh

Basic English Grammar, Fifth Edition
Workbook

Pearson Education, 221 River Street, Hoboken, NJ 07030

Staff credits: The people who made up the *Basic English Grammar,
Fifth Edition, Workbook* team, representing content development,
design, project management, publishing, and rights management, are
Warren Fischbach, Amy McCormick, Mary Rich, Robert Ruvo,
and Joseph Vella.

Production Editor: Jennifer McAliney

Text composition: Page Designs International

Printed in the United States of America
ISBN 13: 978-0-13-672617-3

3 2022

Contents

The titles listed below, for example, *Singular pronouns* + *be,* refer to section names, not practice titles. In general, one section has multiple exercises. The chart numbers refer to the grammar explanations in the *Basic English Grammar* **Student Book**.

Chapter 9 EXPRESSING PAST TIME, PART 2

Chapter 10 EXPRESSING FUTURE TIME, PART 1

Chapter 11 EXPRESSING FUTURE TIME, PART 2

Chapter 12 MODALS, PART 1: EXPRESSING ABILITY AND PERMISSION

Preface

The *Basic English Grammar Workbook* is a self-study textbook. It follows the explanatory grammar charts found in *Basic English Grammar, Fifth Edition*, a classroom teaching text for English language learners. Students can use the *Workbook* independently to enhance their understanding of English structures. Practice ranges from the basic to the more challenging so students can choose from a variety of exercises that will help them use English correctly.

This *Workbook* is also a resource for teachers who need exercise material for additional classwork, homework, testing, or individualized instruction.

The answers to the exercises can be found in the *Answer Key* in the back of the *Workbook*. Its pages are perforated so that they can be detached to make a separate booklet. However, if teachers want to use the *Workbook* as a classroom teaching text, the *Answer Key* can be removed at the beginning of the term.

CHAPTER 1 Using *Be*

PRACTICE 1 ▸ Using *he, she,* or *it.* (Chart 1-1)

Rewrite the sentences using the correct pronouns: **he, she,** or **it.**

1. The bus is here.   *It is here.*
2. Sara is absent.   _____
3. Canada is a country.   _____
4. Mr. Jefferson is sick.   _____
5. Mrs. Jefferson is also sick.   _____
6. Henry is ready.   _____
7. The weather is cold.   _____
8. Ms. Hogan is here.   _____

PRACTICE 2 ▸ Using *am, is,* or *are.* (Chart 1-1)

Write **am, is,** or **are.**

1. She ____*is*____ hungry.
2. I _____ sick.
3. You _____ nice.
4. The weather _____ hot.
5. Mr. Kimura _____ old.
6. Julianna _____ young.
7. It _____ cold.
8. You _____ early.
9. Ms. Rossi _____ here.
10. She _____ late.

PRACTICE 3 ▸ Plural pronouns + *be.* (Chart 1-2)

Choose the correct pronouns.

1. you and Sam   they   (you)
2. Max and Maddie   they   you
3. you and Mr. and Mrs. Lin   they   you
4. Hannah and Dr. Adams   they   we
5. Isabel and I   they   we

PRACTICE 4 ▸ Singular and plural pronouns. (Charts 1-1 and 1-2)
Choose the correct picture.

A

B

1. I am from Canada. _____B_____

2. You are from Brazil. _____A, B_____

3. They are happy. _____

4. He is nice. _____

5. We are here. _____

6. You are late. _____

7. I am ready. _____

PRACTICE 5 ▸ Pronouns + *be*. (Charts 1-1 and 1-2)
Write *am*, *is*, or *are*.

SINGULAR	PLURAL
I _____am_____ cold.	We _____are_____ cold.
You (one) _____ cold.	You (two) _____ cold.
She _____ cold.	They _____ cold.
He _____ cold.	He and she _____ cold.
It _____ cold.	

PRACTICE 6 ▸ Pronoun + *be*. (Charts 1-1 and 1-2)
Complete the sentences with the correct pronouns.

1. Jack and Bruno are homesick. _____They_____ are homesick.

2. Bruno is homesick. _____He_____ is homesick.

3. Julia is homesick. _____ is homesick.

4. Mr. Rivas is homesick. _____ is homesick.

5. Mrs. Rivas is homesick. _____ is homesick.

6. Mrs. Rivas and Mr. Rivas are homesick. _____ are homesick.

7. Mr. Rivas and I are homesick. _____ are homesick.

8. You and I are homesick. _____ are homesick.

9. Jenna is happy. _____ is happy.

10. You and Jenna are happy. _____ are happy.

11. The children are happy. _____ are happy.

12. Dr. Chen is ready. Dr. Greco is ready. _____ are ready.

13. Ella is ready. _____ is ready.

14. Brian is ready. _____ is ready.

15. Ella, Brian, and I are ready. _____ are ready.

PRACTICE 7 ▶ A or *an*. (Chart 1-3)
Write *a* or *an* before each word.

1. ___*an*___ office

2. _____ bank

3. _____ building

4. _____ apple

5. _____ city

6. _____ animal

7. _____ ear

8. _____ street

9. _____ town

10. _____ island

PRACTICE 8 ▶ A or *an*. (Chart 1-3)
Write *a* or *an* before each word. Then choose *yes* or *no*.

1. Chinese is ___*a*___ language. (yes) no

2. Paris is _____ city. yes no

3. Canada is _____ language. yes no

4. Hawaii is _____ island. yes no

5. Africa is _____ city. yes no

6. English is _____ country. yes no

7. French is _____ language. yes no

8. Bali is _____ island. yes no

PRACTICE 9 ▸ Plural nouns. (Chart 1-4)

Write the plural form of the given nouns.

	SINGULAR		PLURAL
1.	a city	→	_____cities_____
2.	a dog	→	_____
3.	a language	→	_____
4.	an animal	→	_____
5.	a country	→	_____
6.	a peanut	→	_____
7.	a berry	→	_____

PRACTICE 10 ▸ Singular and plural nouns. (Charts 1-3 and 1-4)

Complete the sentences with **-s** or **Ø**.

1. Cuba __Ø__ is an island __Ø__ .

2. French and Russian __Ø__ are language _s_ .

3. A lion_____ is an animal_____ .

4. Lion_____ are animal_____ .

5. Spanish_____ is a language_____ .

6. Peanut_____ are snack_____ .

7. A strawberry_____ is a berry_____ .

8. Pea_____ and carrot_____ are vegetable_____ .

a lion

PRACTICE 11 ▸ Be with singular and plural nouns. (Charts 1-3 and 1-4)

Choose the correct verbs.

1. Sodas is / (are) drinks.

2. Onions is / are vegetables.

3. Chinese and Russian is / are languages.

4. Spanish is / are a language.

5. An apple is / are a fruit.

6. Peanuts and pretzels is / are snacks.

7. Bali is / are an island.

8. Japan and Russia is / are countries.

9. A pea is / are a vegetable.

10. Cats and dogs is / are animals.

onions

PRACTICE 12 ▸ Pronoun + *be*. (Charts 1-3 and 1-4)
Complete the sentences. Use a verb (*am, is,* or *are*) and a noun (*a student* or *students*).

1. She ___*is a student*___.

2. I _____.

3. You (one person) _____.

4. You (two persons) _____.

5. They _____.

6. He _____.

7. We _____.

8. Carlos and you _____.

9. He and I _____.

10. Mia and I _____.

PRACTICE 13 ▸ *Be* with singular and plural nouns. (Charts 1-3 and 1-4)
Make sentences using *is/are* and *a/an/Ø* (nothing).

1. cat \ animal ___*A cat is an animal.*___

2. dogs \ animals ___*Dogs are animals.*___

3. elephant \ animal _____

4. China \ country _____

5. Africa \ continent _____

6. Asia and Africa \ continents _____

7. Russian and Spanish \ languages _____

8. Arabic \ language _____

9. Lima \ city _____

10. Lima and Beijing \ cities _____

11. carrot \ vegetable _____

12. carrots \ vegetables _____

an elephant

PRACTICE 14 ▸ Be with singular and plural nouns. (Charts 1-3 and 1-4)
Complete the sentences with *is* or *are* and one of the nouns from the box. Use the correct singular form of the noun (with *a* or *an*) or the correct plural form.

animal	country	language
city	island	vegetable

1. A dog _____*is an animal*_____ .

2. Dogs _____*are animals*_____ .

3. Spanish _____ .

4. Spanish and Chinese _____ .

5. China and Vietnam _____ .

6. France _____ .

7. Hawaii _____ .

8. Hawaii and Vancouver _____ .

9. A carrot _____ .

10. Carrots and onions _____ .

11. Moscow _____ .

12. Moscow and Tokyo _____ .

PRACTICE 15 ▸ Contractions with be. (Chart 1-5)
Rewrite the phrases using contractions.

1. I am _____*I'm*_____   5. it is _____

2. you are _____   6. they are _____

3. he is _____   7. she is _____

4. we are _____

PRACTICE 16 ▸ Contractions with be. (Chart 1-5)
Rewrite the sentences using contractions.

1. I am late.   _____*I'm late.*_____

2. You are busy.   _____

3. They are students.   _____

4. It is cold.   _____

5. She is here.   _____

6. He is absent.   _____

7. We are tired. _____

8. I am a student. _____

PRACTICE 17 ▸ Negative forms of *be*. (Chart 1-6)

Complete the sentences with the negative form of *be*.

1. I _____ *am not* _____ sick.

2. You _____ sick.

3. He _____ sick.

4. She _____ sick.

5. The cat _____ sick.

6. It _____ sick.

7. We _____ sick.

8. They _____ sick.

9. The students _____ sick.

10. Katie and I _____ sick.

11. The teacher _____ sick.

12. The teachers _____ sick.

PRACTICE 18 ▸ Negative forms of *be* and contractions. (Chart 1-6)

Complete the sentences with the negative form of *be*. Then write the contracted form. Give both forms where possible.

BE: NEGATIVE	CONTRACTION
1. You _____ *are not* _____ late.	_____ *aren't* OR *you're not* _____
2. She _____ late.	_____
3. I _____ late.	_____
4. He _____ late.	_____
5. The bus _____ late.	_____
6. It _____ late.	_____
7. We _____ late.	_____
8. You _____ late.	_____
9. They _____ late.	_____

PRACTICE 19 ▸ Using *is, isn't, are,* or *aren't*. (Charts 1-5 and 1-6)

Write *is, isn't, are,* or *aren't*.

1. Canada and Sweden _____ *aren't* _____ continents.

2. Japan _____ a language.

3. Moscow and Beijing _____ cities.

4. France _____ a country.

5. An apple _____ a vegetable.

6. Carrots _____ animals.

7. A sandwich _____ a berry.

8. A bird _____ an animal.

a bird

PRACTICE 20 ▸ Using *be*. (Charts 1-5 and 1-6)
Complete the first sentences with the negative form of *be*. Complete the second sentences with a contraction of *be* and the correct information.

1. Russia _____*isn't*_____ a city. It*'s a country* _____.

2. Cats _____ vegetables. They_____.

3. Asia _____ a country. It_____.

4. Arabic _____ a country. It_____.

5. Peanuts and pretzels _____ sandwiches. They_____.

6. I _____ an English teacher. I_____.

PRACTICE 21 ▸ *Be* + adjective. (Chart 1-7)
Write *is, isn't, are,* or *aren't*.

1. A baby _____*is*_____ small.

2. A car _____ cheap.

3. Cars _____ expensive.

4. Peanuts _____ expensive.

a giraffe

5. A giraffe _____ tall. It _____ short.

6. This exercise _____ difficult. It _____ easy.

7. Flowers _____ ugly. They _____ beautiful.

8. Lemons _____ yellow. They _____ blue.

lemons

PRACTICE 22 ▸ *Be* + adjective. (Charts 1-5 → 1-7)
Make sentences using *is/isn't* or *are/aren't*. Follow the example.

1. apples ... blue \ red

_____*Apples aren't blue. They're red.*_____

2. bananas ... orange \ yellow

_____

3. the sun ... cold \ hot

_____

4. a car … cheap \ expensive

_____

5. Africa … small \ big

_____

6. the exercise … hard \ easy

_____

7. babies … old \ young

_____

PRACTICE 23 ▸ *Be* + a place. (Chart 1-8)
Write the preposition in the blank. Underline the prepositional phrase in each sentence.

PREPOSITION

1. _____*in*_____ David is <u>in his room.</u>

2. _____ Mr. Han is at the library.

3. _____ Karim is from Kuwait.

4. _____ My book is on my desk.

5. _____ The hospital is next to the bank.

6. _____ My feet are under my desk.

a backpack

7. _____ My apartment is on your street.

8. _____ My book is in my backpack.

PRACTICE 24 ▸ Understanding prepositions. (Chart 1-8)
Follow the instructions.

Put an "X" …

1. above circle A.
2. under circle B.
3. in circle A.
4. between circles A and B.
5. next to circle A.

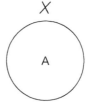
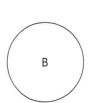

PRACTICE 25 ▶ *Be* + a place. (Chart 1-8)
Make sentences with ***be*** and a preposition if necessary. Some sentences do not need a preposition.

1. Jenny \ the library

   Jenny is at the library.

2. Jenny \ upstairs

   Jenny is upstairs.

3. The students \ downtown

   _____

4. The students \ the bus

   _____

5. The teacher \ here

   _____

6. The teacher \ the room

   _____

7. Sam \ work

   _____

8. Sam \ inside

   _____

PRACTICE 26 ▶ Review: nouns, adjectives, and prepositions. (Chart 1-9)
Write the words from the box in the correct columns.

✓ at	✓ easy	parents
between	happy	sister
✓ city	hungry	small
cold	next to	teacher
country	on	under

NOUNS	ADJECTIVES	PREPOSITIONS (OF PLACE)
city	*easy*	*at*
_____	_____	_____
_____	_____	_____
_____	_____	_____
_____	_____	_____

PRACTICE 27 ▶ Sentence review. (Chart 1-9)
Complete the sentences using the given structure.

1. Dr. Emma Brown is (*noun*) ___*a dentist / a doctor*___ .

   (*place*) ___*here / at home*___ .

   (*adjective*) ___*happy / nice*___ .

2. Anna is (*noun*) _____ .

   (*place*) _____ .

   (*adjective*) _____ .

3. France is (*adjective*) _____ .

   (*place*) _____ .

   (*noun*) _____ .

4. *Basic English Grammar Workbook* is (*place*) _____ .

   (*adjective*) _____ .

   (*noun*) _____ .

PRACTICE 28 ▶ Sentence review. (Chart 1-9)
Make sentences with the given words and a form of *be*.

1. Canada \ not \ a city

   ___*Canada isn't a city.*___

2. Canada \ in North America

   _____

3. France \ next to \ Germany

   _____

4. apples and oranges \ not \ vegetables

   _____

5. airplanes \ fast

   _____

6. vegetables \ healthy

   _____

7. Nora \ doctor

   _____

8. Ben and Sofia \ police officers

   _____

PRACTICE 29 ▸ Review of *be*. (Chapter 1)
Complete the sentences with the correct form of *be*.

Cam and Mai _____*are*_____ from Vietnam. They _____ new students. Mrs.
1   2

Kemper _____ the teacher. She _____ very nice. Fifteen students
3   4

_____ in the class. They _____ friendly. Cam and Mai _____ happy
5   6   7

in this class.

PRACTICE 30 ▸ Review of *be*. (Chapter 1)
Complete the sentences with the correct form of *be*.

MR. QUINN: Hi, I _____*am*_____ Mr. Quinn. Mrs. Kemper _____ not here.
1   2

She _____ sick. I _____ your teacher today.
3   4

CAM: Hi, my name _____ Cam.
5

MR. QUINN: Hi, Cam. It _____ nice to meet you.
6

CAM: It _____ nice to meet you too. This _____ my sister, Mai.
7   8

MR. QUINN: Hi, Mai. I _____ happy to meet you too.
9

PRACTICE 31 ▸ Review. (Chapter 1)
Correct the mistakes.

1. Paris is $\overset{a}{\underset{\wedge}{}}$ city.

2. Hawaii is a island.

3. Peas and carrots are vegetable.

4. The weather warm today.

5. Kate and Leah is late.

6. Michael he is at the library.

7. She is no a teacher.

8. Sam is at here.

2

Using *Be* and *Have*

PRACTICE 1 ▶ *This* or *that*. (Chart 2-1)
Write ***this*** or ***that***.

1. _____*This*_____ is a key.

2. _____ is a pencil.

3. _____ is a stapler.

4. _____ is a pencil sharpener.

5. _____ is a ruler.

6. _____ is a backpack.

7. _____ is a notebook.

8. _____ is an eraser.

PRACTICE 2 ▶ *These* or *those*. (Chart 2-2)
Write ***these*** or ***those***.

1. _____*These*_____ are paper clips.

2. _____ are flash drives.

3. _____ are books.

4. _____ are headphones.

5. _____ are chairs.

PRACTICE 3 ▶ *This, that, these,* and *those*. (Charts 2-1 and 2-2)
Choose the correct answers.

1. This /(These) keys are heavy.

2. That / Those books are old.

3. This / These phone is cheap.

4. That / Those phones are expensive.

5. That / Those computer is new.

6. This / These computers are slow.

7. This / These laptop is fast.

PRACTICE 4 ▶ *This, that, these,* and *those*. (Charts 2-1 and 2-2)
Write ***this, that, these,*** or ***those***.

1. (*This / These*) _____*This*_____ book is inexpensive. (*That / Those*) _____*Those*_____ books
   are expensive.

2. (*This / These*) _____ chairs are comfortable. (*That / Those*) _____ chairs are uncomfortable.

3. (*This / These*) _____ car is fast. (*That / Those*) _____ car is slow.

4. (*This / These*) _____ cats are friendly. (*That / Those*) _____ cat is unfriendly.

5. (*This / These*) _____ pen is new. (*That / Those*) _____ pen is old.

6. (*This / These*) _____ shoes are comfortable. (*That / Those*) _____ shoes are uncomfortable.

7. (*This / These*) _____ exercise is easy. (*That / Those*) _____ exercises are hard.

PRACTICE 5 ▶ *Yes/no* questions with *be*. (Chart 2-3)
Choose the correct answers.

1. _____ you happy?
   a. Am b. Is c. Are

2. _____ they here?
   a. Am b. Is c. Are

3. _____ he absent?
   a. Am b. Is c. Are

4. _____ she a teacher?
   a. Am b. Is c. Are

5. _____ I late?
   a. Am b. Is c. Are

6. _____ we ready?
   a. Am b. Is c. Are

7. _____ you and Paul ready?
   a. Am b. Is c. Are

8. _____ Roberto and Elena at home?
   a. Am b. Is c. Are

9. _____ Emily here?
   a. Am b. Is c. Are

10. _____ you from Canada?
   a. Am b. Is c. Are

PRACTICE 6 ▶ *Yes/no* questions with *be*. (Chart 2-3)
Make *yes/no* questions with the given words and a form of *be*.

1. you \ a student   *Are you a student?*

2. he \ a student   _____

3. they \ students   _____

4. she \ from Vietnam   _____

5. you \ ready   _____

6. we \ ready   _____

7. it \ ready   _____

8. I \ ready   _____

PRACTICE 7 ▸ Yes/no questions with *be*. (Chart 2-3)

Make questions for the given answers.

1. A: _____*Are you a doctor?*_____
   B: Yes, I am a doctor.

2. A: _____
   B: Yes, bananas are healthy.

3. A: _____
   B: Yes, Taka is a nurse.

4. A: _____
   B: Yes, the kids are at school.

5. A: _____
   B: Yes, we are ready for the test.

6. A: _____
   B: Yes, Liz is at school.

7. A: _____
   B: Yes, I am tired.

PRACTICE 8 ▸ Short answers with *be*. (Chart 2-4)

Complete the sentences with short answers.

1. Is Paris a city?   Yes, _____*it is*_____.

2. Are Paris and Tokyo cities?   Yes, _____.

3. Are dogs animals?   Yes, _____.

4. Is Carlos sick today?   Yes, _____.

5. Are peas vegetables?   Yes, _____.

6. Is the sun hot?   Yes, _____.

7. Is Jane a teacher?   Yes, _____.

8. Are you a student?   Yes, _____.

9. Are you students?   Yes, _____.

10. Am I early?   Yes, _____.

PRACTICE 9 ▶ Questions and short answers with *be*. (Chart 2-4)
Complete the questions and answers.

| Anna, a photographer | Mr. Tran, a police officer | Nora, a doctor | Ivan, a firefighter | Mike, a plumber | Ms. Díaz, a teacher | Joe, a student |

1. ____*Is*____ Joe a student? Yes, he ____*is*____ .

2. _____ Anna a photographer? Yes, she _____ .

3. _____ Mike a teacher? No, he _____ .

4. _____ Nora a doctor? Yes, she _____ .

5. _____ Ms. Díaz a student? No, she _____ .

6. _____ Ivan and Mike police officers? No, they _____ .

7. _____ Anna and Nora women? Yes, they _____ .

8. _____ Mr. Tran and Joe men? Yes, they _____ .

9. _____ you a student? Yes, I _____ .

10. _____ you and Joe students? Yes, we _____ .

PRACTICE 10 ▶ Capitalization and punctuation. (Charts 2-3 and 2-4)
Rewrite the sentences. Add capitals letters and the correct punctuation.

1. is Paris a country   no it isn't

    _____*Is Paris a country?*   *No, it isn't.*_____

2. are they students   yes they are

    _____

3. is the library open today   yes it is

    _____

4. are those books expensive   no they aren't

    _____

PRACTICE 11 ▸ Questions and short answers with *be*. (Chart 2-4)
Complete the conversations. Use contractions where possible.

1. A: _____Is_____ Gloria a student?

   B: Yes, ____she is____.

   A: _____ a student?

   B: No, I'm not.

2. A: _____ students?

   B: No, we _____. We _____ teachers.

   A: Is Mr. Ito a teacher?

   B: No, _____. He _____ a student.

PRACTICE 12 ▸ Understanding *where*. (Chart 2-5)
Choose the correct question for each response.

QUESTION	RESPONSE
1. a. Where is Toshi? (b.) Is Toshi at work?	Yes, he is.
2. a. Are the students in the cafeteria? b. Where are the students?	They are in the cafeteria.
3. a. Is my grammar book at home? b. Where is my grammar book?	Yes, it is.
4. a. Where are the headphones? b. Are the headphones in the classroom?	Yes, they are.
5. a. Where are you? b. Are you at home?	I am at home.
6. a. Is the teacher in her office? b. Where is the teacher?	She is in her office.

PRACTICE 13 ▸ Questions with *be* and *where*. (Chart 2-5)
Write ***Is, Are, Where is,*** or ***Where are.***

1. A: _____Is_____ Marco at school?

   B: No, he isn't.

   A: ____Where is____ he?

   B: He's at home.

2. A: _____ the restrooms?

   B: They're near the classroom.

   A: _____ those the restrooms?

   B: Yes, they are.

3. A: _____ Leila?

   B: She's at the gas station.

   A: _____ the gas station?

   B: It's across the street.

4. A: _____ the movie theater nearby?

   B: Yes, it is. It's next to the park.

   A: _____ the park?

   B: It's down the street.

5. A: _____ Mika and Kim?

   B: They're at the bus stop.

   A: _____ the bus stop near school?

   B: No, it isn't.

   A: _____ the bus stop?

   B: It's on 2nd Street.

PRACTICE 14 ▸ Questions with *be* and *where*. (Chart 2-5)
Make questions for each response.

   1. A: ___*Where is the teacher?*_____

      B: In the classroom. (The teacher is in the classroom.)

   2. A: _____

      B: Yes, she is. (The teacher is in the classroom.)

   3. A: _____

      B: At home. (Pablo and Dina are at home.)

   4. A: _____

      B: Yes, they are. (Pablo and Dina are at home.)

   5. A: _____

      B: Yes, it is. (The train station is nearby.)

   6. A: _____

      B: On First Avenue. (The store is on First Avenue.)

7. A: _____

   B: Yes, we are. (We are outside.)

8. A: _____

   B: Outside. (We are outside.)

PRACTICE 15 ▸ Using *have* and *has*. (Chart 2-6)
Choose the correct answers.

1. I (have)/ has a headache.

2. You have / has a cold.

3. She have / has a sore throat.

4. He have / has a backache.

5. We have / has colds.

6. They have / has stomachaches.

7. Mrs. Hong have / has allergies.

8. My son have / has a sore throat.

9. My parents have / has high blood pressure.

10. You have / has a fever.

PRACTICE 16 ▸ Using *have* and *has*. (Chart 2-6)
Write **have** or **has**.

1. You ____*have*____ a ruler on your desk.

2. Eric _____ an eraser on his chair.

3. We _____ grammar books.

4. I _____ a grammar book. It _____ a red cover.

5. Lucy _____ a blue pen. She _____ a blue notebook too.

6. Stella and Dave _____ notebooks. They _____ pencils too.

7. Samir is a student in our class. He _____ a laptop computer.

8. You and I are students. We _____ laptops on our desks.

9. Mike _____ a wallet in his pocket. Mira _____ a wallet in her backpack.

10. Nadia isn't in class today because she _____ a cold.

11. Mr. and Mrs. Collins _____ two daughters.

PRACTICE 17 ▸ Be and have. (Chapter 1 and Chart 2-6)
Write *has, have, is,* or *are*.

The people in the waiting room _____*are*_____ sick. Thomas _____ a stomachache.
_____1_____   2

Mr. and Mrs. Gleason _____ fevers. Mrs. Martinez _____ a headache. Nicole
_____3_____   4

_____ a sore throat. Dr. Lin _____ very busy today.
_____5_____   6

PRACTICE 18 ▸ Be and have. (Chapter 1 and Chart 2-6)
Complete each sentence with the correct form of *be* or *have*.

1. *My apartment …*

    a. _____*has*_____ five rooms.

    b. _____*is*_____ comfortable.

    c. _____ in the city.

    d. _____ twenty years old.

    e. _____ a new kitchen.

    f. _____ expensive.

    g. _____ on the fourth floor.

    h. _____ many windows.

    i. _____ a view of downtown.

2. *My neighbor …*

    a. _____ thirty years old.

    b. _____ brown eyes and brown hair.

    c. _____ tall.

    d. _____ two children.

    e. _____ a small apartment.

    f. _____ friendly.

    g. _____ a student at the university.

    h. _____ very busy.

    i. _____ a busy life.

PRACTICE 19 ▸ Possessive adjectives. (Chart 2-7)
Write *my, your, her, his, our,* or *their*.

1. He has a backpack. _____*His*_____ backpack is heavy.

2. You have a backpack. _____ backpack is heavy.

3. I have a backpack. _____ backpack is heavy.

4. We have backpacks. _____ backpacks are heavy.

5. You have backpacks. _____ backpacks are heavy.

6. They have backpacks. _____ backpacks are heavy.

7. The students have backpacks. _____ backpacks are heavy.

8. Tom has a backpack. _____ backpack is heavy.

9. Kate has a backpack. _____ backpack is heavy.

10. Tom and Kate have backpacks. _____ backpacks are heavy.

11. Kate and I have backpacks. _____ backpacks are heavy.

12. You and I have backpacks. _____ backpacks are heavy.

PRACTICE 20 ▸ Possessive adjectives. (Chart 2-7)
Write *his*, *her*, or *their*. Then label the people in the picture.

1. Paul, Ellen, Tim, and Amy have class today. _____*Their*_____ class is at 2:00.

2. Ellen has on a dress. _____ dress is comfortable.

3. Tim has on a sweater. _____ sweater is warm.

4. Amy has on a jacket. _____ jacket is old.

5. Paul has on a T-shirt. _____ T-shirt is new.

6. Paul, Ellen, Tim, and Amy are in the classroom. _____ teacher is late.

a. _____*Paul*_____   b. _____   c. _____   d. _____

PRACTICE 21 ▸ *Have* and possessive adjectives. (Charts 2-6 and 2-7)
Write *have* or *has* and *my, your, her, his, our,* or *their*.

1. I _____*have*_____ a teenage daughter. _____*My*_____ daughter is busy.

2. Hector _____ a son. _____ son is in college.

3. Maria _____ two grandchildren. _____ grandchildren are friendly.

4. You _____ homework. _____ homework is easy.

5. Peter and Ellen _____ new phones. _____ phones are inexpensive.

6. We _____ an old car. _____ car is slow.

7. Mr. and Mrs. Brown _____ an apartment. _____ apartment is on the top floor.

8. I _____ on a jacket. _____ jacket is brown.

9. The workers _____ on boots. _____ boots are heavy.

10. Nathan _____ a motorcycle. _____ motorcycle is fast.

a motorcycle

PRACTICE 22 ▸ Understanding *who* and *what*. (Chart 2-8)
Choose the correct response for each question.

1. Who is that?
   a. That is Rita.   b. That is a toy.

2. What is that?
   a. That's a flash drive.   b. That's Tom.

3. Who are they?
   a. They are flowers.   b. They are new students.

4. What are they?
   a. They're vegetables.   b. They're Rick and Mira.

5. Who is it?
   a. My neighbor.   b. My car.

6. What is it?
   a. My sister.   b. A butterfly.

a butterfly

PRACTICE 23 ▸ *Who* and *what* + *be*. (Chart 2-8)
Make a question with *who* or *what* for each response.

1. A: _____*What is that?*_____
   B: That is a hospital.

2. A: _____
   B: That is a nurse.

3. A: _____
   B: This is a stethoscope.

a stethoscope

4. A: _____

   B: They are visitors.

5. A: _____

   B: He is Dr. Benson.

6. A: _____

   B: Those are thermometers.

thermometers

PRACTICE 24 ▸ Review: questions and short answers. (Chapter 2)
Answer the questions. Choose from the responses in the box.

Yes, it is.	This is Donna.	Yes, I am.
It's in Canada.	✓ Yes, they are.	No, it isn't.
Yes, he is.	This is a ruler.	Yes, she is.

1. Are the students nice? _____*Yes, they are.*_____

2. Who is this? _____

3. Is Toronto a city? _____

4. Is your sister a doctor? _____

5. Is Canada a continent? _____

6. Is your son a teenager? _____

7. Where is Toronto? _____

8. Are you sick? _____

9. What is this? _____

PRACTICE 25 ▸ Review: *be* and *have*. (Chapters 1 and 2)
Complete the sentences with the correct forms of *be* and *have*.

I ___*have*___ one brother and one sister. My brother _____ a nurse. He _____ a good
          1   2   3
job at a medical clinic. His name _____ Daniel. He _____ thirty years old. My sister
                                       4   5
_____ a doctor. She _____ very busy. She _____ many patients. Her name _____
   6   7   8   9
Monica. She _____ thirty-five years old. My name _____ Martha. I _____
                10   11   12
twenty-eight years old. I _____ an English teacher. We all _____ good jobs. We _____
                            13   14   15
happy with our work.

PRACTICE 26 ▸ Review: be and have. (Chapters 1 and 2)
Complete the sentences. Use the correct form of **be** and the appropriate possessive adjective.

This is the Jackson family. Pat is the grandmother. Bob is _____her_____ husband. They have a son. _____ name is Joe. He is

1

married. _____ wife is Bonnie. Joe and

3

Bonnie have three children. Emma is _____

4

daughter. Tom is _____ big brother. Liam is

5

the baby. Tom, Emma, and Liam are young.

_____ grandparents are Pat and Bob.

6

Joe   Bonnie   Pat   Bob

Tom   Liam   Emma

PRACTICE 27 ▸ Review. (Chapter 2)
Correct the mistakes.

        is
1. Who ~~are~~ that?

2. These phone is expensive.

3. Where my car?

4. Zac has twenty years old.

5. Sofia has sick. She is a cold.

6. What is you phone number?

7. A: Where is Jeff and Kevin?

    B: They at school.

8. A: Is she your sister?

    B: Yes, she's.

9. A: Who are those?

    B: Those are paper clips.

10. A: Where your roommate is from?

    B: His from Mexico.

CHAPTER 3

Using the simple present

PRACTICE 1 ▶ The simple present tense. (Chart 3-1)
Complete the sentences with the correct form of **wake up**.

1. I _____ *wake up* _____ early every day.

2. We _____ early every day.

3. They _____ early every day.

4. He _____ early every day.

5. You _____ early every day.

6. She _____ early every day.

7. The dog _____ early every day.

8. It _____ early every day.

9. Mr. and Mrs. Ito _____ early every day.

10. Mr. Ito _____ early every day.

11. The teacher _____ early every day.

12. The student _____ early every day.

PRACTICE 2 ▶ The simple present tense. (Chart 3-1)
<u>Underline</u> the simple present verbs.

Spiro <u>works</u> at night. He teaches auto mechanics at a school in his town. He leaves his apartment at 5:00. He catches the bus near his home. The bus comes at 5:15. It takes him 40 minutes to get to work. His classes begin at 6:30. He teaches until 10:30. He stays at school until 11:15. A friend drives him home. He gets home around midnight.

PRACTICE 3 ▶ Form of the simple present. (Chart 3-1)
Complete the sentences with the correct form of the verbs in parentheses.

1. My alarm clock (*ring*) _____ *rings* _____ at 5:00 every morning.

2. I (*get*) _____ out of bed slowly.

3. My husband (*make*) _____ breakfast for us.

4. He (cook) _____ a hot breakfast every morning.

5. We (leave) _____ for work at 6:00.

6. I (drive) _____ us to work.

7. We (listen) _____ to the morning news.

8. My husband and I (work) _____ at the same company.

9. We (arrive) _____ at work early.

10. Our two co-workers (come) _____ later.

11. They (take) _____ the bus to the office.

PRACTICE 4 ▸ Form of the simple present. (Charts 3-1)
Complete the sentences with the correct form of the verbs in parentheses.

Joan and I are roommates. We are very different. Joan (wakes / wake) _____*wakes*_____ up

₁

early. I (wakes / wake) _____ up at 11:00. I (eats / eat) _____ breakfast

₂   ₃

at noon. Joan (eats / eat) _____ breakfast at 7:30. She (leaves / leave)

₄

_____ for school at 8:00. I (takes / take) _____ evening classes, so I go

₅   ₆

to school at 5:00. Joan (cooks / cook) _____ an early dinner. She (falls / fall)

₇

_____ asleep around 9:00. I (eats / eat) _____ at midnight and

₈   ₉

(falls / fall) _____ asleep in the early morning. We (sees / see) _____

₁₀   ₁₁

each other on weekends. We (has / have) _____ very different lives, but we are

₁₂

good friends.

PRACTICE 5 ▸ Frequency adverbs. (Chart 3-2)
Rewrite the sentences using the frequency adverb in parentheses.

1. Olga has cream in her coffee. (always)

   _____*Olga always has cream in her coffee.*_____

2. I eat breakfast. (rarely)

   _____

3. The students buy their lunch at school. (seldom)

   _____

4. They bring lunch from home. (usually)

   _____

5. My husband and I go out to a restaurant for dinner. (*often*)

   _____

6. My husband drinks coffee with dinner. (*sometimes*)

   _____

7. We have dessert. (*never*)

   _____

PRACTICE 6 ▸ Frequency adverbs. (Chart 3-2)
Rewrite the sentences using a frequency adverb.

1. Beth has fish for lunch. (50% of the time)

   _____*Beth sometimes has fish for lunch.*_____

2. Roger gets up late. (10% of the time)

   _____

3. Mr. and Mrs. Phillips go to the movies on weekends. (90% of the time)

   _____

4. I clean my apartment. (75% of the time)

   _____

5. My roommate cleans our apartment. (0% of the time)

   _____

6. The students do their homework. (100% of the time)

   _____

7. The teacher corrects papers on weekends. (50% of the time)

   _____

PRACTICE 7 ▸ Frequency adverbs. (Chart 3-2)
Choose *yes* or *no* to agree or disagree with the sentences about your morning activities. If the answer is *no,* write the correct frequency adverb.

1. I always wake up early.   yes   no   _____

2. I sometimes sleep late on weekends.   yes   no   _____

3. I seldom eat a hot breakfast.   yes   no   _____

4. I often listen to a podcast in the morning.   yes   no   _____

5. I usually watch TV during breakfast.   yes   no   _____

6. I rarely study English at home in the morning.   yes   no   _____

7. I never exercise in the morning.   yes   no   _____

PRACTICE 8 ▸ Frequency adverbs. (Chart 3-2)
Complete the sentences about the activities you do in the evening.

1. I always _____

2. I never _____

3. I sometimes _____

4. I often _____

5. I seldom _____

6. I rarely _____

PRACTICE 9 ▸ Other frequency expressions. (Chart 3-2)
Rewrite the sentences using the expressions from the box.

once a day	three times a day
once a month	✓ three times a week
once a week	twice a week
once a year	twice a year

1. I have classes on Mondays, Wednesdays, and Fridays.

    *I have classes three times a week.*_____

2. I pay my phone bill on the first day of every month.

    _____

3. I exercise from 10:00 to 11:00 A.M. every day.

    _____

4. I visit my cousins in December and June every year.

    _____

5. Dr. Williams checks her email at 6:00 A.M., noon, and 10:00 P.M. every day.

    _____

6. The Browns take a long vacation in August.

    _____

7. Cyndi works from home every Friday.

_____

8. Sam buys vegetables at the farmers' market on Mondays and Fridays.

_____

PRACTICE 10 ▶ Position of frequency adverbs. (Chart 3-3)
Complete the sentences with the given frequency adverb. Use Ø if no frequency adverb is needed.

1. *often*   Joan _____Ø_____ is _____often_____ sick.

2. *often*   Joan _____ feels _____ sick.

3. *sometimes* Carly _____ is _____ hungry.

4. *rarely*   It _____ is _____ cold in the summer.

5. *rarely*   It _____ rains _____ in the summer.

6. *usually*   I _____ am _____ in bed at 9:00.

7. *usually*   I _____ go _____ to bed at 9:00.

8. *never*   I _____ sleep _____ late.

9. *never*   I _____ wake up _____ late.

10. *always*   I _____ am _____ up early.

11. *always*   Sam _____ arrives _____ late.

12. *never*   He _____ is _____ on time.

13. *seldom*   Alice _____ goes _____ to the cafeteria.

14. *usually*   She _____ eats _____ in her office.

15. *sometimes* We _____ meet _____ for lunch at a
                restaurant.

PRACTICE 11 ▸ Frequency adverbs. (Charts 3-2 and 3-3)
Make sentences using the given words.

1. The teacher \ clean up the classroom \ usually

   The teacher usually cleans up the classroom.

2. The students \ help the teacher \ often

   _____

3. The classroom \ be clean \ always

   _____

4. The parents \ visit the class \ usually

   _____

5. The parents \ help the students with their work \ sometimes

   _____

6. The parents \ be helpful \ always

   _____

7. The classroom \ be quiet \ seldom

   _____

PRACTICE 12 ▸ Spelling of verbs ending in -s/-es. (Chart 3-4)
Write the correct form of each verb from the box in the appropriate column.

✓ call	eat	fix	listen	talk
✓ catch	finish	kiss	sleep	wish

-s	**-es**
she _____*calls*_____	he _____*catches*_____
he _____	she _____
she _____	he _____
he _____	she _____
she _____	he _____

PRACTICE 13 ▸ Final -s/-es. (Charts 3-1 and 3-4)

Write the correct form of the verbs in parentheses.

1. I (teach) _____ *teach* _____ English.

2. She (teach) _____ English.

3. I (fix) _____ lunch for my kids.

4. He (fix) _____ dinner every night.

5. Sara (miss) _____ her friends.

6. They (miss) _____ their friends.

7. I (brush) _____ my hair.

8. The girl (brush) _____ her hair.

9. She and I (wash) _____ the dishes.

10. He (wash) _____ the dishes.

11. He (cook) _____ dinner.

12. She (read) _____ the news.

13. Richard (watch) _____ movies.

14. Class (begin) _____ early.

15. Many students (come) _____ late.

16. The teacher always (come) _____ on time.

PRACTICE 14 ▸ Spelling of verbs ending in -y. (Chart 3-5)

Complete the sentences with the correct form of **study**.

1. The students _____ *study* _____ every day.

2. I _____ every day.

3. My friend _____ in the evening.

4. You _____ at night.

5. We _____ a lot.

6. She _____ in the morning.

7. They _____ all week.

8. He _____ on weekends.

PRACTICE 15 ▶ Spelling of verbs ending in -y. (Chart 3-5)

Write the correct form of each verb from the box in the appropriate column.

✓buy	✓cry	enjoy	pay	stay	try
copy	employ	fly	play	study	worry

-ies	-s
he _____cries_____	she _____buys_____
she _____	he _____
he _____	she _____
she _____	he _____
he _____	she _____
she _____	he _____

PRACTICE 16 ▶ Simple present tense: spelling. (Charts 3-1, 3-4, and 3-5)

Complete each sentence with the correct form of a verb from the box.

brush	catch	finish	fly	play	study
carry	close	fix	pay	✓start	wash

1. Dr. Lee _____starts_____ work at 6:00 every day.

2. Leah _____ her teeth after every meal.

3. The grocery store _____ at 11:00 every night.

4. An airplane often _____ over my house.

5. Hannah _____ her phone in her backpack.

6. André _____ the bus in the morning.

7. Martha is a mechanic. She _____ cars.

8. My roommate _____ his tuition with a credit card.

9. Inga _____ in the library every afternoon.

10. John _____ video games after school.

11. Max has a new job. He _____ dishes at a restaurant.

12. Amanda is a good student. She always _____ her homework on time.

PRACTICE 17 ▸ *Has, Does, and Goes.* (Chart 3-6)

Make sentences about the people in the chart. Use the correct form of **have class at**, **do homework at**, and **go to work at**.

	JIMI	MARTA	SUSAN	PAUL
9:00	class		homework	homework
10:00	homework	class		
11:00	work	homework	class	class
1:00			work	work
2:00		work		

1. Jimi

    a. He _____*has class at 9:00.*_____

    b. He _____

    c. He _____

2. Marta

    a. She _____

    b. She _____

    c. She _____

3. Susan and Paul

    a. They _____

    b. They _____

    c. They _____

PRACTICE 18 ▸ Simple present tense. (Charts 3-1 → 3-6)

Complete the sentences with the words in parentheses.

Ricardo (*leave*) _____*leaves*_____ his house at 4:30 every morning. He (*catch*)
                              1

_____ the bus near his house. He (*get*) _____ to work at 5:00. He
        2   3

(*work*) _____ in a restaurant. He (*fix*) _____ wonderful dishes from his
            4   5

country. Many people (*come*) _____ to the restaurant for his food. He (*finish*)
                                      6

_____ work at 3:00. Then he (*meet, often*) _____
        7   8

with students from his country and (*help*) _____ them with English. They (*have,*
                                                9

usually) _____ dinner together. After dinner he (*go*) _____ home.
              10   11

Sometimes he (have) _____ a snack. He (be, often) _____ tired at the
                      12   13
end of the day, but he (enjoy) _____ his work and the time with the students from
                                  14
his country.

PRACTICE 19 ▸ Like to, want to, need to. (Chart 3-7)

Think about what you *like to have*, *need to have*, and *want to have*. Write the words from the box in
the correct column.

✓ air	a computer	a leather coat	a phone
a camera	electricity	money	a place to live
a car	food	a motorcycle	water

LIKE TO HAVE	*NEED TO HAVE*	*WANT TO HAVE*
_____	_____ *air* _____	_____
_____	_____	_____
_____	_____	_____
_____	_____	_____
_____	_____	_____

PRACTICE 20 ▸ Like to, need to, want to. (Chart 3-7)

Use the words from the box, or your own words, to complete the sentences. Use an infinitive (*to +
verb*) in each sentence.

buy	eat	listen to	play	talk to	watch
do	✓ go	marry	take	wash	

1. Anna is sleepy. She wants _____ *to go* _____ to bed.

2. Mike likes _____ movies on his laptop.

3. Do you want _____ soccer with us at the park this afternoon?

4. I need _____ Jennifer in person, not on the phone.

5. James doesn't want _____ his homework tonight.

6. My clothes are dirty. I need _____ them.

7. Where is the mall? I need _____ a new coat.

8. John loves Mary. He wants _____ her.

9. Helen needs _____ an English course.

10. Where do you want _____ lunch?

11. Do you like _____ music?

PRACTICE 21 ▸ *Like to, need to, want to, would like to.* (Chart 3-7)

Make sentences using the given words. Pay attention to the final **-s** ending on singular verbs.

1. Emma \ like \ drink coffee

    Emma likes to drink coffee.

2. You \ need \ call your parents

    _____

3. We \ want \ watch a movie

    _____

4. I \ would like \ eat outside

    _____

5. Andrew \ want \ study French

    _____

6. He \ would like \ travel to Africa

    _____

7. Ava \ want \ go to the park

    _____

8. She \ like \ play basketball

    _____

PRACTICE 22 ▸ Simple present tense: negative. (Charts 1-6 and 3-8)

Write the negative form of the verb.

	HAVE	EAT	BE
1. I	don't have	don't eat	am not
2. You	_____	_____	_____
3. He	_____	_____	_____
4. She	_____	_____	_____
5. It	_____	_____	_____
6. We	_____	_____	_____
7. They	_____	_____	_____

PRACTICE 23 ▸ Simple present tense: negative. (Charts 1-6 and 3-8)
Rewrite the sentences. Use the negative form.

1. I have time. _____ *I don't have time.* _____

2. You need more time. _____

3. They eat breakfast. _____

4. Yoshi likes bananas. _____

5. Susan does her homework. _____

6. We save our money. _____

7. The printer works. _____

8. The coffee is good. _____

9. Mr. and Mrs. Costa drive to work. _____

10. They are here today. _____

PRACTICE 24 ▸ Simple present tense: negative. (Charts 1-6 and 3-8)
Use the verbs to make true sentences.

1. *wear* Cows _____ *don't wear* _____ clothes.

2. *be* Bananas _____ *are* _____ healthy.

3. *have* A child _____ gray hair.

4. *fly* Dogs _____ .

5. *grow* Apples _____ on trees.

6. *walk* A newborn baby _____ .

7. *cry* A newborn baby _____ .

8. *have* People _____ twenty fingers.

9. *help* A doctor _____ sick people.

10. *fix* A dentist _____ broken legs.

11. *fix* A dentist _____ broken teeth.

12. *be* The sun _____ cold.

13. *rain* It _____ a lot in London.

14. *rain* It _____ a lot in Saudi Arabia.

PRACTICE 25 ▸ Simple present tense: negative. (Chart 3-8)

Part I. Below is information about the activities Tom, Janet, and Mark do every day. Write sentences using the given words.

	TOM	JANET	MARK
drink coffee	x	x	
watch TV			x
walk to school	x		
study grammar	x	x	x
go shopping		x	
take the bus		x	x
skip lunch	x	x	
eat dinner at home	x		x
eat dinner out*		x	

*eat dinner out = eat dinner at a restaurant.

1. (*drink coffee*) ___Tom and Janet drink coffee.___

2. (*watch TV*) _____

3. (*walk to school*) _____

4. (*study grammar*) _____

5. (*go shopping*) _____

Part II. What don't Tom, Janet, or Mark do every day? Write sentences using the given words.

6. (*take the bus*) ___Tom doesn't take the bus.___

7. (*watch TV*) _____

8. (*skip lunch*) _____

9. (*eat dinner at home*) _____

10. (*eat dinner out*) _____

PRACTICE 26 ▸ Simple present tense: negative. (Chart 3-8)
Complete the sentences using the words in parentheses. Use the simple present tense.

1. Alex (*like*) ___likes___ tea, but he (*like, not*) ___doesn't like___ coffee.

2. Sara (*know*) _____ Ali, but she (*know, not*) _____
Hiroshi.

3. Pablo and Maria (*want*) _____ to stay home tonight. They (*want, not*) _____ to go to a movie.

4. Robert (be, not) _____ hungry. He (want, not) _____ a sandwich.

5. Mr. Smith (drink, not) _____ coffee, but Mr. Jones (drink) _____ twelve cups every day.

6. I (be, not) _____ rich. I (have, not) _____ a lot of money.

7. This pen (belong, not) _____ to me. It (belong) _____ to Pierre.

8. My friends (live, not) _____ in the dorm. They (have) _____ an apartment.

9. It (be) _____ a nice day today. It (be, not) _____ cold. You (need, not) _____ your coat.

10. Today (be) _____ a holiday. We (have, not) _____ class today.

11. Abby (eat, not) _____ breakfast. She (be, not) _____ hungry in the mornings.

12. My roommate (read, not) _____ the newspaper. She (watch) _____ news online.

PRACTICE 27 ▸ Yes/no questions. (Chart 3-9)
Make questions with the given words.

1. she \ study _____ *Does she study?* _____

2. they \ study _____

3. he \ know _____

4. the doctor \ know _____

5. we \ know _____

6. I \ understand _____

7. you \ understand _____

8. the manager \ understand _____

9. your roommate \ work _____

10. the car \ work _____

11. it \ work _____

12. she \ care _____

PRACTICE 28 ▸ *Yes/no* **questions.** (Chart 3-9)

This chart shows the activities that Tom, Sebastian, and Lily do. Make questions for the given answers.

	TOM	SEBASTIAN	LILY
swim			x
run			x
play soccer	x	x	

   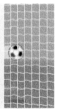

1. Tom

   a. ___*Does he run?*_____ No, he doesn't.

   b. _____ No, he doesn't.

   c. _____ Yes, he does.

2. Lily

   a. _____ Yes, she does.

   b. _____ No, she doesn't.

   c. _____ Yes, she does.

3. Sebastian

   a. _____ Yes, he does.

   b. _____ No, he doesn't.

   c. _____ No, he doesn't.

4. Tom and Sebastian

   a. _____ Yes, they do.

   b. _____ No, they don't.

   c. _____ No, they don't.

PRACTICE 29 ▸ Short answers to *yes/no* questions. (Chart 3-9)
Choose the correct response for each question.

1. Do you like fish?
   (a.) Yes, I do.   b. Yes, I like.

2. Does your husband like fish?
   a. Yes, he does.   b. Yes, he likes.

3. Do you want to go out to dinner?
   a. Yes, I want.   b. Yes, I do.

4. Do you have a question?
   a. Yes, I have.   b. Yes, I do.

5. Do you need help?
   a. Yes, I do.   b. Yes, I need.

6. Does your friend need help?
   a. Yes, she needs.   b. Yes, she does.

7. Do your friends go to school?
   a. Yes, they do.   b. Yes, they go.

8. Does your husband teach English?
   a. Yes, he teaches.   b. Yes, he does.

PRACTICE 30 ▸ *Yes/no* questions and answers. (Chart 3-9)
Make questions. Write a short answer in the negative form.

1. Ann is a doctor. She takes care of children.
   _____*Does she take care of*_____ adults? No, ___*she doesn't*___.

2. Tom is a mechanic. He fixes cars.
   _____ boats? No, _____.

3. I am a cook. I cook Chinese food.
   _____ pizza? No, _____.

4. We are teachers. We teach teenagers.
   _____ young children? No, _____.

5. My sister and I are janitors. We clean offices.
   _____ schools? No, _____.

6. Lynn and Doug are athletes. They play soccer.
   _____ basketball? No, _____.

7. Mrs. Adams is a writer. She writes for a website.
   _____ books? No, _____.

8. I am a nurse. I work at a hospital.

   _____ at a clinic? No, _____.

9. They are construction workers. They build hotels.

   _____ houses? No, _____.

10. Daniel is a student. He studies history.

    _____ chemistry? No, _____.

PRACTICE 31 ▸ Be and do in questions. (Chart 3-9)

Complete the questions with a form of **be** or **do**.

1. _____Are_____ you ready?

2. _____ the bus here?

3. _____ the bus usually come on time?

4. _____ you often ride the bus?

5. _____ the bus comfortable?

6. _____ you do your work on the bus?

7. _____ you read books on the bus?

8. _____ you enjoy the ride?

9. _____ you drive to work sometimes?

10. _____ you tired of my questions?

PRACTICE 32 ▸ Be and do in questions. (Chart 3-9)

Complete the conversations with a form of **be** or **do**. Use contractions where possible.

Conversation 1:

A: _____Are_____ you sick?

B: No, I _____'m_____ not.

A: _____Are_____ you tired?

B: Yes, I _____am_____.

A: _____Do_____ you want to go to bed?

B: No, I _____don't_____.

Conversation 2:

A: _____ you know the time?

B: Yes, I _____. It _____ 5:55.

A: Thanks.

Conversation 3:

A: _____ you hungry?

B: Yes, I _____ .

A: _____ you want some chocolate?

B: Sure. Thanks. Mmm.

A: _____ you like it?

B: No, I _____ . I love it!

Conversation 4:

A: _____ you work at the hospital?

B: Yes, we do.

A: _____ you doctors?

B: No, we aren't.

A: What _____ you?

B: We _____ nurses.

Conversation 5:

A: _____ Mr. Jones here?

B: No, he _____ .

A: Where _____ he?

B: I have no idea.

A: _____ his wife here?

B: No, she _____ .

A: Where _____ she?

B: With Mr. Jones.

Conversation 6:

A: Where _____ my glasses? _____ you know?

B: No. _____ they in your purse?

A: No, they _____ .

B: _____ they in your pocket?

A: No.

B: Oh, I see them! They _____ on your head.

PRACTICE 33 ▸ Questions with *where* and *what*. (Chart 3-10)
Complete the questions with *where* or *what*.

1. _____*Where*_____ does Gino live? He lives in Rome.

2. _____ does Albert work? He works at Valley Hospital.

3. _____ do the kids play after school? They play soccer.

4. _____ do you want for breakfast? I just want toast and coffee.

5. _____ do you want to sit? I want to sit at the table by the window.

6. _____ does Helene like to do for vacation? She likes to travel.

7. _____ does Helene like to go? She likes to go to Hawaii.

8. _____ do you need? I need a vacation.

PRACTICE 34 ▸ Questions with *where* and *what*. (Chart 3-10)
Make questions for the given answers.

1. A: _____*Where does David live?*_____
   B: In Miami. (David lives in Miami.)

2. A: _____
   B: Our email addresses. (The teacher wants our email addresses.)

3. A: _____
   B: At the Plaza Hotel. (Dr. Varma stays at the Plaza Hotel.)

4. A: _____
   B: On First Street. (I catch the bus on First Street.)

5. A: _____
   B: A new job. (Lillian needs a new job.)

6. A: _____
   B: A baby brother. (The children want a baby brother.)

7. A: _____
   B: In the park. (The construction workers eat lunch in the park.)

8. A: _____
   B: Downstairs. (Victoria and Franco are downstairs.)

9. A: _____
   B: Flowers. (Mark brings his wife flowers every week.)

10. A: _____
    B: The flight number. (I need the flight number.)

PRACTICE 35 ▸ Questions with *where* and *what*. (Chart 3-10)
Read the story. Make questions about Paulo with the given answers. Use *where* and *what*.

Paulo is very busy. He works at the university. He is a technician. He fixes computers. After work, he goes to the high school. He coaches soccer. After that, he eats dinner. He usually eats at a restaurant. He doesn't like to cook. During the weekend, he likes to spend time outdoors. He often goes to the river on weekends. He rides his kayak.

1. A: _____Where does he work?_____
   B: At the university.

2. A: _____
   B: Computers.

3. A: _____
   B: To the high school.

4. A: _____
   B: Soccer.

5. A: _____
   B: At a restaurant.

6. A: _____
   B: To the river.

7. A: _____
   B: His kayak.

PRACTICE 36 ▸ *Where*, *what*, and *when* in questions. (Charts 3-10 and 3-11)
Write *where*, *what*, or *when*.

1. _____Where_____ does Tom work?   At the bank.

2. _____When_____ does he leave for work?   At 7:00.

3. _____ does he eat lunch?   At noon.

4. _____ does he eat for lunch?   A sandwich.

5. _____ does he go after work?   To the gym.

6. _____ does he go home?   At 8:00.

7. _____ does he have for dinner?   Chicken or fish.

8. _____ does he do after dinner?   He watches TV.

9. _____ does he get ready for bed?   After dinner.

10. _____ does he sleep?   On his sofa.

PRACTICE 37 ▸ Review: *yes/no* and information questions. (Charts 3-9 → 3-11)
Make questions for the given answers.

1. A: _____*When do you go to bed?*_____
   B: Around 9:00. (I go to bed around 9:00.)

2. A: _____
   B: Yes, I do. (I get up early.)

3. A: _____
   B: At 5:30. (The bus comes at 5:30.)

4. A: _____
   B: Yes, it does. (The bus comes on time.)

5. A: _____
   B: At a hospital. (I work at a hospital.)

6. A: _____
   B: At 6:00. (I start work at 6:00.)

7. A: _____
   B: At 7:00. (I leave work at 7:00.)

8. A: _____
   B: Yes, I do. (I like my job.)

9. A: _____
   B: Yes, it is. (It is interesting work.)

10. A: _____
    B: Yes, I am. (I'm a doctor.)

PRACTICE 38 ▸ Review: *yes/no* and information questions. (Charts 3-9 → 3-11)
Read the message. Then make questions and answers about Dr. Ramos and his schedule.

1. be \ a science teacher?

   _____*Is he a teacher?*_____

   _____*Yes, he is.*_____

2. what \ teach?

   _____

   _____

3. where \ teach \ chemistry?

   _____

   _____

4. when \ be \ in the chemistry lab?

   _____

   _____

5. where \ teach \ biology?

   _____

   _____

6. be \ in his office \ every day?

   _____

   _____

7. be \ in his office \ at 1:00 on Monday?

   _____

   _____

8. teach \ at 8:00?

   _____

   _____

9. when \ teach?

   _____

   _____

> **Dr. Ramos**
>
> **Schedule Change:**
>
> My new office hours are from 1:00–2:00 Monday, Wednesday, and Friday.
>
> I teach biology at 9:00 and 10:00 in the biology lab. I teach chemistry at 12:00 in the chemistry lab.

PRACTICE 39 ▸ Review: Simple present tense. (Charts 3-1 → 3-7)
Add *-s/-es* or Ø (nothing) where necessary.

Sam enjoy__s__ cooking. He and his wife like_____ to invite friends for dinner. They
    1   2

invite_____ me to dinner about once a month. When I arrive_____, we usually go_____ into the
       3   4   5

kitchen, and we talk_____ to Sam while he cook_____. The kitchen always smell_____ wonderful.
              6   7   8

I get_____ very hungry when I sit_____ and talk to Sam. Sometimes he give_____ me a few bites of
   9   10   11

food from the pots. When dinner is ready, we take_____ a long time to eat it. It taste_____ delicious.
                                              12   13

After dinner, Sam clear_____ the table, and his wife serve_____ dessert. These meals are wonderful,
                       14   15

and I always enjoy_____ myself with Sam and his wife.
                  16

PRACTICE 40 ▸ Review: simple present tense. (Chapter 3)
Complete the sentences with the correct form of the verbs in parentheses. Some sentences are
negative, and some are not.

1. Mario likes to talk. He (*be*) _____ *isn't* _____ quiet.

2. Janna isn't quiet. She (*love*) _____ *loves* _____ to talk.

3. Susan is a good student. She (*study*) _____ a lot.

4. The nurses are very busy. They (*have*) _____ time for lunch.

5. John's bedroom is messy. He (*clean*) _____ it often.

6. This soup is delicious. It (*taste*) _____ wonderful.

7. A new car is expensive. It (*cost*) _____ a lot of money.

8. Two students want to answer the question. They (*know*) _____ the answer.

9. Five students don't know the answer. They (*want*) _____ to answer
   the question.

10. Haley lives alone. She (*have*) _____ a roommate.

11. Oliver drives to school. He (*have*) _____ a car.

12. A: Your eyes are red. You (*look*) _____ tired.

    B: Actually, I'm sad. I (*be*) _____ tired.

PRACTICE 41 ▸ Question review. (Chapters 2 and 3)

Make questions. Use the information in the note.

1. A: _____Is Jane at home?_____
   B: No, she isn't. (Jane isn't home.)

2. A: _____
   B: At work. (She is at work.)

3. A: _____
   B: No, they aren't. (Suzie and Jack aren't home.)

4. A: _____
   B: At school. (They are at school.)

5. A: _____
   B: At 6:00. (Dinner is at 6:00.)

6. A: _____
   B: A pizza. (Jane has a pizza for dinner.)

> Ron,
>
> I'm at work. Suzie and Jack are at school. You need to pick them up. Dinner is at 6:00. I have a pizza in the fridge.*
>
> See you soon!
> Jane

fridge = refrigerator

PRACTICE 42 ▸ Review: simple present tense. (Chapter 3)

Choose the correct answers.

1. Alex _____ know French.
   a. isn't   b. doesn't   c. don't

2. _____ Alex speak Russian?
   a. Is   b. Does   c. Do

3. _____ Alex from Canada?
   a. Is   b. Does   c. Do

4. When _____ you usually check your email?
   a. are   b. does   c. do

5. Anita _____ a job.
   a. no have   b. no has   c. doesn't have

6. Omar _____ his new car every Saturday.
   a. wash   b. washs   c. washes

7. Where does Tina _____ to school?
   a. go   b. goes   c. to go

8. Fumiko _____ English at this school.
   a. study   b. studies   c. studys

9. Fumiko and Omar _____ students at this school.
    a. is   b. are   c. be

10. They _____ speak the same language.
    a. aren't   b. doesn't   c. don't

PRACTICE 43 ▶ Review: simple present tense. (Chapter 3)
Correct the mistakes.

1. My sister study *ies* French.

2. Martin usually is late for class.

3. Ivan speak Russian?

4. What time you have class?

5. Where Isabel lives?

6. Kevin and Jeff often eats lunch together.

7. Diana not at home today.

8. Does your apartment has a pool?

9. I need do my homework.

10. Do your roommate work on weekends?

CHAPTER 4

Using the Present Progressive and the Imperative

PRACTICE 1 ▸ The present progressive. (Chart 4-1)
Which sentences are true for you? Choose *yes* or *no*.

At this moment,

1. the sun is shining.	yes	no
2. it is raining.	yes	no
3. I am sitting at a desk.	yes	no
4. I am checking social media.	yes	no
5. I am listening to music.	yes	no
6. friends are texting me.	yes	no
7. my teacher is talking.	yes	no

PRACTICE 2 ▸ The present progressive. (Chart 4-1)
Write *am*, *is*, or *are*.

At this moment,

1. some students __are__ waiting for the bus.

2. their teacher _____ correcting their homework.

3. I _____ doing my homework.

4. Mark _____ doing his homework.

5. Sandra _____ shopping at the mall.

6. her friends _____ shopping with her.

7. Mr. and Mrs. Brown _____ watching TV.

8. their daughter _____ reading a book.

9. you _____ reading this exercise.

10. we _____ learning English.

PRACTICE 3 ▸ The present progressive. (Chart 4-1)

Complete the sentences with the present progressive.

At the airport

An airplane …

1. land _____*is landing*_____ at the airport.

2. park _____ at the gate.

3. wait _____ for passengers.

A pilot …

4. enter _____ the plane.

5. talk _____ to flight attendants.

Some people …

6. stand _____ in line.

7. carry _____ suitcases.

8. eat _____ snacks.

9. watch _____ airplanes.

10. read _____ books.

PRACTICE 4 ▸ The present progressive. (Chart 4-1)

Complete the sentences with the verbs from the box. Use the present progressive.

✓ eat	rain	study	wash
play	sleep	talk	watch

1. Noah and Jessie are in the cafeteria. They _____*are eating*_____ lunch.

2. Ben and Vanessa are in the library. They _____ for a test.

3. I need an umbrella. It _____.

4. Sasha is with her friends. They _____ a movie.

5. I am on the phone. I _____ to my brother.

6. Elena is in the kitchen. She _____ dishes.

7. My roommate is still in bed. He _____.

8. We are at the park. We _____ soccer.

PRACTICE 5 ▸ Spelling of *-ing*. (Chart 4-2)
Write the **-ing** form of each verb.

1. shine _____*shining*_____

2. win _____

3. join _____

4. sign _____

5. fly _____

6. pay _____

7. study _____

8. get _____

9. wait _____

10. write _____

PRACTICE 6 ▸ Spelling of *-ing*. (Chart 4-2)
Write the **-ing** form of each verb.

1. dream _____*dreaming*_____

2. come _____

3. look _____

4. take _____

5. smile _____

6. swim _____

7. help _____

8. clap _____

9. keep _____

10. camp _____

camp

PRACTICE 7 ▸ The present progressive. (Charts 4-1 and 4-2)
Complete each sentence with the correct form of a verb from the box. Use the present progressive.

come	go	read	talk
do	kick	sit	✓ wait

It's 3:00 and the classroom is empty. Some students are outside. They

_____ *are waiting* _____ for the city bus. A few students _____ on
　　　　　　1　　　　　　　　　　　　　　　　　　　　　　　　　　　2

the ground under a tree. They _____ about their plans for the weekend.
　　　　　　　　　　　　　　　　　　3

A girl on a bench _____ her homework. The boy next to her
　　　　　　　　　　　　　　4

_____ a book. A few students _____ a soccer ball.
　　　　5　　　　　　　　　　　　　　　　　　　　　　　6

The bus _____ now. The students _____ home.
　　　　　7　　　　　　　　　　　　　　　　　　　　8

PRACTICE 8 ▸ The present progressive: negative forms. (Chart 4-3)
Complete the sentences with the negative form of the verbs in bold. Use contractions.

1. Oliva **is speaking** Spanish. She _____ *isn't speaking* _____ French.

2. I **am drinking** coffee. I _____ tea.

3. They **are eating** sandwiches. They _____ pizza.

4. She **is watching** the news. She _____ a movie.

5. James **is wearing** a shirt. He _____ a sweater.

6. They **are playing** basketball. They _____ soccer.

7. We **are buying** a used car. We _____ a new car.

8. You **are working** from home today. You _____ at the office.

PRACTICE 9 ▸ The present progressive: affirmative and negative. (Chart 4-3)
Part I. Tony is an engineer. He is a very hard worker. Right now he is in his office. What do you think he is doing? Check (✓) all the possible activities. Make possible sentences for the given phrases.

___✓___ work on an assignment　　　_____ talk on the phone

_____ repair his car　　　　　　　　_____ ride a horse

_____ look at his computer　　　　　_____ buy food for dinner

1. ___ *He is working on an assignment.* ___

2. ___ *He isn't repairing his car.* ___

3. _____

4. _____

5. _____ 55

6. _____

Part II. Anita and Ben are nurses. They are at the hospital. Check (✓) all the possible activities. Make a sentence for each phrase.

_____ talk to patients   _____ work with doctors

_____ wash cars   _____ give medicine to patients

_____ watch movies

1. _____

2. _____

3. _____

4. _____

5. _____

Part III. What are you doing right now? Check (✓) the activities and make true sentences for the given phrases.

_____ listen to music   _____ study in the library

_____ sit at a desk   _____ wait for a friend

_____ work at home   _____ ride on a bus

1. _____

2. _____

3. _____

4. _____

5. _____

6. _____

PRACTICE 10 ▶ The present progressive: affirmative and negative. (Chart 4-3)

Use the verb in parentheses to make a true sentence in the present progressive. Use an affirmative or negative form.

1. I (*think*) *am thinking / am not thinking* about my family right now.

2. I (*write*) _____ in a classroom right now.

3. I (*listen*) _____ to music right now.

4. I (*travel*) _____ in another country today.

5. A cat (*sit*) _____ beside me right now.

6. A bird (*sing*) _____ outside my window right now.

7. My phone (*ring*) _____ at this moment.

8. My computer (*make*) _____ noise right now.

PRACTICE 11 ▸ The present progressive: questions. (Chart 4-4)
Make questions with the given words. Use the present progressive.

1. he \ study English? ___*Is he studying English?*___

2. you \ work? _____

3. they \ leave? _____

4. she \ stay home? _____

5. we \ go to school? _____

6. the computer \ work? _____

7. it \ work? _____

8. I \ drive? _____

9. your friend \ come? _____

10. the students \ laugh? _____

11. Mr. Kim \ sleep? _____

12. Monica \ dream? _____

PRACTICE 12 ▸ The present progressive: questions and negatives. (Chart 4-4)
Make questions and answers. Use the verbs in parentheses.

1. Anna is in the kitchen. (*cook, sleep*)

   A: ___*Is she sleeping*___ ?

   B: No, ___*she isn't*___ . She ___*is cooking*___ .

2. Pablo is in the car. (*drive, run*)

   A: _____ ?

   B: No, _____ . He _____ .

3. Terry and Tony are in the swimming pool. (*swim, study*)

   A: _____ ?

   B: No, _____ . They _____ .

4. Mrs. Ramírez is at the supermarket. (*teach, shop*)

   A: _____ ?

   B: No, _____ . She _____ .

5. Marta is in her bedroom. (*sleep, fish*)

A: _____?

B: No, _____. She _____.

6. Some teenagers are in the park with their soccer ball. (*play, work*)

A: _____?

B: No, _____. They _____.

7. I am on a plane. (*wash dishes, read a book*)

A: _____?

B: No, _____. I _____.

PRACTICE 13 ▸ The present progressive: statements, negatives, and questions. (Charts 4-1 → 4-4)

Complete the sentences with the correct form of the verb **work**.

Part I. Statement Forms

1. I ____*am working*_____ right now.

2. They _____ right now.

3. She _____ right now.

4. You _____ right now.

5. He _____ right now.

Part II. Negative Forms

6. I ____*am not working*_____ right now.

7. They _____ right now.

8. She _____ right now.

9. You _____ right now.

10. He _____ right now.

Part III. Question Forms

11. ____*Are*____ you ____*working*____ right now?

12. _____ he _____ right now?

13. _____ they _____ right now?

14. _____ we _____ right now?

15. _____ she _____ right now?

PRACTICE 14 ▸ The simple present: statements, negatives, and questions. (Chapter 3)

Complete the sentences with the correct form of the verb **work**.

Part I. Statement Forms

1. I _____ work _____ every day.

2. They _____ every day.

3. She _____ every day.

4. You _____ every day.

5. He _____ every day.

Part II. Negative Forms

6. I _____ do not work _____ every day.

7. They _____ every day.

8. She _____ every day.

9. You _____ every day.

10. He _____ every day.

Part III. Question Forms

11. _____ Do _____ you _____ work _____ every day?

12. _____ he _____ every day?

13. _____ they _____ every day?

14. _____ we _____ every day?

15. _____ she _____ every day?

PRACTICE 15 ▸ Simple present vs. the present progressive. (Chart 4-5)

Choose the correct answers.

1. I send text messages now / (every day.)

2. I am not sending a text message now / every day.

3. I receive text messages now / every day.

4. I post to social media now / every day.

5. I'm reading a book now / every day.

6. It's raining now / every day.

7. My kids play outside now / every day.

8. My kids are playing outside now / every day.

9. My computer isn't working now / every day.

10. I work at my computer now / every day.

PRACTICE 16 ▸ Simple present vs. the present progressive. (Chart 4-5)
Check (✓) the sentences that describe activities happening right now.

1. __✓__ The phone is ringing.

2. _____ I'm talking to my sister.

3. _____ We talk two or three times a week.

4. _____ Ruth exercises in the mornings.

5. _____ She rides her bike.

6. _____ The baby is crying.

7. _____ She cries when she is hungry.

8. _____ Her mother is feeding her.

9. _____ We are listening to music.

10. _____ We listen to music in the car.

PRACTICE 17 ▸ Simple present vs. the present progressive. (Chart 4-5)
Complete the sentences with the correct form of the verbs in parentheses.

Right now the sun (*shine*) _____*is shining*_____. I (*look*)
                                        1

_____ out my window at the lake. A man and a young boy
                2

(*fish*) _____ from a small boat. A mother and her baby (*sit*)
                    3

_____ on the grass. They (*play*) _____ with
                4   5

a ball. Two girls (*swim*) _____ near the shore. A teenage boy
                                            6

(*jump*) _____ in the water.
                    7

   I (*swim*) _____*swim*_____ in the lake every day in the summer for exercise.
                          8

In the winter, I usually (*walk*) _____ around the lake, or I
                                                9

(*go*) _____ to a gym.
            10

   Today I (*work*) _____ at home. I usually (*work*)
                                11

_____ at home three days a week. I (*teach*) _____
            12   13

English at a college. Right now I (*teach*) _____ a class online.
                                                            14

PRACTICE 18 ▸ Simple present vs. the present progressive. (Chart 4-5)
Complete the sentences with the correct form of the words in parentheses.

1. Ahmed (*talk*) _____talks_____ to his classmates every day in class. Right now he
   (*talk*) _____is talking_____ to Yoko. He (*talk, not*) _____ to
   his friend Omar right now.

2. It (*rain*) _____ a lot in this city, but it (*rain, not*)
   _____ right now. The sun (*shine*) _____.
   (*it, rain*) _____ a lot in your hometown?

3. Hans and Anna (*sit*) _____ next to each other in class every day, so
   they often (*help*) _____ each other with their grammar exercises.
   Right now Anna (*help*) _____ Hans with an exercise on verbs.

4. Alberto (*cook*) _____ his own dinner every evening. Right now he is
   in his kitchen. He (*cook*) _____ rice and beans. (*he, cook*)
   _____ meat for his dinner tonight too? No, he is a vegetarian. He
   (*eat, never*) _____ meat. (*you, eat*) _____
   meat? (*you, be*) _____ a vegetarian?

PRACTICE 19 ▸ Simple present vs. the present progressive. (Chart 4-5)
Write **Do, Does, Is,** or **Are**.

1. _____Do_____ you study every day?

2. _____ you working hard now?

3. _____ the student working hard now?

4. _____ you learning a lot of English?

5. _____ you memorize vocabulary every day?

6. _____ your teacher helping you now?

7. _____ your teacher help you after class?

8. _____ you do your homework every day?

9. _____ the homework take a long time?

10. _____ you understand your classmates?

11. _____ your teacher understand you?

12. _____ you ask a lot of questions?

13. _____ you studying with friends right now?

14. _____ you often study with friends?

PRACTICE 20 ▸ Non-action verbs. (Chart 4-6)

Choose the correct answers.

1. (Do you know)/ Are you knowing the names of all the students in your class?

2. Mmm. I smell / am smelling something good in the oven.

3. The baby cries / is crying right now. She is wanting / wants her mother.

4. This coffee is tasting / tastes wonderful. I like / am liking strong coffee.

5. The cat and dog are running / run outside right now. The dog likes / is liking the cat, but the cat is hating / hates the dog.

PRACTICE 21 ▸ Non-action verbs. (Chart 4-6)

Complete the sentences with the correct form of the verbs in parentheses.

1. A: Mmm. This bread (*taste*) _____*tastes*_____ delicious.

   B: Thank you. I (*think*) _____ it has honey in it.

2. A: What (*Jan, want*) _____ for her birthday?

   B: Well, she (*need*) _____ a winter coat, but she

   (*want*) _____ leather boots.

3. A: Jackie (*love*) _____ Carl.

   B: What? I (*believe, not*) _____ you. Carl

   (*love*) _____ me!

4. A: Shhh. (*you, hear*) _____ a siren?

   B: I (*hear*) _____ it, but

   I (*see, not*) _____ it.

a siren

PRACTICE 22 ▸ *See, look at, watch, hear,* and *listen to.* (Chart 4-7)

Circle the correct sentence in each pair.

1. a. I am hearing the neighbor's TV. It's very loud.
   (b.) I hear the neighbor's TV. It's very loud.

2. a. Annette isn't listening to me right now.
   b. Annette doesn't listen to me right now.

3. a. Shhh. I watch a movie.
   b. Shhh. I'm watching a movie.

4. a. I look at the clock. We are late.
   b. I'm looking at the clock. We are late.

5. a. Mary, what are you looking at?
   b. Mary, what do you look at?

6. a. Do you hear that noise? It sounds like an earthquake.
   b. Are you hearing that noise? It sounds like an earthquake.

7. a. I am listening to music at night. It helps me fall asleep.
   b. I listen to music at night. It helps me fall asleep.

8. a. I hear my phone. I need to answer it right now.
   b. I am hearing my phone. I need to answer it right now.

9. a. Look! I see a squirrel.
   b. Look! I am seeing a squirrel.

a squirrel

PRACTICE 23 ▶ See, look at, watch, hear, and listen to. (Chart 4-7)
Complete the sentences with the correct form of the verbs in parentheses.

Andy is sitting in his living room right now. He (*watch*) _____*is watching*_____ a
                                                              1
football game on TV. His favorite team (*play*) _____. He (*listen, also*)
                                                         2
_____ to a sports podcast and (*look*) _____ at
            3   4
social media posts on his phone. He (*wear*) _____ headphones. His wife
                                                       5
(*talk*) _____ to him. She (*tell*) _____ him about
              6   7
her plans for the day. He (*listen, not*) _____ because he (*hear, not*)
                                                    8
_____ her. Suddenly, she turns off the TV. Now Andy (*listen*)
            9
_____ very carefully.
            10

PRACTICE 24 ▶ See, look at, watch, hear, and listen to. (Chart 4-7)
Circle the correct verb in each sentence.

1. In the evenings, I like to sit in front of the TV and (watch) / see old movies.

2. The neighbors are having a party. I hear / listen to a lot of loud noise.

3. Shhh. I hear / listen to something. Is someone outside?

4. I love rock music. When I'm at home, I put on my headphones, sit down, and hear / listen to
   rock music.

5. A: Let's go shopping. I want to look at / watch clothes.

   B: Okay. You can look at / see clothes. I want to sit on a bench and see / watch the
      people at the mall.

6. A: Look out the window. Do you see / Do you watch the storm clouds?

   B: I see / look at several dark rain clouds.

PRACTICE 25 ▸ Review. (Charts 4-6 and 4-7)

Write true sentences with the given verbs.

Right now I ...

1. (*look at*) _____.

2. (*see*) _____.

3. (*hear*) _____.

4. (*listen to*) _____.

5. (*watch*) _____.

6. (*want*) _____.

7. (*need*) _____.

PRACTICE 26 ▸ *Think about* and *think that*. (Chart 4-8)

Circle the correct sentence in each pair.

1. a. You are very quiet. What do you think about?
   (b.) You are very quiet. What are you thinking about?

2. a. I am thinking about my plans for today.
   b. I think about my plans for today.

3. a. I am thinking that grammar is difficult.
   b. I think that grammar is difficult.

4. a. What are you thinking? Does this shirt look okay?
   b. What do you think? Does this shirt look okay?

5. a. Joe, do you think that sports stars get too much money?
   b. Joe, are you thinking that sports stars get too much money?

PRACTICE 27 ▸ *Think about* and *think that*. (Chart 4-8)

Complete each sentence with the correct form of ***think that*** or ***think about***.

1. A: What _____*are*_____ you _____*thinking about*_____ right now?

   B: I _____ my family. I miss them.

   A: You have a nice family. I _____ you are lucky.

2. A: Some people _____ English is an easy language.

   B: I (*not*) _____ it is easy to learn. I _____ it

   is difficult.

3. A: I have a new game. I _____ an animal. It is very long and

   sometimes dangerous. Do you know the animal? Can you guess?

   B: _____ you _____ a snake?

   A: Yes!

   B: I _____ snakes make nice pets, but many people are afraid of them.

   A: I'm afraid of them. I _____ they are scary.

PRACTICE 28 ▸ Imperative sentences. (Chart 4-9)
Underline the imperative verbs in the conversation.

PROFESSOR: We have an exam today. Please <u>put</u> your books, notes, and phones away.

STUDENT: Do we need a pen or a pencil?

PROFESSOR: Use a pencil. Please write your answers on the answer sheet. Don't write in the
exam booklet.

STUDENT: Do we need a calculator for the exam?

PROFESSOR: No, you don't.

STUDENT: When do we start?

PROFESSOR: Right now. Please open the exam booklet. The questions begin on page 2. Don't talk
during the exam. You have one hour to complete it. Don't forget your name. Please
write your name at the top of the answer sheet. Good luck, everyone!

PRACTICE 29 ▸ Imperative sentences. (Chart 4-9)
Write the correct imperative sentence from the box for each icon.

Connect to Bluetooth.	Download the file.	Send the message.
Don't bring pets inside.	Fasten your seatbelt.	Stop.
Don't eat here.	Please be quiet.	Throw away your trash.
Don't run.	Recycle your trash.	✓ Wash your hands.

1. ___*Wash your hands.*___   2. _____   3. _____

4. _____ 5. _____ 6. _____

7. _____ 8. _____ 9. _____

10. _____ 11. _____ 12. _____

PRACTICE 30 ▸ Verb review. (Chapters 3 and 4)

Complete the sentences with the correct form of the verbs in parentheses.

1. Tony (*eat*) _____ *eats* _____ dinner with his family every evening. During dinner,
his phone sometimes (*ring*) _____. Tony (*answer, not*)
_____ it. His parents (*want, not*) _____
him to talk on the phone during dinner. They (*believe*) _____ dinner
is an important time for the family.

2. Olga Burns is a pilot for an airline company in Alaska. She (*fly*) _____
almost every day. Today she (*fly*) _____ from Juneau to Anchorage.

3. A: Excuse me. (*you, wait*) _____ for the downtown bus?

   B: Yes, I (*be*) _____ .

   A: What time (*the bus, stop*) _____ here?

   B: 10:35.

   A: (*be, usually, it*) _____ on time?

   B: Yes. It (*come, rarely*) _____ late.

4. A: What (*your teacher, do, usually*) _____

   at lunchtime every day?

   B: I (*think*) _____ she (*correct*) _____ papers

   in the classroom and (*have*) _____ lunch.

   A: What (*she, do*) _____ right now?

   B: She (*talk*) _____ to a student.

5. A: (*you, know*) _____ the capital of Australia?

   B: I (*think*) _____ that it (*be*) _____ Vienna.

   A: Not Austria. Australia!

   B: Oh. Wait a minute. Let me think. I (*know*) _____. It's Canberra.

PRACTICE 31 ▸ Verb review. (Chapters 3 and 4)

Complete the sentences with the words in parentheses. Use the simple present or the present progressive. Use an infinitive where necessary.

The Lind family is at home. It is evening. Jens (*sit*) _____*is sitting*_____ on the

couch. He (*look at*) _____ a weather report on his phone. Brita

(*work*) _____ at her desk. She (*study*) _____ and

(*listen to*) _____ music. Jens (*hear*) _____ the

music, but he (*listen to, not*) _____ it right now. He (*think about*)

_____ the weather report. Axel is in the living room. He is nine years

old. He (*play*) _____ with a toy train. In the corner of the living room,

their cat (*sleep*) _____.

   Brita (*learn*) _____ chemistry

formulas. She (*like*) _____ chemistry.

She (*think*) _____ that chemistry is

easy. She (*understand*) _____ it.

Chemistry (*be*) _____ her favorite course.

She (*like, not*) _____ history.

chemistry formulas

   Mr. Lind is in the kitchen. He (*cook*) _____ dinner. He (*cook*)

_____ three or four times a week. He (*cut*) _____

vegetables for a salad. Mrs. Lind (*stand*) _____ near the front door. She

(*take off*) _____ her jacket. She (*wear*) _____
                    21   22

exercise clothes because she (*exercise, usually*) _____ after work. She
                                                                    23

(*think about*) _____ dinner. She (*be*) _____
                        24   25

very hungry, and the food (*smell*) _____ good. After dinner, she (*want*)
                                            26

_____ (*watch*) _____ a movie with her family.
            27   28

PRACTICE 32 ▸ Review. (Chapter 4)

Correct the mistakes.

      are eating
1. We ~~eat~~ lunch right now.

2. I'm not needing an umbrella. It isn't rain today.

3. What you are doing right now?

4. The soup is tasting wonderful.

5. John is think about his next vacation.

6. Why are you standing? Please you have a seat.

7. What's that noise? Are you hearing it?

8. What you think about this homework? I'm thinking that it is easy.

CHAPTER 5

Nouns and Pronouns

PRACTICE 1 ▶ Identifying nouns. (Chart 5-1)
Check (✓) each noun (person, place, or thing).

1. __✓__ father
2. _____ happy
3. _____ choose
4. _____ old
5. _____ snacks
6. _____ radio
7. _____ Beijing
8. _____ Mary
9. _____ hospital
10. _____ eat

Beijing
CHINA

PRACTICE 2 ▶ Nouns: Singular and plural forms. (Chart 5-1)
Complete the lists with the correct forms of the given nouns.

SINGULAR	PLURAL
1. box	_boxes_
2. tomato	_____
3. zoo	_____
4. _____	pens
5. baby	_____
6. key	_____
7. _____	cities
8. _____	wives
9. dish	_____
10. thief	_____

PRACTICE 3 ▸ Spelling of plural nouns. (Chart 5-1)

Write the plural form of each noun in the correct column.

baby	girl	✓ leaf	tax
brush	glass	life	thief
✓ cat	key	party	tomato
country	knife	sandwich	tray
city	lady	shoe	wife

-s	-ies	-ves	-es
cats		leaves	

PRACTICE 4 ▸ Spelling of plural nouns. (Chart 5-1)

Complete the sentences with the plural form of the nouns in parentheses.

1. (*Potato*) _____ Potatoes _____ are my favorite vegetable.

2. Where are the car (*key*) _____?

3. My English (*class*) _____ meet in the afternoon.

4. The police want to catch the car (*thief*) _____ soon.

5. The students are studying for their (*test*) _____.

6. (*Baby*) _____ don't like loud noises.

7. I need two (*box*) _____ for these gifts.

8. Why does Richard have three (*clock*) _____ in his kitchen?

9. During the holidays, we go to many (*party*) _____.

10. Miriam has ten (*cat*) _____ in her apartment.

11. They make good (*sandwich*) _____ at that restaurant.

12. How many (*textbook*) _____ do you need for your English class?

13. Do you think cats have nine (*life*) _____?

14. The wind is blowing the (*leaf*) _____ off the trees.

PRACTICE 5 ▸ Irregular plural nouns. (Chart 5-2)
Complete each sentence with the plural form of the appropriate noun from the box.

child	foot	mouse	tooth
fish	man	sheep	woman

1. A dentist fixes _____ *teeth* _____.

2. In your culture, do _____ and women have the same freedoms?

3. Andrea has three _____. She has one daughter and two sons.

4. Many different kinds of _____ are in the sea.

5. We put shoes on our _____.

6. Cats like to catch _____.

7. Are men and _____ very different?

8. Baby lambs become _____.

a lamb

PRACTICE 6 ▸ Identifying nouns and adjectives. (Chart 5-3)
Write "N" over the nouns and "A" over the adjectives.

     N   A   N
1. Sarah lives in a new apartment.

2. It is very bright.

3. The rooms are large and have tall ceilings.

4. The building is next to a Japanese restaurant.

5. I love food from other countries.

6. Mexican food is spicy and delicious.

7. We have a wonderful café in our neighborhood.

8. The café serves good coffee.

9. Henry works for a large company.

10. Henry's job is interesting.

11. We have a difficult test today.

12. The students are nervous about the test.

PRACTICE 7 ▸ Identifying nouns and adjectives. (Chart 5-3)

Identify each word in the box as a noun or an adjective. Write the words in the correct column.

✓ bright	easy	job	poor	tree
✓ car	food	leg	quiet	wet
chair	fresh	nervous	rain	

NOUNS	ADJECTIVES
car	_bright_
_____	_____
_____	_____
_____	_____
_____	_____
_____	_____
_____	_____

PRACTICE 8 ▸ Adjectives. (Chart 5-3)

Write the adjective that has the opposite meaning.

1. happy _____ _sad_ _____
2. new _____
3. soft _____
4. beautiful _____
5. young _____
6. boring _____
7. fast _____
8. tall _____
9. easy _____
10. noisy _____

PRACTICE 9 ▸ Adjectives. (Chart 5-3)

Some nationality adjectives are listed below. Write the country next to each adjective.

NATIONALITY	COUNTRY
1. American	_USA / America_
2. Australian	_____
3. Canadian	_____
4. Chinese	_____

NATIONALITY	COUNTRY
5. Egyptian	_____
6. Indian	_____
7. Indonesian	_____
8. Italian	_____
9. Japanese	_____
10. Korean	_____
11. Malaysian	_____
12. Mexican	_____
13. Russian	_____
14. Saudi Arabian	_____

Write two more nationalities and countries.

15. _____   _____

16. _____   _____

PRACTICE 10 ▸ Identifying subjects. (Chart 5-4)

<u>Underline</u> the subject in each sentence.

1. The <u>weather</u> is very cold today.

2. Snow is falling.

3. The sun isn't shining.

4. Some people are throwing snowballs.

5. Some teenagers are building a huge snowman.

6. The kids and their parents are playing

   outside in the snow.

PRACTICE 11 ▸ Subjects and objects. (Chart 5-4)

Complete each sentence diagram with the subject, verb, and object.

1. Aiden likes coffee.

Aiden	*likes*	*coffee*
subject	verb	object

2. I drink tea.

subject	verb	object

3. Kylie is working.

subject	verb	object

4. She has a job.

subject	verb	object

5. Zac and Brandon are running.

subject	verb	object

6. They are playing soccer.

subject	verb	object

PRACTICE 12 ▸ Identifying objects. (Chart 5-4)
Which sentences have objects? Check (✓) them. Then <u>underline</u> the objects.

1. a. __✓__ I read the <u>news</u>.

   b. _____ I read every morning.

   c. __✓__ I read the <u>news</u> every morning.

2. a. _____ The kids play every day.

   b. _____ The kids play at the park.

   c. _____ The kids play soccer.

3. a. _____ My father cooks several times a week.

   b. _____ My father cooks eggs.

   c. _____ My father cooks eggs several times a week.

4. a. _____ Dogs chew bones.

   b. _____ Dogs chew furniture.

   c. _____ Dogs chew with their sharp teeth.

a dog with a bone

5. a. _____ We are eating.

   b. _____ We are eating lunch.

6. a. _____ Jan teaches English.

   b. _____ Jan teaches at a private college.

   c. _____ Jan teaches three days a week.

   d. _____ Jan teaches English three days a week.

7. a. _____ Joe is staying with his cousins.

   b. _____ Joe is staying with his cousins for one week.

8. a. _____ Pedro helps with the housework.

   b. _____ Pedro helps Maria with the housework.

PRACTICE 13 ▸ Complete/incomplete sentences. (Chart 5-4)

Check (✓) the incomplete sentences and correct them. Remember: A *complete sentence* is a group of words that has a subject and a verb. An *incomplete sentence* is a group of words that does not have a subject and a verb.

1. _✓_ I *work* in my home office in the morning.

2. _____ My parents work at a university.

3. _____ My father in the library.

4. _____ Is a teacher.

5. _____ My mother a professor.

6. _____ Is an excellent professor.

7. _____ I study at the university.

8. _____ The university many interesting and useful classes.

9. _____ Education is important for my family.

PRACTICE 14 ▸ Subject and object pronouns. (Chart 5-5)

Write *I, me, he, him*, etc.

1. Susan knows Thomas. _____*She*_____ knows _____*him*_____ well.

2. Thomas knows Susan. _____ knows _____ well.

3. Susan helps her co-workers. _____ helps _____ a lot.

4. Thomas helps his co-workers. _____ helps _____ a lot.

5. Susan and Thomas help their co-workers. _____ help _____ a lot.

6. Thomas and Susan rarely see Mr. Jones. _____ don't know _____ well.

7. Thomas and Susan rarely see Mrs. Jones. _____ don't know _____ well.

8. Susan and Thomas don't talk to their neighbors very much. _____ don't know _____ well.

9. The neighbors don't talk to Susan and Thomas very much. _____ don't know _____ well.

PRACTICE 15 ▸ Subject and object pronouns. (Chart 5-5)

Complete the sentences with the correct subject or object pronouns.

1. Grandpa John is in the picture. Do you see _____*him*_____?

2. Grandma Ella is in the picture. Do you see _____?

3. My son and daughter are in the picture. Do you see _____?

4. Your brother is in the picture. Do you see _____?

5. I am in the picture. Do you see _____?

6. Your brother and I are in the picture. Do you see _____?

7. King, our dog, is in the picture. Do you see _____?

8. Queen, our cat, is in the picture. Do you see _____?

9. I don't see your sister. Where is _____?

10. I don't see King. Where is _____?

11. I don't see the dog and cat. Where are _____?

12. I don't see my son. Where is _____?

13. I don't see my brother and you. Where are _____?

14. I don't see you. Where are _____?

PRACTICE 16 ▸ Object pronouns. (Chart 5-5)

Choose the correct response for each question.

1. Where do you buy apples?
   a. I buy at the farmers' market.   (b.) I buy them at the farmers' market.

2. When do you see the manager, Mr. Owens?
   a. I see him on Mondays.   b. I see on Mondays.

3. Where do you keep your phone?
   a. I keep in my pocket.   b. I keep it in my pocket.

4. Where do you watch TV?
   a. I watch in the living room.   b. I watch it in the living room.

5. What time do you set your alarm clock for?
   a. I set it for 7:00 A.M.   b. I set for 7:00 A.M.

PRACTICE 17 ▸ Object pronouns. (Chart 5-5)

Write *her*, *him*, *it*, or *them*.

1. A: When do you take your children to school?

   B: I take _____*them*_____ at 8:30.

2. A: When do you have breakfast?

   B: I have _____ at 9:00.

3. A: When do you call your friends?

   B: I call _____ in the evening.

4. A: When do you call your husband?

   B: I call _____ during lunch.

5. A: When do you visit your parents?

   B: I visit _____ on weekends.

6. A: When do you check your email?

   B: I check _____ when I wake up.

7. A: When do you listen to music?

   B: I listen to _____ in the car.

8. A: When do you talk to your teacher, Mrs. Davis?

   B: I talk to _____ after class.

9. A: When do you see Mr. Gómez?

   B: I see _____ in class.

PRACTICE 18 ▸ Subject and object pronouns. (Chart 5-5)

Use pronouns to complete the sentences.

1. A: How are Mr. and Mrs. Carson?

   B: _____*They*_____ are fine. _____*They*_____ are taking care of their grandchildren

   right now. They enjoy taking care of _____*them*_____.

2. A: Do you know Nathan and Vince?

   B: Yes, I do. _____ are in my chemistry class. I sit behind _____.

   _____ help me with my homework. The class is really hard, and I don't

   always understand _____.

3. A: That's Ms. Williams. Do you know _____?

   B: Yes, I do. _____ is the kindergarten teacher. The kids love

   _____.

4. A: Would you like to join Paul and me for dinner this evening?

   B: Yes, _____ would. Thank you. Can I bring something? Do you want

   _____ to bring a salad?

   A: No, thanks. Paul is cooking, and _____ has everything he needs.

PRACTICE 19 ▸ Review: subject and object pronouns and possessive adjectives. (Charts 2-7 and 5-5)

Review the information. Complete the sentences.

SUBJECT PRONOUNS	POSSESSIVE ADJECTIVES	OBJECT PRONOUNS
I	my	me
you	your	you
she	her	her
he	his	him
it	its	it
we	our	us
they	their	them

1. I have a book. _____My_____ book is red. Please give it to _____me_____.

2. You have a book. _____Your_____ book is red. I'm giving it to _____you_____.

3. She has a book. _____ book is red. Please give it to _____.

4. He has a book. _____ book is red. Please give it to _____.

5. We have books. _____ books are red. Please give them to _____.

6. They have books. _____ books are red. Please give them to _____.

7. I have a female cat. _____ fur is black. I like to play with _____.

8. I have a male cat. _____ fur is brown. I like to play with _____.

9. My new car is blue. _____ seats are red. I love driving _____.

PRACTICE 20 ▸ Review: subject and object pronouns and possessive adjectives. (Charts 2-7 and 5-5)

Complete the sentences with the correct words.

1. Hi. (*I* / *My* / *Me*) _____My_____ name is Kathy. How are you?

2. This isn't my textbook. It doesn't belong to (*I* / *my* / *me*) _____.

3. Where is Jon? I don't see (*he* / *his* / *him*) _____. I don't see (*he* / *his* / *him*)

   _____ bike.

4. Your dress is beautiful. Is (*it / your / she*) _____ new?

5. Do (*you / your / you're*) _____ have a charger? My phone is dead.

6. We have two children. (*We / Our / Us*) _____ son is three, and (*we / our / us*) _____ daughter is five.

7. Dogs like to hide (*it / their / them*) _____ bones.

PRACTICE 21 ▶ Review: subject and object pronouns and possessive adjectives. (Charts 2-7 and 5-5)

Complete the sentences with the correct words.

1. Frederick is an artist. (*He / His / Him*) _____He_____ draws cartoons. (*He / His / Him*) _____ cartoons are very funny. I like to watch (*he / his / him*) _____ when he draws.

2. The kids are doing (*they / them / their*) _____ homework. (*They / Them / Their*) _____ are working hard. Sometimes I help (*they / them / their*) _____ with (*they / them / their*) _____ homework.

3. Mary is a surgeon. (*She / Her*) _____ works long hours. (*She / Her*) _____ family doesn't see (*she / her*) _____ very much.

4. Mr. and Mrs. Cook are on vacation. I am taking care of (*they / them / their*) _____ dog and cat. (*They / Them / Their*) _____ dog likes to play, but (*they / them / their*) _____ cat likes to sleep.

5. My husband and (*I / me / my*) _____ own a restaurant together. We enjoy (*we / our / us*) _____ work. Sometimes (*we / our / us*) _____ friends and family help (*we / our / us*) _____ at the restaurant.

PRACTICE 22 ▶ Prepositions. (Chart 5-6)
Underline the prepositions.

1. Marta talks <u>to</u> her sister every day.

2. Jenna is leaving with her roommate.

3. Is this gift for me?

4. Michael is sitting between Bill and Luisa.

5. I live near my parents.

PRACTICE 23 ▸ Objects of prepositions. (Chart 5-6)
Choose the correct answers.

1. My sister lives in New York. I talk to she /(her) on the phone every week.

2. We are going out for coffee. Would you like to come with we / us?

3. What is this package? Is it for I / me?

4. I have two classes on Monday. I take a lunch break between they / them.

5. This gift is for you / your. It is from my brother and I / me.

6. Where is my backpack? My phone is in it / him.

7. I know Bill very well. I live near he / him and his wife.

8. I don't know Professor Li, but I know about she / her. She teaches chemistry at my college.

PRACTICE 24 ▸ Possessive adjectives and possessive pronouns. (Chart 5-7)
Complete the sentences with possessive adjectives and possessive pronouns.

1. It's his car. It's _____his_____.

2. It's her car. It's _____.

3. They're our cars. They're _____.

4. It's my car. It's _____.

5. It's your car. It's _____.

6. It's their car. It's _____.

7. The car belongs to her. It's _____her_____ car.

8. The car belongs to me. It's _____ car.

9. The car belongs to him. It's _____ car.

10. The car belongs to them. It's _____ car.

11. The car belongs to you. It's _____ car.

12. The car belongs to us. It's _____ car.

PRACTICE 25 ▸ Possessive adjectives and possessive pronouns. (Chart 5-7)
Choose the correct answers.

1. A: Is this (my)/ mine book?

   B: No, it's not your / yours. It's my / mine.

   A: Where's my / mine?

   B: It's in your / yours backpack.

2. A: Ingrid is here today. Is that her / hers car?

   B: No, it's not her / hers. She doesn't have a car. She always rides her / hers bike

   to school.

3. A: Don't forget your / yours jacket.

   B: That jacket is not my / mine.

   A: Michael has a blue jacket. I think that it is him / his.

4. A: We need to get off the bus now.

   B: No, not yet. This isn't our / ours bus stop.

   A: Are you sure?

   B: Yes. This stop is next to the museum. Our / Ours is by the library.

5. A: I'm calling the neighbors. Their / Theirs cat is in our backyard.

   B: That cat isn't their / theirs. That cat is gray. Our / Ours neighbors have a black and

   white cat.

PRACTICE 26 ▶ Possessive nouns. (Chart 5-8)
Complete the sentences with the correct nouns.

1. Jim's dog is active.

   The _____*dog*_____ belongs to _____*Jim*_____ .

2. Bill's car is new.

   The _____ belongs to _____ .

3. The teacher's desk is next to mine.

   The _____ belongs to the _____ .

4. The students' schedules are ready.

   The _____ belong to the _____ .

5. I'm going to buy my parents' truck.

   The _____ belongs to my _____ .

6. Where are the professors' offices?

   The _____ belong to the _____ .

PRACTICE 27 ▶ Possessive nouns. (Chart 5-8)
Choose the meaning of each noun in **bold**: *one* or *more than one*.

	HOW MANY?	
1. My **friend's** parents are very friendly.	one	more than one
2. Where is your **parents'** house?	one	more than one

3. The **doctors'** offices are near the hospital.	one	more than one
4. The **doctor's** office is near the hospital.	one	more than one
5. Our **co-worker's** schedule changes every week.	one	more than one
6. Your **daughters'** bedroom is very large.	one	more than one
7. The **dog's** toys are all over the yard.	one	more than one

PRACTICE 28 ▸ Possessive nouns. (Chart 5-8)
Add an apostrophe (') where necessary.

1. Where is Ben's calculator?

2. Dans daughter is a university professor.

3. Who has the teachers pen?

4. My sisters baby doesn't sleep very much.

5. Dr. Smiths nurse is very helpful.

6. My pets names are Ping and Pong.

7. All our neighbors yards have flower and vegetable gardens.

8. What is your mothers maiden* name?

PRACTICE 29 ▸ Possessive nouns. (Chart 5-8)
Add **'s** where necessary or **Ø** (nothing).

1. Tom_'s___ job is very interesting.

2. Tom_Ø__ works for a large airline.

3. Tom_____ buys airplanes.

4. Tom_____ wife, Olga, works at home.

5. Olga_____ designs web pages.

6. Olga_____ is artistic.

7. Olga_____ websites are very creative.

Maiden name is a married woman's last name (family name) before she got married.

PRACTICE 30 ▸ Possessive nouns. (Chart 5-8)
Read the story. Then complete the sentences with the correct possessive names.

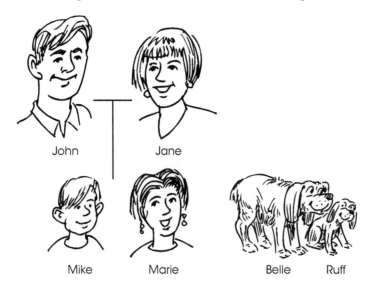

John   Jane

Mike   Marie   Belle   Ruff

Jane and John are married. They have one son and one daughter. Their son is Mike and their daughter is Marie. They also have two dogs: Belle and her puppy, Ruff.

1. Jane is _____ John's _____ wife.

2. John is _____ husband.

3. Marie is _____ sister.

4. Belle is _____ mother.

5. Mike is _____ brother.

6. Ruff is _____ son.

7. Mike is Jane and _____ son.

8. Marie is John and _____ daughter.

PRACTICE 31 ▸ Possessive noun or *is*. (Chart 5-8)
Choose the meaning of *'s*: possessive or *is*.

1. Bob's happy.   possessive   (is)

2. Bob's family is happy.   possessive   is

3. My teacher's not at school today.   possessive   is

4. The substitute teacher's nice.   possessive   is

5. Bill's manager went on vacation.   possessive   is

6. Bill's managing the office.   possessive   is

7. Bill's a good manager.   possessive   is

8. Bill's co-workers like him.   possessive   is

PRACTICE 32 ▸ Whose. (Chart 5-9)
Make questions with **Whose**.

1. book \ this _____Whose book is this?_____

2. glasses \ these _____

3. toy \ this _____

4. keys \ these _____

5. shoes \ these _____

6. shirt \ this _____

7. phone \ this _____

8. pens \ these _____

PRACTICE 33 ▸ Whose. (Chart 5-9)
Make questions with the given words.

1. is \ project \ that \ whose

    _____Whose project is that?_____

2. whose \ are \ children \ those

    _____

3. who \ next \ is

    _____

4. are \ whose \ shoes \ in the middle of the floor

    _____

5. today \ absent \ is \ who

    _____

6. package \ whose \ this \ is

    _____

PRACTICE 34 ▸ Whose and who's. (Chart 5-9)
Choose the correct response for each sentence.

1. Whose are these?
   a. Pat's.   b. Pat.

2. Who's on the phone?
   a. Mr. Smith.   b. Mr. Smith's.

3. Who's coming?
   a. Some teachers.   b. Some teachers'.

4. Whose sweater is on the chair?
   a. Pam.   b. Pam's.

5. Who's going to help you with your homework?
   a. Andy.   b. Andy's.

6. Whose schedule do you have?
   a. Mark.   b. Mark's.

7. Whose is this?
   a. My.   b. Mine.

PRACTICE 35 ▸ *Whose* and *who's*. (Chart 5-9)
Write **Whose** or **Who's**.

1. _____*Who's*_____ that?

2. _____ is that?

3. _____ coming?

4. _____ ready?

5. _____ glasses are these?

6. _____ lunch is this?

7. _____ car is in the driveway?

8. _____ working tomorrow?

9. _____ outside?

10. _____ work is this?

PRACTICE 36 ▸ Regular and irregular possessives. (Charts 5-8 and 5-10)
Choose the meaning of each noun in **bold**: *one* or *more than one*.

		HOW MANY?
1. The **dogs'** food is in the kitchen.	one	(more than one)
2. The **cat's** dishes are in the garage.	one	more than one
3. The **teachers'** office is near the classrooms.	one	more than one
4. That **woman's** grandchildren are noisy.	one	more than one
5. Where is the **women's** clothing department?	one	more than one
6. I'm looking for the **men's** restroom.	one	more than one
7. The **man's** children are waiting outside.	one	more than one
8. The **child's** toys are on the floor.	one	more than one
9. The **children's** toys aren't in the closet.	one	more than one

PRACTICE 37 ▸ Regular and irregular possessives. (Charts 5-8 and 5-10)
Make possessive phrases with the given words.

1. (one)   *boy \ truck*   the ___boy's truck___
2. (five)   *boys \ trucks*   the ___boys' trucks___
3. (three) *girls \ bikes*   the _____
4. (one)   *girl \ bike*   the _____
5. (four)   *children \ toys*   the _____
6. (six)   *students \ passwords*   the _____
7. (one)   *woman \ books*   the _____
8. (five)   *women \ books*   the _____
9. (two)   *people \ ideas*   some _____
10. (one)   *person \ ideas*   a _____
11. (three) *men \ coats*   the _____
12. (one)   *man \ coats*   the _____

PRACTICE 38 ▸ Regular and irregular possessives. (Charts 5-8 and 5-10)
Check (✓) the incorrect sentences and correct them.

1. _✓_ The ~~childrens'~~ school is down the street.   *children's*

2. _____ Several student's parents help at school.

3. _____ I have one brother. I like my brother's friends'.

4. _____ My brother's friend is very funny.

5. _____ I offered to fix my neighbor's computer.

6. _____ I like hearing other peoples' opinions.

7. _____ Womans' opinions are frequently different from men's opinions.

8. _____ Do you and your husband's agree very often?

PRACTICE 39 ▸ Review. (Chapter 5)
Choose the correct answers.

1. Where do _____ live?
   a. she   b. he   c.) you   d. them

2. New York and Toronto are big _____.
   a. citys   b. cities   c. city's   d. cities'

3. Dr. Ruíz is my dentist and neighbor. _____ is very helpful.
   a. We   b. She   c. They   d. You

4. This is our apartment. _____ is very comfortable.
   a. It   b. We   c. She   d. He

5. These are our seats. Do you want to sit next to _____?
   a. we   b. our   c. it   d. us

6. The students are going to the movies. Their teacher is taking _____.
   a. we   b. us   c. they   d. them

7. Many _____ in the neighborhood work from their homes.
   a. womens   b. woman   c. women   d. womans

8. You and _____ like to read the same books and listen to the same music.
   a. me   b. I   c. him   d. her

9. Paul is an active child. Children like to play with _____.
   a. her   b. he   c. him   d. she

10. _____ bird has a vocabulary of fifteen words.
    a. Our   b. We   c. I   d. Us

11. I love _____.
    a. China food   b. food Chinese   c. food China   d. Chinese food

12. _____ car is in the driveway?
    a. Whose   b. Who is   c. Who's   d. Who

PRACTICE 40 ▶ Review. (Chapter 5)
Choose the correct answers.

1. These _____ are delicious.
   a. strawberry   b. strawberrys   c. strawberries   d. strawberry's

2. Twenty _____ are in our class.
   a. people   b. peoples   c. person   d. people's

3. You need to wear _____ today. It's very cold.
   a. clothes warm   b. warm clothes   c. warms clothes   d. clothes warms

4. Please give this package to Ben and Vanessa. It is a gift for _____.
   a. they   b. them   c. their   d. theirs

5. This book is yours. That book is _____.
   a. my   b. mine   c. mine's   d. ours'

6. My _____ name is Ernesto.
   a. father   b. fathers   c. fathers'   d. father's

7. _____ keys are these?
   a. Who's   b. Whose   c. Who   d. Who are

8. _____ coming to the party?
   a. Who's   b. Whose   c. Who   d. Who are

9. I found two _____ backpacks in the park.
   a. girls   b. girl's   c. girls'   d. girl

10. My _____ are older than me.
    a. brother   b. brother's   c. brothers   d. brothers'

11. My _____ teacher is very patient.
    a. children's   b. childrens'   c. childs'   d. children

12. This is our hotel room and that room is _____.
    a. theirs'   b. their's   c. their   d. theirs

PRACTICE 41 ▸ Review. (Chapter 5)
Correct the mistakes.

               tomatoes
1. I need two ~~tomato~~ for the salad.

2. The babys are sleeping.

3. Tom is my neighbor. Me and him are goods friends.

4. We are going to the cafeteria. Would you like to join we?

5. Jenny lives near my husband and I.

6. Is this you book? It isn't my.

7. The English teachers share an office. The teachers office is in Room 119. Theirs office

   is large.

8. Luca brothers' live in Italy.

9. Who's keys are these? They aren't mine keys.

10. A pediatrician is a childrens' doctor.

CHAPTER 6

Count and Noncount Nouns

PRACTICE 1 ▶ Count and noncount nouns. (Chart 6-1)
Look at the <u>underlined</u> noun. Is it count or noncount?

1. My parents always give me good <u>advice</u>.	count	(noncount)
2. Do you want <u>sugar</u> in your coffee?	count	noncount
3. This is an interesting <u>book</u>.	count	noncount
4. I have a lot of <u>homework</u> today.	count	noncount
5. I need some <u>furniture</u> for my apartment.	count	noncount
6. I need a table and some <u>chairs</u>.	count	noncount
7. Why do you have three <u>phones</u>?	count	noncount
8. My sister wears a lot of <u>jewelry</u>.	count	noncount
9. She is wearing five <u>bracelets</u>.	count	noncount
10. My favorite snacks are popcorn and <u>ice cream</u>.	count	noncount

PRACTICE 2 ▶ Count and noncount nouns. (Chart 6-1)
Write "C" for count or "NC" for noncount.

1. __C__ girls
2. _____ girl
3. _____ children
4. _____ traffic
5. _____ cars
6. _____ rice
7. _____ money
8. _____ coin

9. _____ help
10. _____ teacher
11. _____ fruit
12. _____ apple
13. _____ salt
14. _____ words
15. _____ vocabulary
16. _____ mail

PRACTICE 3 ▶ Count and noncount nouns. (Chart 6-1)
Match the noncount noun with the count noun that is close in meaning.

COUNT	NONCOUNT
1. a job __d__	a. furniture
2. an assignment for school _____	b. vocabulary
3. a song _____	c. music
4. words _____	✓ d. work
5. some facts _____	e. jewelry
6. a suggestion _____	f. information
7. a chair, a desk, a table _____	g. money
8. a banana, an apple _____	h. fruit
9. a dollar _____	i. homework
10. some letters and bills _____	j. advice
11. a lot of cars _____	k. mail
12. a bracelet, a necklace, a ring _____	l. traffic

a bracelet

a necklace

a ring

PRACTICE 4 ▶ Singular and plural count and noncount nouns. (Chart 6-1)
Complete each word with **-s** or **Ø** (nothing).

1. a book __Ø__, one book_____, two book_____, fifty book_____

2. a job_____, one job_____, five job_____, a lot of job_____

3. information_____, some information_____, a lot of information_____

4. a fact_____, one fact_____, three fact_____, a lot of fact_____

PRACTICE 5 ▶ Count and noncount nouns. (Chart 6-1)
Choose all the words that can come in front of each noun.

1. a   one   (five)   (a lot of)   phones
2. a   one   five   a lot of   phone
3. a   one   five   a lot of   assignments
4. a   one   five   a lot of   homework

5. a	one	five	a lot of	mistakes
6. a	one	five	a lot of	advice
7. a	one	five	a lot of	food
8. a	one	five	a lot of	salt
9. a	one	five	a lot of	bowl
10. a	one	five	a lot of	soup

PRACTICE 6 ▸ Count and noncount nouns. (Chart 6-1)
Write all the words from the box for each noun.

| a | a lot of | one | ten | twenty |

1. _____*a, one*_____ coin

2. _____ coins

3. _____ money

4. _____ water

5. _____ book

6. _____ information

7. _____ teacher

8. _____ students

PRACTICE 7 ▸ Noun review. (Charts 5-1 and 5-2)
Complete each sentence with a word from the box. Make the word plural when necessary. Use each word only once.

child	foot	help	✓ money	traffic
city	fruit	horse	monkey	weather
country	furniture	man	tomato	work

1. I have a lot of _____*money*_____ in my wallet. I'm going shopping.

2. Cowboys ride _____.

3. I would like to visit many _____ in Canada. I'd like to visit Vancouver, Victoria, Quebec City, Toronto, and some others.

4. Canada, the United States, and Mexico are _____ in North America.

5. _____ live in trees.

6. Barbara has four suitcases. She can't carry all of them. She needs some
_____.

7. The bridge has a lot of _____ during rush hour.

8. My _____ are seven years old. They are twins.

9. We need a new bed, a new couch, and some new chairs. We need some
_____.

a monkey

10. People wear shoes on their _____.

11. I like pears, oranges, and bananas. I eat a lot of _____.

12. I would like a salad with lettuce and _____ for dinner.

13. When the temperature is around 35°C (77°F), I'm comfortable. I don't like very hot _____.

14. I'm not busy today. I don't have much _____ to do.

15. Some _____ have mustaches.

a pear

PRACTICE 8 ▸ A vs. an. (Chart 6-2)
Write *a* or *an*.

1. __*an*__ idea

2. _____ office

3. _____ elephant

4. _____ university

5. _____ uncle

6. _____ interesting idea

7. _____ hour

8. _____ house

9. _____ hungry animal

10. _____ upset child

PRACTICE 9 ▸ A vs. an. (Chart 6-2)
Write *a* or *an*.

1. I need to see __*a*__ doctor.

2. I have _____ headache.

3. I have _____ appointment in _____ hour.

4. _____ healthy person gets regular exercise.

5. The Browns own _____ house.

6. Gary and Joel are having _____ argument in the cafeteria. It is _____ uncomfortable situation.

7. Are you _____ hard worker?

8. Janet is _____ professor. She works at _____ university.

9. The store manager is talking to _____ angry woman.

10. Bill is _____ uncle. He has _____ niece and two nephews.

PRACTICE 10 ▶ A/an and some. (Chart 6-3)
Write each word from the box in the correct column.

advice	dog	hour	letter	umbrella
✓ aunt	elevator	house	mail	umbrellas
cousin	furniture	idea	suggestion	university

A	*AN*	*SOME*
_____	_____*aunt*_____	_____
_____	_____	_____
_____	_____	_____
_____	_____	_____
_____	_____	_____
_____	_____	_____

an elevator

PRACTICE 11 ▶ A/an and some. (Chart 6-3)
Write **a/an** or **some**. Are the nouns singular or plural?

1. Bob has _____*a*_____ book on his desk. (singular) plural

2. Bob has ____*some*____ books on his desk. singular (plural)

3. I see _____ desk in this room. singular plural

4. I see _____ desks in this room. singular plural

5. I would like _____ apple. singular plural

6. The kids want _____ apples too. singular plural

7. Do you have _____ mail for me? singular plural

8. I need to move _____ furniture downstairs. singular plural

9. Did you eat _____ sandwich? singular plural

10. Did you cook _____ rice? singular plural

PRACTICE 12 ▸ A/an and some. (Chart 6-3)
Write *a/an* or *some*.

1. Here is _____*a*_____ letter for you.

2. Here is _____ mail for you.

3. _____ teachers give a lot of homework.

4. I have _____ long assignment.

5. The teacher has _____ interesting idea for today's discussion.

6. _____ ideas take several days to discuss.

7. Dr. Roberts is _____ very special teacher.

8. He gives _____ interesting lectures.

9. Are _____ students working on their projects?

10. Is _____ assistant teacher helping them?

PRACTICE 13 ▸ Review. (Charts 6-1 → 6-3)
Choose all the correct sentences.

1. (a.) We are learning a lot of vocabulary.
   (b.) We are learning some vocabulary.
   c. We are learning some vocabularies.

2. a. Our teacher gives a lot of homeworks.
   b. Our teacher gives a lot of homework.
   c. Our teachers gives a lot of assignment.

3. a. Let's listen to music.
   b. Let's listen to some music.
   c. Let's listen to a music.

4. a. Do you have some advice for me?
   b. Do you have an advice for me?
   c. Do you have a suggestion for me?

5. a. I have job.
   b. I have a job.
   c. I have some job.

6. a. I would like interesting job.
   b. I would like an interesting job.
   c. I would like some interesting job.

PRACTICE 14 ▸ Measurements with noncount nouns. (Chart 6-4)

Write the name of the item for each picture. Use the expressions in the box.

✓ a bag of	a box of	a carton of
a bar of	a bunch of	a jar of
a bottle of	a can of	a tube of

1. _____*a bag of rice*_____

2. _____

3. _____

4. _____

5. _____

6. _____

7. _____

8. _____

9. _____

PRACTICE 15 ▸ Units of measure. (Chart 6-4)

What can you find at a store or restaurant? Complete each phrase with nouns from the box. You may use some nouns more than once.

bananas	cheese	lettuce	rice
bread	honey	oil	toothpaste
cereal	ice cream	paper	water

1. a box of _____*cereal, rice, paper*_____

2. a sheet of _____

3. a head of _____

4. a piece of _____

5. a loaf of _____

6. a bunch of _____

7. a bowl of _____

8. a bottle of _____

9. a jar of _____

honey

10. a tube of _____

PRACTICE 16 ▸ Review: *A/an* or *some*, and measurements. (Charts 6-3 and 6-4)
Write *a/an* or *some*.

1. *I'm hungry. I'd like ...*

    a. _____*a*_____ piece of chicken.

    b. _____ fruit.

    c. _____ food.

    d. _____ bowl of ice cream.

    e. _____ apple.

    f. _____ can of soup.

    g. _____ rice.

    h. _____ strawberries.

2. *I'm thirsty. I'd like ...*

    a. _____*some*_____ water.

    b. _____ bottle of water.

    c. _____ juice.

    d. _____ glass of milk.

    e. _____ cup of coffee.

    f. _____ strong coffee.

    g. _____ tea.

    h. _____ milk.

PRACTICE 17 ▸ *Much/many*. (Chart 6-5)
Write *much* or *many*.

I need to go to the store. I don't have ...

1. _____*much*_____ coffee.

2. _____ bananas.

3. _____ fruit.

4. _____ eggs.

5. _____ rice.

6. _____ sugar.

7. _____ bread.

8. _____ food.

9. _____ cans of soup.

10. _____ peaches.

11. _____ orange juice.

12. _____ potatoes.

peaches

PRACTICE 18 ▸ A few/a little. (Chart 6-5)

Write *a few* or *a little*.

I need to go shopping. I need ...

1. ____*a little*____ salt.

2. _____ strawberries.

3. _____ pens.

4. _____ cheese.

5. _____ flour.

6. _____ rolls of toilet paper.

7. _____ bottles of water.

8. _____ tomatoes.

9. _____ tea.

10. _____ teabags.

a cup of tea
with a teabag

PRACTICE 19 ▸ Much/many/a few/a little. (Chart 6-5)

Choose the correct words. Add **-s** or **Ø** (nothing) to the nouns where necessary.

1. The teacher needs a few /(a little) information *Ø* about her students.

2. Do the students have much /(many) question *s* ?

3. Here are a few / a little new pen____ for you.

4. Do you have a few / a little minute____ to talk?

5. Andy doesn't drink much / many coffee____. He drinks a few / a little tea____.

6. You have much / many beautiful flower____ in your garden.

7. I have a few / a little flower____ in my garden and much / many vegetable____.

PRACTICE 20 ▸ How much/how many. (Chart 6-5)

Rick is going shopping. His roommate gives him a list. He needs to know the amount to buy.
Write questions with the words in the box. Use ***How much/How many ... do we need?***

✓carrots	cheese	eggs	flour	fruit	potatoes

1. ____*How many carrots do we need?*_____

2. _____

3. _____

4. _____

5. _____

6. _____

PRACTICE 21 ▸ Using *the*. (Chart 6-6)
Write *the* or **Ø** (nothing).

1. I'm going to __*the*__ store. I need to buy __Ø__ milk and __Ø__ bread.

2. Please put _____ milk in _____ refrigerator.

3. _____ moon is full tonight.

4. I love our new apartment. _____ kitchen is nice, and _____ bedrooms are big.

5. I have two sons. _____ boys want _____ new bicycles.

6. The kids are playing outside. _____ weather is beautiful.

PRACTICE 22 ▸ *The* vs. *a*. (Chart 6-6)
Write *the* or *a*.

1. These pants and shirts don't fit. __*The*__ pants are too big, and _____ shirts are too tight.

2. Here's some chicken. Be careful! _____ chicken is very spicy.

3. Rudy wants to give his wife _____ ring for their anniversary. _____ ring has three diamonds, and _____ diamonds are very large.

4. Rachel is looking at _____ picture of _____ dog and _____ baby. _____ baby is sleeping, and _____ dog is watching her.

5. Tommy is getting _____ new bike for his birthday. _____ bike is very fast, and he is excited to ride it.

6. Dr. Olsson is speaking with _____ new patient. _____ patient is scared because she needs emergency surgery.

7. Do you have _____ minute? I have _____ problem and would like your advice.

8. Andrew drives _____ company truck. _____ truck is big and uses a lot of gas. His company pays for _____ gas.

PRACTICE 23 ▸ General vs. specific. (Chart 6-7)
Does the word in *italics* have a general meaning or a specific meaning? Choose the correct word.

1. *Clothes* are expensive.	(general)	specific
2. The *clothes* in Jan's closet are expensive.	general	specific
3. *Lemons* are sour.	general	specific
4. I love *vegetables*.	general	specific
5. The *vegetables* on the counter are from my garden.	general	specific

6. How are the *carrots* in your salad? Are they sweet?   general   specific

7. *Computers* are important in our lives.   general   specific

8. I like the new *computers* at our office.   general   specific

PRACTICE 24 ▸ General vs. specific. (Charts 6-3 and 6-7)
Write *a/an*, *the*, or *Ø* (nothing).

1. I need _____Ø_____ sugar for my coffee.

2. _____ sugar is in the cupboard.

3. Dentists say _____ sugar is not good for our teeth.

4. I'd like _____ glass of water.

5. Ann would like _____ orange for a snack.

6. _____ oranges grow on trees.

7. Ken has _____ egg every day for lunch.

8. Are _____ eggs healthy?

9. _____ eggs in _____ refrigerator are old.

10. I'm going shopping. I need _____ bread and _____ cheese.

11. Jack is having _____ rice, _____ fish, and _____ bowl of soup for dinner.

12. Johnny, please feed _____ cat. He's hungry.

13. Do you like _____ cats?

14. Would you like _____ cat for a pet?

15. _____ cat in our driveway belongs to our neighbor.

PRACTICE 25 ▸ Article review. (Charts 6-3, 6-6, and 6-7)
Choose the sentence that is closest in meaning to the situation.

1. Mark is at a toy store. He sees five fire trucks. He buys one for his son.
   a. He buys a fire truck.   b. He buys the fire truck.

2. Pat is at a pet store. One turtle is for sale. She buys it.
   a. She buys a turtle.   b. She buys the turtle.

a turtle

3. Martha is leaving her apartment. Three bags are near the door. She takes one.
   a. She takes the bag.   b. She takes a bag.

4. Jane is sitting outside in her garden. It is midnight. She is looking up at the sky.
   a. She sees the moon.   b. She sees a moon.

5. I love ice cream. Vanilla ice cream is my favorite.
   a. I love the vanilla ice cream.   b. I love vanilla ice cream.

6. Alice is picking apples from an apple tree. It has only five apples. She picks all five.
   a. She takes the apples home.   b. She takes apples home.

7. Paul drives a small car. He wants to save gas.
   a. He doesn't like to drive big cars.   b. He doesn't like to drive the big cars.

8. Riley wants to go to the beach. The weather is nice.
   a. A sky is clear.   b. The sky is clear.

PRACTICE 26 ▸ *Some/any.* (Chart 6-8)

Choose the correct word. In some cases, both words may be correct.

1. Let's go outside. I need (some) / any fresh air.

2. I don't see some / any clouds in the sky.

3. There is some / any wind.

4. I don't feel some / any wind.

5. Do you have some / any time?

6. Sorry, I don't have some / any time right now.

7. I have some / any time tomorrow.

8. I need some / any money for the store.

9. Do you have some / any money?

10. Some / Any people carry a lot of money in their wallets.

PRACTICE 27 ▸ *Some/any.* (Chart 6-8)

Think about shopping. Write sentences about what you need and don't need. Use *some*/*any* and the words from the box. Add *-s/-es* where necessary. You can also use your own words.

avocado	egg	fruit	potato	soup
banana	fish	grape	rice	toothpaste
coffee	flour	meat	soap	vegetable

an avocado

1. I need _____, _____,

   _____, _____, and _____.

2. I don't need _____, _____, _____,

   _____, or _____.

PRACTICE 28 ▸ A/an or any. (Charts 6-3 and 6-8)

Choose *a*, *an*, or *any*. Remember, use *any* with noncount nouns and plural count nouns. Use *a* with singular count nouns.

I don't want …

1. (a)   an   any   low grade on my test.
2. a   an   any   low grades this year.
3. a   an   any   pets.
4. a   an   any   pet.
5. a   an   any   ice cream for dessert.
6. a   an   any   bowl of ice cream for dessert.
7. a   an   any   cup of coffee.
8. a   an   any   help.
9. a   an   any   homework.
10. a   an   any   assignment.
11. a   an   any   assignments.

PRACTICE 29 ▸ A/any. (Charts 6-3 and 6-8)

Write *a* or *any*. Use *a* with singular count nouns. Use *any* with noncount nouns and plural count nouns.

1. I don't have ___*any*___ money.
2. I don't have ___*a*___ job.
3. I don't have ___*any*___ brothers or sisters.
4. We don't need to buy _____ new furniture.
5. Mr. and Mrs. Kelly don't have _____ children.
6. We don't have _____ coffee in the house.
7. Ann doesn't want _____ cup of coffee.
8. I don't like this room because it doesn't have _____ windows.
9. Amanda has good grades. She doesn't need _____ tutor.
10. I don't need _____ help. I can finish my homework by myself.
11. I don't have _____ comfortable chair in my dorm room.
12. I'm getting along fine. I don't have _____ problems.
13. Joe doesn't have _____ car, so he takes the bus to school.
14. I don't have _____ homework to do tonight.

15. I don't need _____ new clothes.

16. I don't need _____ new suit.

PRACTICE 30 ▸ Review. (Chapter 6)
Draw a line through the expressions that <u>cannot</u> complete the sentences.

1. I need to buy ____ white sugar.
   a. ~~a~~
   b. ~~an~~
   c. some
   d. ~~any~~
   e. ~~two~~
   f. a lot of
   g. a bag of
   h. Ø

2. I don't need ____ brown sugar.
   a. some
   b. much
   c. a
   d. a lot of
   e. any
   f. two
   g. three bags of
   h. Ø

3. Do you need ____ flour?
   a. an
   b. any
   c. a
   d. a bag of
   e. some
   f. two bags of
   g. a lot of
   h. Ø

4. We need to buy ____ apples.
   a. a
   b. an
   c. some
   d. any
   e. two
   f. a lot of
   g. a bag of
   h. Ø

PRACTICE 31 ▸ Review. (Chapter 6)
Correct the mistakes.

1. Korea and Japan are ~~country~~ *countries* in Asia.

2. Does this town have many traffics at 5:00 P.M.?

3. Are you a hungry? Do you want some food?

4. My children come home every day with a lot of homeworks.

5. Michael is a vegetarian. He doesn't eat the meat or the fish.

6. My eggs and coffee don't taste very good. Eggs are very salty, and coffee is weak.

7. Claire is looking for new job. She has a little interviews this week.

8. I wear dresses for work and the jeans at home.

9. I'm going to bank. I need a money.

10. We need to get any furniture. Do you know good furniture store?

CHAPTER 7

More About the Present Tense

PRACTICE 1 ▸ Using *it* with time and dates. (Chart 7-1)
Read the message. Make questions for the answers. Begin each question with ***What***.

Course	**Beginning Grammar** ▾
To	Students
Date	Tuesday, March 2, 2021, 2:00 P.M.
Subject	Reminder

Hello everyone,

Your homework is due this afternoon. Please turn in your assignments as soon as possible.

Prof. Kamm

1. _____*What day is it?*_____ It's Tuesday.

2. _____ It's 2:00 P.M.

3. _____ It's March.

4. _____ It's 2021.

5. _____ It's March 2.

6. _____ It's two o'clock.

7. _____ It's the 2nd of March.

PRACTICE 2 ▸ Using *it* with time and dates. (Chart 7-1)
Choose the correct response to each question.

1. What's the date today?
   a. It's April 1.　　　　b. It's Monday.

2. What day is it?
   a. It's February 2.　　b. It's Friday.

3. What month is it?
   a. It's January 2nd.　　b. It's December.

4. What time is it?

   a. It's 9:55.   b. It's 9:55 o'clock.

5. What's the date today?

   a. It's Monday.   b. It's the 2nd of May.

PRACTICE 3 ▸ Prepositions of time. (Chart 7-2)

Complete each sentence with the correct preposition.

1. *I wake up …*

   a. _____*in*_____ the morning.

   b. _____ 7:00.

2. *My husband goes to work …*

   a. _____ 1:00 P.M.

   b. _____ the afternoon.

   c. _____ Mondays, Wednesdays, and Thursdays.

3. *I work …*

   a. _____ the evening.

   b. _____ night.

   c. _____ 5:00 _____ midnight.

   d. _____ Saturday.

   e. _____ Saturdays.

4. *My daughter was born …*

   a. _____ December.

   b. _____ December 26.

   c. _____ the afternoon.

   d. _____ 1:00, _____ the afternoon.

   e. _____ December 26, 2019.

   f. _____ 2019.

PRACTICE 4 ▸ Prepositions of time. (Chart 7-2)

Write *in, on, at, from*, or *to*.

1. I have English class _____*in*_____ the morning.

2. My first class begins _____ 9:00 A.M.

3. The class meets _____ 9:00 _____ 9:55.

4. I don't have class _____ Fridays.

5. My math class meets _____ the evenings.

6. I don't like to study _____ night.

7. I prefer to study _____ the afternoon.

8. There is no class _____ May 1st.

9. Summer vacation is _____ June _____ September.

PRACTICE 5 ▶ Talking about the weather. (Chart 7-3)
Look at the weather information in the chart.

CITY	TODAY'S TEMPERATURE		TODAY'S WEATHER
Moscow	0°C	32°F	partly cloudy, snow
Sydney	24°C	75°F	clear, dry
Seoul	5°C	41°F	heavy rain, strong winds
Cairo	38°C	100°F	sunny, dry

Part I. Make questions for the answers.

1. _How's the weather / What's the weather like in Seoul?_ It's stormy.

2. _____ It's 75°F.

3. _____ It's hot and sunny.

4. _____ It's freezing.

Part II. Choose *yes* or *no*.

5. It's chilly in Moscow.   (yes)   no

6. It's humid in Cairo.   yes   no

7. It's freezing in Seoul.   yes   no

8. It's nice in Sydney.   yes   no

PRACTICE 6 ▶ Asking about the weather. (Chart 7-3)
Complete the questions with the words from the box.

how's	it's	like	temperature	the weather

1. What's the weather _____ in your hometown?

2. _____ the weather in your hometown?

3. What's the average _____ in the summer?

4. How's _____ in Singapore right now?

5. Did Alice say _____ going to be hot and humid today?

PRACTICE 7 ▸ Questions: time and weather. (Chart 7-1 and 7-3)
Choose the correct answers.

1. What _____ the weather like today?
   a. is it   (b.) is

2. What month _____?
   a. is it   b. is

3. What _____ the date today?
   a. is it   b. is

4. What day _____?
   a. is it   b. is

5. What time _____?
   a. is it   b. is

6. How _____ the weather?
   a. is it   b. is

7. What year _____?
   a. is it   b. is

PRACTICE 8 ▸ *There + be.* (Chart 7-4)
Look at the picture of the business class. What do you see? Choose the correct verb. Then choose *yes* or *no*.

1. There is / are a professor.   yes   no

2. There is / are four students.   yes   no

3. There is / are a laptop.   yes   no

4. There is / are five tables.   yes   no

5. There is / are some chairs.   yes   no

6. There is / are a clock.   yes   no

7. There is / are a bookshelf.   yes   no

8. There is / are a TV.   yes   no

9. There is / are a board.   yes   no

10. There is / are two windows.   yes   no

PRACTICE 9 ▸ *There + be.* (Chart 7-4)

Make sentences about the picture. Use **there is** or **there are** and the words in parentheses.

1. (*some pictures*)   *There are some pictures.*

2. (*a couch*) _____

3. (*one table*) _____

4. (*four pillows*) _____

5. (*one lamp*) _____

6. (*two plants*) _____

7. (*a TV*) _____

8. (*some curtains*) _____

PRACTICE 10 ▸ *There + be: yes/no* questions. (Chart 7-5)

Write **is** or **are**.

1. A: _____ there two sandwiches in the picnic basket?

   B: Yes, there _____.

2. A: _____ there some pretzels?

   B: No, there _____.

3. A: _____ there a banana?

   B: No, there _____.

4. A: _____ two apples?

   B: Yes, there _____.

5. A: _____ there a bottle of mustard?

   B: Yes, there _____.

6. A: _____ there a carton of milk?

   B: No, there _____.

a picnic basket

PRACTICE 11 ▸ There + be: yes/no questions. (Chart 7-5)

You are new to a town. Make questions about the places in parentheses. Begin with **Is there** or **Are there**.

1. (a subway)   ___Is there a subway?_____

2. (a bus station)   _____

3. (good restaurants) _____

4. (an art museum)   _____

5. (nice parks)   _____

6. (a zoo)   _____

7. (movie theaters) _____

8. (a library)   _____

PRACTICE 12 ▸ There + be: questions with how many. (Chart 7-6)

Choose the correct nouns.

1. How many country / (countries) are there in the world?

2. How many lake / lakes are there in the world?

3. How many car / cars are there in the world?

4. How many word / words are there in a dictionary?

5. How many minute / minutes are there in a day?

6. How many second / seconds are there in a day?

7. How many star / stars are there in the sky?

8. How many airplane / airplanes are there in the sky?

PRACTICE 13 ▸ There + be: questions with how many. (Chart 7-6)

Complete each question with a word or phrase from the box. Begin with **How many**.

colors	✓ continents	days	letters	main languages	meters

1. ___How many continents are there_____ in the world? There are seven.

2. _____ in a year? There are 365.

3. _____ on the Thai flag? There are three.

4. _____ in a kilometer? There are 1,000.

5. _____ in the English alphabet? There are 26.

6. _____ in Canada? There are two: French and English.

PRACTICE 14 ▸ Prepositions of place. (Chart 7-7)
Write *in, on,* or *at*.

1. Marco lives ___in___ Italy.

2. Tina lives _____ Vancouver, Canada.

3. Tina works _____ Robson Street.

4. Margaret lives _____ 6456 Oak Street.

5. Margaret lives _____ Oak Street.

6. Jeffrey lives _____ Australia.

7. Jeffrey works _____ Park Street.

8. Jeffrey works _____ 5725 Park Street.

PRACTICE 15 ▸ Prepositions of place. (Chart 7-7)
Write *at* or *in*.

Ben is ...

1. ___at___ home.

2. _____ school for a meeting.

3. _____ work.

4. _____ the bedroom.

5. _____ the living room.

6. _____ the hospital visiting a friend.

7. _____ the post office.

8. _____ class.

9. _____ his hometown of Mountain View.

10. on the phone with someone _____ jail.

PRACTICE 16 ▸ Prepositions of place. (Chart 7-7)
Write *at, in,* or *on*.

1. Renata is sleeping. She is _____ her bedroom.

2. Jack is very sick. He is a patient. He is _____ the hospital.

3. Mrs. Nelson is a university professor. Her students are _____ class. They are sitting _____ the classroom.

4. Everyone in class is listening to the teacher. They are _____ school right now.

5. Kellen is absent today. He is _____ home.

6. His wife is not _____ home. She is _____ work.

7. Your shoes are _____ the hall.

8. My laptop is _____ my desk.

9. The teacher's books are _____ her desk _____ school.

10. Your keys are _____ the table _____ the kitchen.

PRACTICE 17 ▸ Prepositions of place. (Chart 7-7)
Complete the sentences about the Johnson family. Write *at* or *in*.

It's 10:00 A.M. Where is everyone?

1. Mr. Johnson is _____*in*_____ his office _____*at*_____ work.

2. Mrs. Johnson is _____ the library with her first-grade class.

3. Joe is _____ class _____ school.

4. Beth is sick _____ home _____ bed.

5. Rita is on vacation _____ Hawaii.

6. Bob is _____ work. He is working _____ a bookstore.

7. Grandma Johnson is _____ the hospital. She is very sick.

PRACTICE 18 ▸ More prepositions of place. (Chart 7-8)
Look at the kitchen. Choose the correct preposition for each sentence.

1. The teapot is in / on / under the stove.

2. The refrigerator is above / next to / below the microwave.

3. The plates are at / in / on the cabinet.

4. The microwave is between / behind / in front of the refrigerator and stove.

5. The plants are above / far from / near the clock.

6. The sink is above / below / between the clock.

7. The bread and olive oil are inside / far away from / on top of the counter.

PRACTICE 19 ▸ More prepositions of place. (Chart 7-8)
Complete each sentence with a preposition. There may be more than one possible completion.

1. The rabbit is _____*in / inside*_____ the hat.

2. The rabbit is _____ the hat.

3. The rabbit is _____ the hat.

4. The rabbit is _____ the hat.

5. The rabbit is _____ the hat.

6. The rabbit is _____ the hat.

7. The rabbit is _____ the hat.

8. The rabbit is _____ the hats.

PRACTICE 20 ▸ More prepositions of place. (Chart 7-8)
Complete each sentence with a preposition. There may be more than one possible answer.

1. The pencils are _____*in / inside*_____ the cup.

2. The pencils are _____ the lamp and the books.

3. The lamp is _____ the desk.

4. The bookshelf is _____ the desk.

5. The desk is _____ the bookshelf.

6. The clock is _____ the bookshelf.

PRACTICE 21 ▸ *Would like.* (Chart 7-9)

Complete the sentences with **would like**.

1. I _____ would like _____ to leave.

2. You _____ to leave.

3. He _____ to leave.

4. She _____ to leave.

5. The cat _____ to leave.

6. Mrs. Jones _____ to leave.

7. We _____ to leave.

8. They _____ to leave.

9. The students _____ to leave.

10. Their teacher _____ to leave.

11. My friend _____ to leave.

12. My parents _____ to leave.

PRACTICE 22 ▸ *Would like* vs. *like.* (Chart 7-10)

Decide the meaning of each sentence. Choose *want* or *like*.

1. I would like a cup of coffee.   (want)   like

2. I enjoy coffee in the morning.   want   like

3. Daniel enjoys video games.   wants   likes

4. Aisha would like to play a game.   wants   likes

5. I don't enjoy cold weather.   want   like

6. I would like to stay inside today.   want   like

PRACTICE 23 ▸ *Would like* vs. *like.* (Chart 7-10)

Choose the correct answer for each question.

1. A: Does Mark want to have a large family?
   B: Yes, he do / does / would.

2. A: Would you like something to drink?
   B: Yes, I do / does / would. Thank you.

3. A: Does your baby like vegetables?
   B: No, she do / doesn't / wouldn't, but she likes fruit.

4. A: Would you like to go to the football game?
   B: No, I don't / doesn't / wouldn't. I don't like sports, and I need to study today.

5. A: What would Claudia like for her birthday?
   B: She'd like / likes / liking some books.

6. A: Do you have any pets?
   B: No, I don't.
   A: Do you want a pet?
   B: Yes. I like / likes / would like animals. I like / likes / would like a pet dog.

PRACTICE 24 ▸ Verb review. (Chapters 1 → 5 and 7)
Complete the sentences with the correct form of the words in parentheses.

Sara *(not, have)* _____ a car. There *(be)* _____ a bus stop next to
                                    1   2

her apartment. On Mondays and Wednesdays, she *(take)* _____ the bus to school. On
                                                                          3

Tuesdays and Thursdays, she *(ride)* _____ with her roommate. Her roommate
                                              4

(have) _____ a new car. Today *(be)* _____ Tuesday. Sara *(ride)*
              5   6

_____ to school with her roommate right now. They usually *(listen)*
              7

_____ to music in the car, but right now they *(not, listen)* _____ to
       8   9

music. They *(talk)* _____ about their math class. There *(be)* _____ a
                              10   11

math test today. They *(be)* _____ nervous about the test.
                                      12

PRACTICE 25 ▸ Review. (Chapter 7)
Choose the correct answer for each sentence.

1. There _____ in our classroom.
   a. is twenty desks   b. are twenty desks   c. is twenty desk   d. are twenty desk

2. What _____ today?
   a. day is it   b. is day   c. day it   d. is it day

3. How many _____ there in your class?
   a. students are   b. student is   c. students   d. student

4. Dr. Smith is tired. She _____ to go home and sleep now.
   a. likes   b. would likes   c. would like   d. like

5. There _____ in a minute.
   a. is sixty second   b. are sixty second   c. is sixty seconds   d. are sixty seconds

6. The students _____ finish their work.
   a. needs to   b. need   c. needs   d. need to

7. What _____ the weather like in Bangkok?
   a. is   b. does   c. do   d. are

8. Philip lives _____ Dexter Avenue.
   a. in   b. at   c. on   d. next

9. Jason likes to sit _____ the room.
   a. in middle of   b. in the middle of   c. middle of   d. in middle

10. How _____ in Tokyo?
    a. the weather   b. is the weather   c. weather   d. is weather

11. Pam works _____ 1300 Lexington Avenue.
    a. next   b. at   c. in   d. on

12. I'm getting my hair cut _____ 2:45.
    a. in   b. on   c. from   d. at

13. The weather in my country is very hot _____ August.
    a. from   b. in   c. at   d. on

PRACTICE 26 ▶ Review. (Chapter 7)
Correct the mistakes.

1. There's three cars in the driveway. *(are written above "'s")*

2. What time it is?

3. Carolina was born in January 1, 2020.

4. I have class at 9:00 to 10:00.

5. Terry works on the afternoon.

6. My family always travels on June.

7. How the weather is in London?

8. What's the weather likes today?

9. There are a lot of traffic today.

10. Is there good restaurants in your city?

11. How many chapters is there in this book?

12. Julia lives on 107 Maple Street.

13. Chris is not in home right now.

14. He'd likes to watch a movie.

CHAPTER 8

Expressing Past Time, Part 1

PRACTICE 1 ▸ Simple past tense: *be.* (Chart 8-1)
Write the correct form of *be*.

NOW	AN HOUR AGO
1. I am here.	I ____was____ outside.
2. We are here.	We _____ outside.
3. She is here.	She _____ outside.
4. They are here.	They _____ outside.
5. He is here.	He _____ outside.
6. The cat is here.	The cat _____ outside.
7. My kids are here.	My kids _____ outside.
8. Al and Todd are here.	Al and Todd _____ outside.
9. Our teacher is here.	Our teacher _____ outside.
10. You are here.	You _____ outside.

PRACTICE 2 ▸ Simple past tense: *be.* (Chart 8-1)
Choose the correct form of the verb in each sentence.

1. My parents was /(were) at home last night.

2. Our next-door neighbors was / were at work.

3. I was / were at the library.

4. My roommate was / were there too.

5. She was / were across the table from me.

6. Our teacher was / were at the table next to us.

7. He was / were half-asleep.

8. We was / were at the library until closing time.

9. The library was / were open until 9:00 P.M.

10. My roommate and I was / were the last people to leave.

PRACTICE 3 ▸ Simple past tense of *be*: negative. (Chart 8-2)
Write *wasn't* or *weren't*.

Absent from School

1. I _____wasn't_____ at school yesterday.

2. You _____ at school yesterday.

3. Some students _____ at school yesterday.

4. They _____ at school yesterday.

5. Toshi _____ at school yesterday.

6. He _____ at school yesterday.

7. My teacher _____ at school yesterday.

8. Beth and Mark _____ at school yesterday.

9. Sarah _____ at school yesterday.

10. She and I _____ at school yesterday.

11. We _____ at school yesterday.

12. Our teacher _____ at school yesterday.

PRACTICE 4 ▸ Simple past tense of *be*: negative. (Chart 8-2)
Write *wasn't* or *weren't*.

A Bad Hotel

1. The hotel _____wasn't_____ nice.

2. My room _____ clean.

3. The beds _____ comfortable.

4. The pillows _____ soft.

5. The shower water _____ warm.

6. The elevators _____ fast.

7. The restaurant _____ good.

8. The food _____ fresh.

9. The hotel clerks _____ polite.

10. The pool _____ big.

PRACTICE 5 ▸ Simple past tense of *be*: negative. (Chart 8-2)
Make sentences about the people in the chart.

	MIKE	LORI	RICARDO	EVA
at work	x			
at school				
on vacation			x	
out-of-town		x		x

Where were they yesterday?

1. Mike *wasn't out-of-town yesterday. He was at work.*

2. Ricardo _____

3. Lori _____

4. Lori and Eva _____

PRACTICE 6 ▸ Simple past tense of *be*: negative. (Chart 8-2)
Make sentences about yourself when you were a child. Use **was** or **wasn't**.

1. (*shy*)   *I was / wasn't shy.*   4. (*active*) _____

2. (*happy*) _____   5. (*serious*) _____

3. (*quiet*) _____   6. (*noisy*) _____

PRACTICE 7 ▸ Simple past tense of *be*: questions. (Chart 8-3)
Make questions. Write **was** or **were**.

1. ___*Were*___ you home yesterday evening?

2. _____ your roommate home yesterday evening?

3. _____ he home yesterday evening?

4. _____ your parents home last weekend?

5. _____ they home last weekend?

6. _____ I home last weekend?

7. _____ the teacher home last night?

8. _____ your teacher home last night?

9. _____ Jan and I home yesterday evening?

10. _____ we home last weekend?

PRACTICE 8 ▸ Simple past tense of *be:* questions. (Chart 8-3)

Make two questions for each situation. The first question is a *yes/no* question, and the second is a *where* question. Give the answers for both questions. Use the places from the box.

✓ at the grocery store	at the library	at the train station
at home	at the mall	at the zoo

1. Jake and Kevin \ at a swimming pool

   A: _____Were Jake and Kevin at a swimming pool?_____

   B: _____No, they weren't._____

   A: _____Where were they?_____

   B: _____They were at the grocery store._____

2. Ellen \ at the library

   A: _____

   B: _____

   A: _____

   B: _____

3. you \ at a party

   A: _____

   B: _____

   A: _____

   B: _____

4. Thomas \ at the airport

   A: _____

   B: _____

   A: _____

   B: _____

5. your kids \ at school

   A: _____

   B: _____

   A: _____

   B: _____

6. you and Liz \ at the park

A: _____

B: _____

A: _____

B: _____

PRACTICE 9 ▶ Simple past tense of *be:* questions. (Chart 8-3)
Your friend was at a movie last night. Ask questions about the movie. Write **was** or **were**.

1. _____*Was*_____ it scary?

2. _____ you afraid?

3. _____ the characters interesting?

4. _____ the movie funny?

5. _____ the main actor good?

6. _____ she or he a good actor?

7. _____ the actors good?

8. _____ they good?

PRACTICE 10 ▶ Simple past tense: regular verbs. (Chart 8-4)
Write the simple past form of the verbs.

EVERY DAY	YESTERDAY
1. I study English.	I _____*studied*_____ English.
2. He studies English.	He _____ English.
3. We walk in the park.	We _____ in the park.
4. You work hard.	You _____ hard.
5. They smile.	They _____ .
6. The baby smiles.	The baby _____ .
7. Sonja talks on the phone.	Sonja _____ on the phone.
8. Tim helps his parents.	Tim _____ his parents.
9. I help my parents.	I _____ my parents.
10. She listens carefully.	She _____ carefully.
11. They listen carefully.	They _____ carefully.

PRACTICE 11 ▸ Simple past tense: regular verbs. (Chart 8-4)

Look at the activities and write simple past tense sentences about the people.

YESTERDAY	RUTH	DEB	BILL	STUART
cook breakfast	x		x	
watch TV		x	x	
text a friend	x			
exercise at a gym				x

1. Deb _____watched TV._____

2. Stuart _____

3. Ruth and Bill _____

4. Ruth also _____

5. Bill also _____

PRACTICE 12 ▸ Simple past tense: regular verbs. (Chart 8-4)

Complete each sentence with the simple past form of a verb from the box.

carry	cry	✓ finish	rub	stay	taste
clap	fail	learn	smile	stop	wait

1. I _____finished_____ my homework at nine o'clock last night.

2. We _____ some new vocabulary yesterday.

3. I _____ the soup before dinner last night. It was delicious.

4. Linda _____ for the bus at the corner yesterday.

5. The bus _____ at the corner. It was on time.

6. Ann _____ her suitcases to the bus station yesterday. They weren't heavy.

7. The baby _____ her eyes because she was sleepy.

8. I _____ home and watched a sad show on TV last night.

   I _____ at the end of the show.

9. Mike _____ his math test last week. He got most answers wrong.

10. Jane _____ at her kids. She was happy to see them.

8-A Summary of Spelling Rules for -ed Verbs

	END OF VERB → -ED FORM
RULE 1	CONSONANT + -e → ADD -d. smile → smiled erase → erased
RULE 2	ONE VOWEL + ONE CONSONANT → DOUBLE THE CONSONANT.* ADD -ed. stop → stopped rub → rubbed
RULE 3	TWO VOWELS + ONE CONSONANT → ADD -ed. DO NOT DOUBLE THE CONSONANT. rain → rained need → needed
RULE 4	TWO CONSONANTS → ADD -ed. DO NOT DOUBLE THE CONSONANT. count → counted help → helped
RULE 5	CONSONANT + -y → CHANGE -y TO -i. ADD -ed. study → studied carry → carried
RULE 6	VOWEL + -y → ADD -ed. DO NOT CHANGE -y TO -i. play → played enjoy → enjoyed

*EXCEPTIONS: Do not double *x* (*fix* + *-ed* = *fixed*). Do not double *w* (*snow* + *-ed* = *snowed*).

PRACTICE 13 ▶ Spelling rules: -ed verbs. (Chart 8-A)
Study each rule and the examples. Then write the simple past form of the verbs.

Rule 1. CONSONANT + -e → ADD -d.

1. like   → _____

2. close   → _____

3. shave   → _____

4. love   → _____

5. hate   → _____

6. exercise   → _____

Rule 2. ONE VOWEL + ONE CONSONANT → DOUBLE THE CONSONANT. ADD -ed.

7. plan   → _____

8. drop   → _____

9. clap   → _____

Rule 3. TWO VOWELS + ONE CONSONANT → ADD *-ed*. DO NOT DOUBLE THE CONSONANT.

10. join → _____

11. shout → _____

12. wait → _____

Rule 4. TWO CONSONANTS → ADD *-ed*. DO NOT DOUBLE THE CONSONANT.

13. point → _____

14. touch → _____

15. jump → _____

Rule 5. CONSONANT + *-y* → CHANGE *-y* TO *-i*. ADD *-ed*.

16. marry → _____

17. try → _____

18. hurry → _____

19. reply → _____

20. dry → _____

Rule 6. VOWEL + *-y* → ADD *-ed*. DO NOT CHANGE *-y* TO *-i*.

21. stay → _____

22. enjoy → _____

NOTE: Spelling rules for the two-syllable verbs *visit, answer, happen, occur, listen, open,* and *enter* are in Appendix 5 of this Workbook.

PRACTICE 14 ▸ Spelling practice: -ed. (Chart 8-A)
Write the *-ed* forms of these verbs.

	-ed			*-ed*
1. count	_counted_		7. close	_____
2. rain	_____		8. yawn	_____
3. help	_____		9. study	_____
4. plan	_____		10. worry	_____
5. dream	_____		11. drop	_____
6. erase	_____			

PRACTICE 15 ▸ Simple past tense: regular verbs. (Chart 8-4)
Complete each sentence with the simple past form of a verb from the box.

At School

ask	erase	finish	help	laugh	✓ walk	watch

1. Anna missed the bus yesterday, so she _____*walked*_____ to school.

2. I was ready for school yesterday. I _____ my homework before class.

3. We _____ a video in class yesterday.

4. The professor _____ the board with an eraser.

5. My classmate shared a joke. We _____ at the funny story.

6. Olivia _____ a question in class.

7. I had a problem with my homework. My teacher _____ me after class.

About the Weather

arrive	close	enjoy	play	rain	snow	stay

8. It's winter. The ground is white because it _____ yesterday.

9. There was a storm last week. My flight _____ at the airport two hours late.

10. It was sunny last weekend. The kids _____ basketball outside.

11. We _____ the beautiful weather.

12. The window was open. I _____ the window because it was cold outside.

13. The streets were wet this morning because it _____ last night.

14. The weather was terrible last night. We _____ home.

At Home

cook	invite	visit	want	wash	work

15. I have an office at home. I _____ from home yesterday.

16. After work, Dan _____ me. He is my friend.

17. Dan is a good cook. He _____ some delicious food last night.

18. I _____ my neighbors to my house. They had dinner with us.

19. The kids _____ ice cream after dinner.

20. I _____ the dirty dishes after dinner last night.

PRACTICE 16 ▸ Yesterday, last, and ago. (Chart 8-5)

Write *yesterday*, *last*, or *ago*.

My soccer team played …

1. _____last_____ night.
2. _____ afternoon.
3. _____ Wednesday.
4. _____ week.
5. _____ summer.
6. _____ month.
7. _____ evening.
8. three months _____.
9. two weeks _____.
10. one year _____.
11. _____ morning.
12. _____ weekend.

PRACTICE 17 ▸ Yesterday, last, and ago. (Chart 8-5)

Rewrite each *italicized* sentence. Use a time expression with *yesterday*, *last*, or *ago*.

1. It's 7:00. *At 6:55, Tim brushed his teeth.*

   _____Tim brushed his teeth five minutes ago._____

2. It's 3:00 in the afternoon. *The day before at 3:00, Bonnie walked to the park.*

   _____

3. This week Tom is on vacation. *The week before, he worked.*

   _____

4. It's 2021. *In 2016, Sam graduated from high school.*

   _____

5. It's Saturday. *The Thursday before, Jan worked 12 hours.*

   _____

6. It's March. *The January before, Martin stayed with his parents.*

   _____

7. It's 10:00 P.M. *The night before at 10:00, we streamed a movie.*

   _____

PRACTICE 18 ▸ Irregular verbs, Part I: Group 1. (Chart 8-6)

Write the simple past form of the verb.

EVERY DAY	YESTERDAY
1. I do my homework.	I _____ my homework.
2. He does his homework.	He _____ his homework.
3. Nora has a lot of homework.	She _____ a lot of homework.
4. You have cereal for breakfast.	You _____ cereal for breakfast.

EVERY DAY	YESTERDAY
5. The cat hides under the bed.	The cat _____ under the bed.
6. My roommate makes coffee.	My roommate _____ coffee.
7. The students pay for lunch.	They _____ for lunch.
8. We hear our neighbor play the drums.	We _____ our neighbor play the drums.

drums

PRACTICE 19 ▸ Irregular verbs, Part I: Group 2. (Chart 8-6)
Write the simple past form of the verbs in parentheses.

1. Greta (*become*) _____*became*_____ a nurse last year.

2. Paul (*sing*) _____ in the shower this morning.

3. I (*give*) _____ my sister a birthday gift.

4. My roommate (*drink*) _____ all the milk.

5. The phone (*ring*) _____ four times.

6. The kids (*begin*) _____ school last month.

7. We (*see*) _____ a rainbow yesterday afternoon.

8. I (*run*) _____ to the train station.

9. The teacher (*come*) _____ to class late today.

10. We (*sit*) _____ on a bench in the park.

PRACTICE 20 ▸ Irregular verbs, Part I: Group 3. (Chart 8-6)
Complete each sentence with the simple past form of a verb from the box. Use each verb one time.

✓ break	forget	speak	wear	write
choose	ride	wake	win	

1. Zac dropped his phone on the sidewalk. He _____*broke*_____ the screen.

2. Our basketball team _____ every game last month.

3. I don't have my phone with me. I _____ it at home.

4. The restaurant had a lot of desserts. I _____ chocolate cake.

5. That is my book. I _____ my name inside it.

6. Our teacher _____ a motorcycle to work yesterday.

7. It was cold and windy, so Terry _____ a jacket.

8. I called the clinic and _____ to the nurse.

9. Sara _____ up an hour late this morning. She missed her first class.

PRACTICE 21 ▸ Irregular verbs, Part I. (Chart 8-6)
Write the simple past form of the verbs in the box. Put the verbs in the correct place in the chart.

✓ become	do	give	make	sell	take
begin	drink	have	ride	sit	understand
break	eat	hear	run	speak	wake
choose	get	hide	see	stand	write

THE FINAL SOUND CHANGES TO *d*.	VOWELS CHANGE TO *a*.	VOWELS CHANGE TO *o*.	THE VOWEL CHANGES TO *oo*.
	became		

PRACTICE 22 ▸ Irregular verbs, Part I. (Chart 8-6)
Write the present form of the verbs in italics.

	PRESENT FORM
1. I *hid* my son's birthday gift in the closet.	*hide*
2. They *did* their homework in the library.	
3. We *paid* for our train tickets.	
4. I *had* a headache last night.	
5. We *made* sandwiches for lunch.	
6. The kids *swam* in the pool.	
7. Classes *began* an hour ago.	
8. We *saw* our teacher at the coffee shop.	
9. Jeff and Kevin *came* to class ten minutes late.	
10. They *forgot* their homework.	

11. We *sat* outside for lunch. _____

12. I *rang* the doorbell twice. _____

13. You *ran* to the bus stop. _____

14. We *heard* a funny story this morning. _____

15. I *rode* a horse last year. _____

16. We *drove* to New York last summer. _____

17. I *spoke* to the manager. _____

18. They *understood* the problem. _____

PRACTICE 23 ▸ Simple past: negative. (Chart 8-7)

Write the negative form of the verb. Use a contraction.

1. I came home late today.   I _____*didn't come*_____ home late yesterday.

2. You did your homework last night.   You _____ your homework last week.

3. He cleaned his room on Monday.   He _____ his room last weekend.

4. She woke up late this morning.   She _____ up late yesterday.

5. We watched a movie yesterday.   We _____ a movie last week.

6. I ate lunch today.   I _____ breakfast.

7. They drank tea this afternoon.   They _____ coffee.

8. The kids played soccer.   They _____ baseball.

9. She spoke to a nurse.   She _____ to a doctor.

10. I forgot my book at home.   I _____ my homework.

11. We went to the park.   We _____ to the zoo.

12. I took the bus to school.   I _____ a taxi.

PRACTICE 24 ▸ Simple past: negative. (Chart 8-7)

Make sentences that are true for you.

1. eat \ a big dinner \ last night

    _____*I ate a big dinner last night.* OR *I didn't eat a big dinner last night.*_____

2. drive \ to school \ this morning

    _____

3. write \ a long email \ last night

    _____

4. walk \ to school \ yesterday

_____

5. get \ groceries \ last week

_____

6. go \ on vacation \ last month

_____

7. do \ housework \ last weekend

_____

8. work \ outside \ yesterday

_____

9. pay \ some bills \ yesterday

_____

10. stop \ at a café \ yesterday afternoon

_____

PRACTICE 25 ▸ Review of *yes/no* questions: past and present. (Charts 3-9 and 8-8)
Make *yes/no* questions.

1. _____*Do they play*_____ tennis?　　Yes, they do. They play tennis.

2. _____*Did they play*_____ tennis?　　Yes, they did. They played tennis.

3. _____ tennis?　　Yes, she does. She plays tennis.

4. _____ tennis?　　Yes, she did. She played tennis.

5. _____ to work?　　Yes, he does. He walks to work.

6. _____ to work?　　Yes, he did. He walked to work.

7. _____ from home?　　Yes, she does. She works from home.

8. _____ from home?　　Yes, she did. She worked from home.

9. _____ your new job?　Yes, I do. I like my new job.

10. _____ your old job?　　Yes, I did. I liked my old job.

tennis

PRACTICE 26 ▸ Yes/no questions. (Charts 8-3 and 8-8)
Make questions. Write *did*, *was*, or *were*.

Tell me about your trip.

1. _____Did_____ you have a good time?

2. _____ it fun?

3. _____ you see a lot of interesting sights?

4. _____ you meet many people?

5. _____ the people friendly?

6. _____ you learn a lot?

7. _____ the trip long enough?

8. _____ you want to come home?

9. _____ you ready to come home?

PRACTICE 27 ▸ Review: questions and negatives. (Charts 3-9, 8-7, and 8-8)
Make questions and negative sentences from the given sentences.

	QUESTION	NEGATIVE
1. a. They study.	*Do they study?*	*They don't study.*
b. They studied.	*Did they study?*	*They didn't study.*
2. a. They understand.	_____	_____
b. They understood.	_____	_____
3. a. She drives.	_____	_____
b. She drove.	_____	_____
4. a. He works.	_____	_____
b. He worked.	_____	_____
5. a. The baby cries.	_____	_____
b. The baby cried.	_____	_____
6. a. We are sick.	_____	_____
b. We were sick.	_____	_____

PRACTICE 28 ▸ Review: *Yes/no* questions. (Charts 3-9, 8-2, 8-3, 8-7, and 8-8)
Make *yes/no* questions. Give short answers.

1. A: _____*Were you at home last night?*_____

   B: _____*No, I wasn't.*_____ (I wasn't at home last night.)

   A: _____*Did you go to a lake last weekend?*_____

   B: _____*Yes, I did.*_____ (I went to a lake last weekend.)

2. A: _____

   B: _____ (It isn't cold today.)

3. A: _____

   B: _____ (I come to class every day.)

4. A: _____

   B: _____ (Roberto was absent yesterday.)

5. A: _____

   B: _____ (Roberto stayed home yesterday.)

6. A: _____

   B: _____ (Phillip doesn't change his passwords often.)

7. A: _____

   B: _____ (Mohammed isn't in class today.)

8. A: _____

   B: _____ (He was here yesterday.)

9. A: _____

   B: _____ (He came to class the day before yesterday.)

10. A: _____

    B: _____ (He usually comes to class every day.)

PRACTICE 29 ▸ Irregular verbs, Part II: Group 1. (Chart 8-9)
Check (✓) the sentences that are true for you. Write the present form for the verb in *italics*.

		PRESENT FORM

1. _____ I *cut* something with a sharp knife yesterday.   _____*cut*_____

2. _____ I *shut* a window last night.   _____

3. _____ I *read* the news yesterday.   _____

PRESENT FORM

4. _____ I *hurt* my back last year.   _____

5. _____ I *put* my phone on the charger last night.   _____

6. _____ I once *hit* my finger with a hammer.   _____

7. _____ Ice-cream cones *cost* a lot when I was a child.   _____

a hammer   an ice-cream cone

PRACTICE 30 ▶ Irregular verbs, Part II: Groups 2 and 3. (Chart 8-9)
Check (✓) the sentences that are true for you. Write the present form for each verb in *italics*.

PRESENT FORM

1. _____ I *felt* happy all day yesterday.   _____ *feel*

2. _____ I *fell* down last week.   _____

3. _____ I *spent* money on snack food yesterday.   _____

4. _____ I *met* a famous person at a party.   _____

5. _____ I *slept* eight hours last night.   _____

6. _____ I *lost* my keys last week.   _____

7. _____ I *left* my house early this morning.   _____

8. _____ I *built* a sandcastle last summer.   _____

a sandcastle

PRACTICE 31 ▶ Irregular verbs, Part II: Groups 1, 2, and 3. (Chart 8-9)
Complete the second sentence with the affirmative verb. Use the simple past form.

1. I didn't meet Ivan's brother. I _____ *met* _____ his sister.

2. Sarah didn't hurt her arm. She _____ her hand.

3. The book didn't cost 30 euros. It _____ 20 euros.

4. Jacob didn't fall in the parking lot. He _____ on the sidewalk.

5. Daniel didn't sleep on the sofa. He _____ on his bed.

6. I didn't read my email. I _____ the news.

7. Sam didn't put his keys in his pocket. He _____ them on the table.

8. We didn't leave early. We _____ late.

9. Ava didn't lose her phone. She _____ her laptop.

10. The kids didn't build a doghouse. They _____ a birdhouse.

a birdhouse

PRACTICE 32 ▶ Irregular verbs, Part II: Groups 4, 5, 6, and 7. (Chart 8-9)
Check (✓) the sentences that are true for you. Write the present form for each verb in *italics*.

                                                  PRESENT FORM

1. _____ When I was young, I sometimes *fought* with my brother or sister.   *fight*

2. _____ I *knew* all the answers in the last exercise.   _____

3. _____ I *threw* away some mail yesterday.   _____

4. _____ I *flew* in an airplane last month.   _____

5. _____ I *grew* vegetables in a garden last year.   _____

6. _____ I *bought* some shoes last month.   _____

7. _____ I *caught* a taxi last week.   _____

8. _____ My teacher *taught* me something new today.   _____

9. _____ I *brought* my phone to class yesterday.   _____

PRACTICE 33 ▶ Irregular verbs, Part II: Groups 4, 5, 6, and 7. (Chart 8-9)
Write the simple past tense form of the verbs in parentheses.

1. Gabi (*bring*) _____*brought*_____ her son to work yesterday.

2. Her son (*grow*) _____ a lot last year.

3. I (*throw*) _____ a ball to my dog. The dog (*catch*) _____ the ball in his mouth.

4. Our professor (*teach*) _____ us some new vocabulary.

5. I lost my keys, but I (*find*) _____ them this morning.

6. Alicia (*fly*) _____ to Mexico last week.

7. I enjoyed the movie. I (*think*) _____ it was very funny.

8. We (*buy*) _____ some new furniture for our apartment.

PRACTICE 34 ▸ Irregular verbs, Parts I and II. (Charts 8-6 and 8-9)
Complete each sentence with the simple past form of a verb from the box.

break	cost	have	hurt	shut
come	forget	hit	pay	✓ wake

Jonathan had a bad day yesterday.

1. He _____ *woke* _____ up early because a dog was barking outside.

2. He _____ his bedroom window too hard, and he _____ the glass.

3. He missed the bus, so he walked to school. He _____ to class fifteen minutes late.

4. He _____ to bring his homework to class. His teacher wasn't happy.

5. He left his lunch at home, so he _____ for food in the cafeteria. It _____ a lot of money.

6. He used all his money for lunch, so he _____ no money for the bus. He walked home.

7. He played soccer with his friends. Someone kicked the ball, and it _____ him in the face.

8. He couldn't open his eye, and his face _____ the rest of the day.

PRACTICE 35 ▸ Irregular verbs, Parts I and II. (Charts 8-6 and 8-9)
Complete each sentence with the simple past form of a verb from the box. Use each verb one time.

feel	get	hear	leave	ring	take
✓ fly	go	hurt	meet	speak	wake

1. It was 7:00 A.M. Jerry was asleep. A bird _____ *flew* _____ into his open bedroom window.

2. Jerry _____ a noise.

3. The noise _____ him up. He saw the bird.

4. The bird looked hurt. Jerry _____ the bird to the veterinarian.*

5. A nurse _____ Jerry in the parking lot and helped him with the bird.

6. Jerry _____ the bird at the vet's office. Then he _____ to work.

7. An hour later, Jerry's phone _____ . It was the vet.

8. The vet _____ to Jerry about the bird.

---

*veterinarian (vet) = an animal doctor

9. The bird _____ its wing, but it was okay.

10. The vet took care of the bird for a week. Then she put the bird outside, and it flew away. Jerry _____ happy.

PRACTICE 36 ▸ Review: -ed spelling. (Chapter 8)
Write the correct spelling of the **-ed** form.

	-ed FORM		-ed FORM
1. wait	_____waited_____	9. point	_____
2. spell	_____spelled_____	10. pat	_____
3. kiss	_____	11. shout	_____
4. plan	_____	12. reply	_____
5. join	_____	13. play	_____
6. hope	_____	14. touch	_____
7. drop	_____	15. end	_____
8. add	_____	16. dance	_____

PRACTICE 37 ▸ Verb review: simple past tense. (Chapter 8)
Complete the sentences with the verbs in parentheses.

1. Last night I (*find*) _____found_____ some interesting articles online.

2. Mari and I (*go*) _____ to the grocery store yesterday. I (*buy*) _____ some bread and milk.

3. I had to go downtown yesterday. I (*catch*) _____ the bus in front of my apartment and (*ride*) _____ to Grand Avenue. Then I (*get off*) _____ the bus and transferred to another one. It (*be*) _____ a long trip.

4. Sue (*eat*) _____ popcorn and (*drink*) _____ a soft drink at the movie theater last night. I (*eat, not*) _____ anything. Movie theater food prices are too high.

5. Maria (*ask*) _____ the teacher a question in class yesterday. The teacher (*think*) _____ about the question for a few minutes before he (*answer*) _____ the question.

6. I (*want*) _____ to go to the basketball game last night, but I (*stay*) _____ home and (*study*) _____ for my grammar test.

7. Rita (*pass, not*) _____ the test yesterday. She (*fail*) _____ it.

8. Last summer my family (*drive*) _____ to Colorado for vacation. We (*sleep*)
_____ in a camper by a lake. The kids (*swim*) _____ in the lake.
We (*go*) _____ fishing every day. We (*catch*) _____ a lot of fish.
We (*cook*) _____ the fish for dinner. It (*be*) _____ delicious. We
all (*enjoy*) _____ our vacation.

a camper

PRACTICE 38 ▸ Verb review: past and present. (Chapters 1–4 and 8)
Complete the sentences with the words in parentheses. Use the simple present, present progressive,
or simple past. The sentence may need an affirmative statement, a negative statement, or a
question form.

1. Tom (*walk*) _____ *walks* _____ to work almost every day.

2. I see Tom from my window. He's on the street below. He (*walk*) _____.

3. (*Tom, walk*) _____ to work every day?

4. (*you, walk*) _____ to work every day?

5. I usually take the bus to work, but yesterday I (*walk*) _____ to
my office.

6. On my way to work yesterday, I (*see*) _____ an accident.

7. Alex (*see, not*) _____ the accident.

8. (*you, see*) _____ the accident yesterday?

9. Tom (*walk, not*) _____ to work last week. The weather was too cold.
He (*take*) _____ the bus.

10. I (*walk, not*) _____ to work last week either.

PRACTICE 39 ▸ Verb review: past and present. (Chapters 1–4 and 8)
Complete the sentences. Use the words in parentheses. Use any appropriate verb form.

1. I (*finish, not*) _____ *didn't finish* _____ my chores last night. I (*fall*)
_____ asleep very early.

2. Jasmin (*stand, not*) _____ up right now. She (*sit*)
_____ down.

3. The weather (*be, not*) _____ cold today, but it (*be*)

   _____ cold yesterday.

4. It (*rain, not*) _____ right now. The rain (*stop*)

   _____ a few minutes ago.

5. I (*write*) _____ a paragraph for my history class last night, but I

   (*spend, not*) _____ much time on it.

6. We (*be*) _____ late for a meeting at our son's school last night. The

   meeting (*start*) _____ at 7:00, but we (*arrive, not*)

   _____ until 7:15.

7. Olga (*ask*) _____ Hamid a question a few minutes ago, but he

   (*answer, not*) _____ her.

8. When Ben and I (*go*) _____ to the mall yesterday, I (*buy*)

   _____ some new shoes. Ben (*buy, not*) _____

   anything.

9. I (*lose*) _____ my grammar book yesterday, but I (*find*)

   _____ it later.

10. I (*go, not*) _____ to work yesterday. My daughter (*feel, not*)

    _____ well, so I (*stay*) _____ home with her.

    She's fine now. She (*be*) _____ at school.

PRACTICE 40 ▶ Review. (Chapter 8)
Correct the mistakes.

       was
1. Our teacher ~~is~~ late yesterday.

2. Did you call me last morning?

3. I payed my rent a few days ago.

4. Sebastian hurted his hand. He was cut it on a piece of glass.

5. Nicole no drove to work yesterday.

6. Did you went on vacation last week?

7. Ryan was no at home last night.

8. The test were difficult. I didn't knew the answers.

9. Did you ready for the test yesterday?

10. I texted you before an hour. Did you got my message?

CHAPTER 9

Expressing Past Time, Part 2

PRACTICE 1 ▶ *Where, why, when, and what time.* (Chart 9-1)
Make simple past questions and answers. Use ***Where ... go?***, ***When/What time ... leave?***,
Why ... go there? and the given information.

> *Oscar's travel plans*
>
> *To Mexico City*
> *Leave on March 22*
> *To visit family*

> *Serena's travel plans*
>
> *the Canary Islands*
> *Leave at 6 AM*
> *For vacation*

Oscar's Plans

1. A: _Where did Oscar go?_
   B: _He went to Mexico City._

2. A: _____
   B: _____

3. A: _____
   B: _____

Serena's Plans

4. A: _____
   B: _____

5. A: _____
   B: _____

6. A: _____
   B: _____

PRACTICE 2 ▸ *Where, why, when,* and *what time.* (Chart 9-1)

Write the letter of the correct response next to each question.

1. Who did you invite to your party? __*b*__   a. It started at 7:30.

2. When did your plane arrive? _____   ✓b. My best friends.

3. Why did you eat two sandwiches? _____   c. In 2018.

4. When did you travel to Peru? _____   d. In Toronto.

5. Where did you live during high school? _____   e. Because I was very hungry.

6. What time was the soccer game? _____   f. A few minutes ago.

PRACTICE 3 ▸ *Where, why, when,* and *what time.* (Chart 9-1)

Make questions for the given answers.

1. A: _____*Where did you study last night?*_____
   B: At the library. (I studied at the library last night.)

2. A: _____
   B: At 10:00. (I left the library at 10:00.)

3. A: _____
   B: Because it closed at 10:00. (I left because the library closed at 10:00.)

4. A: _____
   B: To the park. (My friends and I went to the park yesterday afternoon.)

5. A: _____
   B: Two days ago. (Sandra got back from Brazil two days ago.)

6. A: _____
   B: Because he was sick. (Bobby was in bed because he was sick.)

7. A: _____
   B: Because he didn't get enough sleep. (Bobby was sick because he didn't get enough sleep.)

8. A: _____
   B: Online. (I bought my sandals online.)

sandals

PRACTICE 4 ▸ *Why didn't.* (Chart 9-1)

Make questions. Begin with *Why didn't*.

1. A: I looked for you at the meeting, but you didn't come. _____*Why didn't you come?*_____
   B: Because I had to work late.

2. A: You needed help, but you didn't ask the teacher. _____
   B: Because no one else had questions, and I felt shy.

3. A: The homework is due today, and you didn't bring it. _____

   B: Because I fell asleep while I was studying last night.

4. A: You told a lie. You didn't tell me the truth. _____

   B: Because I didn't want to upset you.

5. A: Sharon looked sad. You didn't go to her party. _____

   B: Because I forgot it was her birthday.

6. A: Look at this mess! You didn't clean the kitchen. _____

   B: Because I was too tired.

PRACTICE 5 ▶ Questions with *what*. (Chart 9-2)

Make questions. Pay attention to verb tenses.

1. A: _____*What did you buy?*_____

   B: A camera. (We bought a camera.)

2. A: _____*Did you buy a camera?*_____

   B: Yes, we did. (We bought a camera.)

3. A: _____

   B: Math. (I studied math.)

4. A: _____

   B: Yes, I did. (I studied math.)

5. A: _____

   B: Some pictures. (They're looking at pictures.)

6. A: _____

   B: Yes, they are. (They're looking at pictures.)

7. A: _____

   B: His country. (David talked about his country.)

8. A: _____

   B: Yes, he did. (David talked about his country.)

9. A: _____

   B: My homework. (I am thinking about my homework.)

10. A: _____

    B: Yes, I am. (I am thinking about my homework.)

11. A: _____

    B: English grammar. (I dreamed about English grammar last night.)

12. A: _____

    B: Yes, I did. (I dreamed about English grammar last night.)

13. A: _____

    B: Spiders. (I'm afraid of spiders.)

14. A: _____

    B: Yes, I am. (I'm afraid of spiders.)

a spider

PRACTICE 6 ▸ Questions with *who*. (Chart 9-3)
Make questions and short answers for the given sentences.

1. Julie called the police.

    a. Who called _____*the police*_____?   Julie.

    b. Who did _____*Julie call*_____?   The police.

2. The nurse checked Lea.

    a. Who checked _____?   The nurse.

    b. Who did _____?   Lea.

3. Felix helped the new assistant.

    a. Who did _____?   The new assistant.

    b. Who helped _____?   Felix.

4. Professor Jones taught the advanced students.

    a. Who taught _____?   _____.

    b. Who did _____?   _____.

5. The police caught the criminal.

    a. Who did _____?   _____.

    b. Who caught _____?   _____.

6. Oliver spoke to the manager.

    a. Who spoke to _____?   _____.

    b. Who did _____?   _____.

PRACTICE 7 ▸ Questions with *who*. (Chart 9-3)
Make questions with **who**.

1. Ron helped Judy.

    a. ___Who helped Judy?_____ Ron.

    b. ___Who did Ron help?_____ Judy.

2. The doctor examined the patient.

    a. _____ The patient.

    b. _____ The doctor.

3. Miriam called the supervisor.

    a. _____ Miriam.

    b. _____ The supervisor.

4. The students surprised the teacher.

    a. _____ The students.

    b. _____ The teacher.

5. Andrew and Catherine waited for Mrs. Allen.

    a. _____ Mrs. Allen.

    b. _____ Andrew and Catherine.

PRACTICE 8 ▸ Questions with *who*. (Chart 9-3)
There were some parties last week. Write questions for the given answers. Use the words from the box.

Questions: Who had a ____ party?
Who did ____ invite?

HOST*	PARTY	GUESTS
Mrs. Adams	birthday party for her son	her son's friends
Dr. Martin	New Year's party	her employees
Professor Brown	graduation party	his students

1. ___Who had a birthday party?_____ Mrs. Adams.

2. ___Who did Mrs. Adams invite?_____ Her son's friends.

3. _____ Professor Brown.

4. _____ His students.

---

* *host* = the person who gives a party

5. _____ Dr. Martin.

6. _____ Her employees.

PRACTICE 9 ▸ Questions with *who*. (Chart 9-3)
Make questions with ***who***.

1. A: ___*Who did you see?*_____
   B: Ken. (I saw Ken.)

2. A: _____
   B: Ken. (I talked to Ken.)

3. A: _____
   B: Nancy. (I visited Nancy.)

4. A: _____
   B: Ahmed. (Ahmed answered the phone.)

5. A: _____
   B: Mr. Lee. (Mr. Lee taught the English class.)

6. A: _____
   B: Carlos. (Carlos helped me.)

7. A: _____
   B. Gina. (I helped Gina.)

8. A: _____
   B: My brother. (My brother carried my suitcases.)

9. A: _____
   B: Yuko. (Yuko called.)

PRACTICE 10 ▸ Question review. (Charts 9-1 → 9-3)
Make simple past questions with the given words.

1. A: Where \ you \ go ___*Where did you go?*_____
   B: To the cafeteria.

2. A: Who \ go \ with you _____
   B: Sara. (Sara went with me.)

3. A: Why \ you \ go \ there _____
   B: Because we met some friends for lunch.

4. A: Who \ you \ meet _____
   B: Noah and Leo. (We met Noah and Leo.)

5. A: What \ you \ have \ for lunch _____
   B: A sandwich.

6. A: What time \ you \ go _____
   B: Around noon.

7. A: When \ you \ get back _____
   B: A few minutes ago.

PRACTICE 11 ▸ Question review. (Charts 9-1 → 9-3)
Make questions. Use any appropriate question word: *where, when, what time, why, who,* or *what*.

1. A: _____*Where did Simone go?*_____
   B: To a meeting. (Simone went to a meeting.)

2. A: _____
   B: Last month. (Simone went to a meeting last month.)

3. A: _____
   B: Simone. (Simone went to a meeting.)

4. A: _____
   B: Ali. (I saw Ali.)

5. A: _____
   B: At the train station. (I saw Ali at the train station.)

6. A: _____
   B: At 10:00. (I saw Ali at the train station at 10:00.)

7. A: _____
   B: Grammar. (The teacher is talking about grammar.)

8. A: _____
   B: Because the weather was hot. (The kids played in the pool because the weather was hot.)

9. A: _____
   B: The doctor's office. (The doctor's office called.)

10. A: _____
    B: Yesterday afternoon. (They called yesterday afternoon.)

11. A: _____

    B: The nurse. (I talked to the nurse.)

12. A: _____

    B: At home. (I was at home last night.)

13. A: _____

    B: "Very old." (*Ancient* means "very old.")

14. A: _____

    B: In an apartment. (I live in an apartment.)

15. A: _____

    B: Coffee. (I have coffee in my thermos.)

a thermos

PRACTICE 12 ▸ Complete and incomplete sentences. (Chart 9-4)
Write the phrases or sentences from the box in the correct column. Add capitalization and punctuation where necessary.

✓ we slept	before school starts
✓ when we ate lunch	before school starts, I help the teacher
they left	we ate at a restaurant
after they left	after we finish dinner
after several minutes	we were at home

INCOMPLETE SENTENCE	COMPLETE SENTENCE
when we ate lunch	*We slept.*
_____	_____
_____	_____
_____	_____
_____	_____

PRACTICE 13 ▸ *After.* (Chart 9-4)
Look at the pairs of sentences. Decide which action happened first and which action happened second. Write "1" for the first action and "2" for the second action. Then write sentences with *after*. Pay special attention to the punctuation.

1. __*1*__ My computer crashed.

   __*2*__ I lost my information.

   After my computer crashed, I lost my information. _____ OR

   I lost my information after my computer crashed. _____

2. _____ I closed the freezer door.

   _____ I looked in the freezer.

   _____ OR

   _____

3. _____ We ate dinner.

   _____ We washed the dishes.

   _____ OR

   _____

4. _____ I exercised.

   _____ I put on my exercise clothes.

   _____ OR

   _____

5. _____ The alarm rang at the fire station.

   _____ The firefighters got in their truck.

   _____ OR

   _____

PRACTICE 14 ▸ *Before* and *after.* (Chart 9-4)
Look at the pairs of sentences. Which action happened first and which action happened second?
Choose the two sentences that have the same meaning.

1. __1__ Joan washed the dishes.

   __2__ Joan dried the dishes.

   (a.) After Joan washed the dishes, she dried them.
   b. Before Joan washed the dishes, she dried them.
   c. After Joan dried the dishes, she washed them.
   (d.) Before Joan dried the dishes, she washed them.

2. _____ It rained.

   _____ The rain clouds came.

   a. After it rained, the rain clouds came.
   b. Before it rained, the rain clouds came.
   c. After the rain clouds came, it rained.
   d. Before the rain clouds came, it rained.

3. _____ Luis drove away.

   _____ Luis started the car.

   a. Before Luis drove away, he started the car.
   b. Before Luis started the car, he drove away.
   c. After Luis drove away, he started the car.
   d. After Luis started the car, he drove away.

4. _____ I opened my eyes.

   _____ I looked around the room.

   a. Before I opened my eyes, I looked around the room.
   b. After I opened my eyes, I looked around the room.
   c. Before I looked around the room, I opened my eyes.
   d. After I looked around the room, I opened my eyes.

PRACTICE 15 ▸ *Before* and *after*. (Chart 9-4)

Combine the two ideas into one sentence by using ***before*** or ***after*** in a time clause. Make four sentences for each item.

1. They put on their jackets. They went outside.

   After they put on their jackets, they went outside.

   They went outside after they put on their jackets.

   Before they went outside, they put on their jackets.

   They put on their jackets before they went outside.

2. He packed his bags. He left.

   _____

   _____

   _____

   _____

3. She sat down. She ordered some food.

_____

_____

_____

_____

PRACTICE 16 ▸ When in questions and time clauses. (Chart 9-5)
In each of the following pairs, one is a question and one is a time clause. Add punctuation: a question mark or a comma.

1. a. When you called,

   b. When did you call?

2. a. When did the movie start

   b. When the movie started

3. a. When you were in high school

   b. When were you in high school

4. a. When it snowed

   b. When did it snow

5. a. When was Dave sick

   b. When Dave was sick

PRACTICE 17 ▸ When in questions and time clauses. (Chart 9-5)
Add punctuation: a question mark or a comma. Then make each time clause a complete sentence by adding another clause from the box.

| we felt sad. | everyone clapped. | ✓I met them at the airport. | I woke up. |

1. When was the Smiths' party?

2. When the Browns came, *I met them at the airport.*

3. When did you hear the good news

4. When Mr. King died

5. When were you here

6. When did we meet

7. When my alarm clock rang

8. When our team won

9. When was Ms. Allen a teacher

PRACTICE 18 ▶ *When* in questions and time clauses. (Chart 9-5)
Use the given words to make (a) a simple past question and (b) a simple past time clause. Then use the words in the box to complete the sentence in (b).

we had a great time	I called the vet*	✓ I went inside	we used flashlights

1. when \ rain \ it

   a. _____ When did it rain? _____

   b. _____ When it rained, I went inside. _____

2. when \ get sick \ the dog

   a. _____

   b. _____

3. when \ go out \ the electricity

   a. _____

   b. _____

a flashlight

4. when \ visit \ my parents

   a. _____

   b. _____

PRACTICE 19 ▶ Forms of the present and past progressive. (Chart 9-6)
Complete the sentences. Use a form of *be* + *sit*.

1. I _____ am sitting _____ in class right now.

2. I _____ was sitting _____ in class yesterday too.

3. You _____ in class right now.

4. You _____ in class yesterday too.

5. Tony _____ in class right now.

---

*vet = an animal doctor

6. He _____ in class yesterday too.

7. We _____ in class today.

8. We _____ in class yesterday too.

9. Rita _____ in class now.

10. She _____ in class yesterday too.

11. Rita and Tony _____ in class today.

12. They _____ in class yesterday too.

PRACTICE 20 ▸ Forms of the past progressive. (Chart 9-6)
Complete the sentences. Use *study* and the correct form of the past progressive.

1. I ____*was studying.*_____

2. You _____

3. He _____

4. She _____

5. Ray and I _____

6. Several students _____

7. We (*not*) _____

8. My children (*not*) _____

9. Dr. Roberts (*not*) _____

10. My friends and I (*not*) _____

11. Your friends (*not*) _____

12. I (*not*) _____

PRACTICE 21 ▸ *While* + past progressive. (Chart 9-7)
Combine the sentences in each pair and add the correct punctuation. Use *while*.

1. We felt an earthquake.
   We were sitting in our living room last night.

   a. _____*We felt an earthquake while we were sitting in our living room last night.*_____

   b. _____*While we were sitting in our living room last night, we felt an earthquake.*_____

2. I was talking to the teacher.
   Another student interrupted us.

   a. _____

   b. _____

3. A police officer stopped me for speeding.
   I was driving to work.

   a. _____

   b. _____

4. We were walking in the forest.
   A dead tree fell over.

   a. _____

   b. _____

5. I was talking to my neighbor.
   My dog began to bark at a squirrel.

   a. _____

   b. _____

a squirrel

PRACTICE 22 ▸ Simple past vs. past progressive. (Chart 9-8)
Complete the sentences with the correct form of the verbs in parentheses.

1. My roommate came home late last night. I (sleep) _____*was sleeping*_____ when she
   (get) _____*got*_____ home.

2. When Gina (call) _____ last night, I (take)
   _____ a shower.

3. I (eat) _____ lunch with my brother when I suddenly (remember)
   _____ my promise to pick my cousin up at school.

4. When the president (begin) _____ to speak, everyone (become)
   _____ quiet.

5. While I (drive) _____ to the airport, I (see)
   _____ an accident.

6. While Joan (exercise) _____, a salesperson (come)
   _____ to the door.

7. Pete (text) _____ his friend while his teacher (talk)

_____ . She (tell) _____ him to put his

phone away.

8. When Albert (hear) _____ the police siren, he (stop)

_____ on the side of the road.

PRACTICE 23 ▸ Using *while* and *when*. (Chart 9-8)
Read the story. Complete the sentences with information from the story.

A Nonstop Talker

    While I was riding the train, a man sat down next to me.
I was reading a book, and he asked me about it. I didn't want
to talk, but I answered his question. While I was talking, he
interrupted me. He told me about his job, his boss, and his
family. When I looked away, he continued to talk. When I
looked at my watch, he continued to talk. Finally, I told him
I wasn't feeling well. He began to tell me about his health.
While he was giving me details about his doctor visits, I stood
up. I excused myself and walked to the back of the train.
When I looked ten minutes later, he was talking to another
passenger. I'm sure he is talking to someone right now!

1. While the woman was riding the train, ____*a man sat down next to her.*____

2. When she was talking, _____

3. When she looked away, _____

4. When she told him she wasn't feeling well, _____

5. While he was talking about doctors, _____

6. When she looked at him later, _____

PRACTICE 24 ▸ Simple past vs. past progressive. (Chart 9-8)
Complete the sentences with the correct form of the verbs in parentheses.

    While Tom (drive) _____*was driving*_____ yesterday, his phone (ring)
                               1

_____ . He (answer, not) _____ it because he
         2   3

(want) _____ to be careful. He (notice) _____
         4   5

many drivers with phones. While he (slow) _____ down to make a turn,
                                               6

the driver in front of him suddenly (drive) _____ off the road. Tom
                                               7

(see) _____ a phone in her hand.
         8

PRACTICE 25 ▶ Simple past vs. past progressive. (Chart 9-8)

Complete the sentences with the correct form of the verbs in parentheses.

A: My husband and I (be) _____*were*_____ at my cousin's last night.
   1

While we (sit) _____ outside in the garden after dinner, her cat
   2

(come) _____ up to us with a snake in its mouth. I
   3

(scream) _____ when I (see) _____ the snake.
   4   5

B: What (your cousin, do) _____?
   6

A: She (yell) _____.
   7

B: (your husband, do) _____ something?
   8

A: He (run) _____ into the house. While he (run)
   9

_____, the cat (run) _____ after him. The cat
   10   11

(drop) _____ the snake on the kitchen floor. Then my husband
   12

(yell) _____ "Help!" Fortunately, the snake (go) _____
   13   14

back into the garden.

PRACTICE 26 ▶ Review: irregular verbs. (Chapters 8 and 9)

Choose a sentence from the box that best completes each idea.

It sold in three days.	He ate too much for lunch.
He lost his wallet.	I took a taxi.
She finished after midnight.	She caught a cold yesterday.
✓ He said they were too noisy.	Sam picked it up for her.
She had a job interview after class.	I grew up there.
Some students came to class without their homework.	She found it under her bed.

1. The teacher told the students to work more quietly. _____*He said they were too noisy.*_____

2. Laurie doesn't feel good. _____

3. Beth lost her grammar book. _____

4. Jack had no money. _____

5. Peter didn't want dinner. _____

6. Susan didn't want to sell her car, but she needed money. _____

7. Maria wore her best clothes to school. _____

8. Shelley began her homework at 9:00 P.M. _____

9. Kathy dropped her pen on the floor. _____

10. I missed the bus for the airport yesterday. _____

11. The teacher was unhappy. _____

12. My hometown is Ames, Iowa. _____

PRACTICE 27 ▸ Review: irregular verbs. (Chapters 8 and 9)
Complete the sentences. Use the simple past form of the verbs from the box.

break	fall	lose	meet	spend	tell
cost	know	make	put	take	✓ throw

1. The baseball player _____*threw*_____ the ball to the catcher.

2. Rick _____ his arm when he fell on the ice.

3. Maggie didn't tell a lie. She _____ the truth.

4. We _____ a lot of money at the restaurant last night. The food was good but expensive.

5. I _____ some mistakes on my homework, so I did it again.

6. I _____ on my winter jacket yesterday because the weather was cold.

7. Tom bought a new phone. It _____ a lot.

8. Leo read the story. It was easy because he _____ the vocabulary in the story.

9. I know Amanda Clark. I _____ her at a party a couple of weeks ago.

10. I dropped my book. It _____ to the floor.

11. Jack couldn't get into his apartment because he _____ his keys.

12. Someone _____ my bike, so I called the police.

PRACTICE 28 ▸ Review: irregular verbs. (Chapters 8 and 9)
Complete the sentences. Use the simple past form of the verbs from the box.

✓ begin	cut	fight	leave	understand
build	eat	fly	sing	win

1. We were late for the party. It _____*began*_____ at 7:00, but we didn't get there until 7:15.

2. We _____ songs at the party last night and had a good time.

3. I _____ to Chicago last week. The plane was only five minutes late.

4. My plane _____ at 6:00 and arrived at 8:45.

5. We played a soccer game yesterday. The other team _____. We lost.

6. The homework was hard, but our teacher helped us. We _____ the assignment when our teacher explained it.

7. My daughter _____ a website for her class in high school.

8. Mike _____ spaghetti for dinner last night.

9. The kids wanted the same toy. They _____ for a few minutes. Then they decided to share it.

10. I _____ my hand on the glass. It hurt a lot.

PRACTICE 29 ▸ Review. (Chapter 9)
Correct the mistakes.

1. Who ~~did~~ called you?

2. What time you came home last night?

3. What did you bought at the store?

4. Why the teacher did leave early yesterday?

5. Where did Claire works last year?

6. When you texted me, I was sit in class.

7. I forgot to lock the door when I leave this morning.

8. Vanessa called me while she waiting for the bus.

9. I fell asleep before the movie was ending.

10. I was washing dishes when I was breaking a plate.

CHAPTER 10

Expressing Future Time, Part 1

PRACTICE 1 ▶ Forms of *be going to*. (Chart 10-1)
Write the correct form of ***be going to***.

TOMORROW

1. I _____*am going to*_____ go downtown.

2. We _____ go downtown.

3. She _____ go downtown.

4. You _____ go downtown.

5. They _____ go downtown.

6. Tim and I _____ go downtown.

7. Mr. Han _____ go downtown.

8. Mr. Han and you _____ go downtown.

9. He _____ go downtown.

10. Rick and Sam _____ go downtown.

PRACTICE 2 ▶ *Be going to*. (Chart 10-1)
Complete the sentences with the correct form of ***be going to***. Use the verbs in parentheses.

1. A: (*you, be*) _____*Are you going to be*_____ at home tomorrow morning around ten?

   B: No. I (*be*) _____ out.

2. A: (*Albert, fix*) _____ the bathroom faucet soon? It's still dripping.

   B: He already tried. I (*call*) _____ a plumber in the morning.

3. A: (*you, apply*) _____ for the job at the mall?

   B: Yes. I (*complete*) _____ the online application tomorrow.

4. A: (*Ed and Nancy, join*) _____ us at the restaurant for dinner?

   B: Yes, they (*meet*) _____ us there at 7:00.

PRACTICE 3 ▸ Be going to. (Chart 10-1)

Read the story. Rewrite the second paragraph using **be going to**.

Mondays are always very busy for Antonia. She is the project manager for a construction company, and she has a long day. Here is her schedule.

She wakes up at 5:00. She has a quick breakfast of toast and coffee. She catches the 5:45 train to work. At 6:30, she has a weekly meeting with her employees. For the rest of the morning, she is at her desk. She answers phone calls and emails. She answers a lot of questions. She has a big lunch at 11:00. In the afternoon, she visits job sites. She meets with builders and architects. She finishes by 7:00 and is home by 8:00.

Today is Monday. What is Antonia going to do?

_____ *She is going to wake up at 5:00. She* _____

_____

_____

_____

_____

_____

_____

_____

PRACTICE 4 ▸ Be going to. (Chart 10-1)

Complete the sentences. Use **be going to** and the expressions from the box.

call the neighbors	✓ go back to bed	take it back to the store
check the lost-and-found	move to a big house	take some medicine
eat a big lunch	rain this afternoon	

1. It's 6:00 A.M. and I'm very tired.

   I _____ *am going to go back to bed.* _____

2. I'm hungry. I didn't have breakfast.

   I _____

3. Sam has a stomachache.

   He _____

4. The dog next door is barking loudly.

   We _____

5. Bring an umbrella.

   It _____

6. The Smiths have a new baby. Their apartment is too small.

They _____

7. Diane left her backpack in the classroom.

She _____

8. The zipper broke on my new dress.

I _____

a zipper

PRACTICE 5 ▸ *Be going to.* (Chart 10-1)
Write answers to the question *What are you going to do?* Use **be going to** in your answers.

1. You're thirsty. _____*I am going to get a drink of water.*_____

2. You have a sore throat. _____

3. You broke a tooth. _____

4. Your alarm didn't go off. You are in bed, and class starts in fifteen minutes.

_____

5. It's midnight. You are wide awake, and you want to go to sleep.

_____

6. You are at school. You locked your bike in a bike rack, and now it's not there.

_____

PRACTICE 6 ▸ *Be going to:* negative and question forms. (Chart 10-1)
Create your own chart by rewriting the given sentences as negatives and questions.

	NEGATIVE	QUESTION
1. I am going to eat.	*I am not going to eat.*	*Am I going to eat?*
2. You are going to eat.		
3. He is going to eat.		
4. She is going to eat.		
5. We are going to eat.		
6. They are going to eat.		
7. My friend is going to eat.		
8. The students are going to eat.		

PRACTICE 7 ▸ *Be going to: negative and question forms.* (Chart 10-1)

Complete the sentences with the correct form of the verbs in parentheses. Use **be going to**.

1. A: What (*you, do*) _____*are you going to do*_____ next weekend?

   B: We (*go*) _____ fishing at a lake in the mountains.

   A: (*you, stay*) _____ overnight?

   B: No. We (*come*) _____ back the same day.

2. A: Where (*Sally, work*) _____ this summer?

   B: She (*work, not*) _____. She (*take*)
   _____ summer school classes.

3. A: (*the students, have*) _____ an end-of-
   the-year party?

   B: Yes, they are. They (*have*) _____ a picnic at
   the park near the beach.

4. A: (*Joan and Bob, move*) _____ next
   month?

   B: Yes. Joan (*start*) _____ a new job in the city.

   A: (*they, look for*) _____ a house?

   B: No, they (*look for, not*) _____ a house. They
   (*rent*) _____ an apartment.

PRACTICE 8 ▸ Using the present progressive for future time. Chart 10-2

Write "P" if the sentence has a present meaning. Write "F" if the sentence has a future meaning.

1. __P__ Wait! I'm coming.

2. _____ I'm coming at 8:00 tonight.

3. _____ Wait—what are you doing?

4. _____ Ron is taking us to the airport soon.

5. _____ I'm returning this library book. I'm sorry it's late.

6. _____ We're flying to Madrid in a few weeks.

7. _____ A: Joe, are you leaving?

   _____ B: No, I'm not going. I'm staying.

8. _____ Claude isn't here. He is hiking in the mountains.

9. _____ Claude and Marie are spending their next vacation in the mountains.

PRACTICE 9 ▸ Using the present progressive for future time. (Chart 10-2)
Rewrite the sentences using the present progressive for the future verbs.

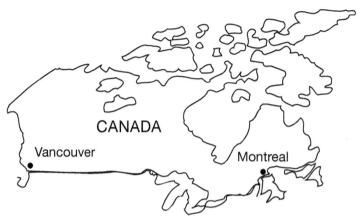

A Trip Across Canada

1. The Johnsons are going to take a camping trip across Canada this summer.

    The Johnsons are taking a camping trip across Canada this summer.

2. They are going to take their teenage grandchildren with them.

    _____

3. They are going to stay in parks and campgrounds.

    _____

4. They are going to leave from Vancouver in June.

    _____

5. They are going to arrive in Montreal in August.

    _____

6. Mr. and Mrs. Johnson are going to drive back home.

    _____

7. Their grandchildren are going to fly home.

    _____

8. Their parents are going to meet them at the airport.

    _____

PRACTICE 10 ▸ Using *yesterday, last, tomorrow, next, in,* or *ago.* (Chart 10-3)
Write *yesterday, last, tomorrow, next, in,* or *ago*.

1. I went to Hawaii _____*last*_____ year.

2. I went to Hawaii a year _____.

3. My sister went to Singapore a week _____.

4. My sister went to Singapore _____ week.

5. Our neighbors are going to Iceland _____ Friday.

6. We're going to Morocco _____ two weeks.

7. My parents went to Costa Rica _____ afternoon.

8. Their friends are going to Costa Rica _____ morning.

9. My cousins are going to Kenya _____ three weeks.

10. Were you home _____ afternoon around 4:00?

11. Were you home _____ night around 9:00?

12. Are you going to be in the office _____ afternoon around 3:00?

13. I wasn't at work two days _____ .

14. I'm not going to be at work _____ Thursday.

PRACTICE 11 ▸ Using *yesterday, last, tomorrow, next, in,* or *ago*. (Chart 10-3)
Complete the phrases with the appropriate time word.

1. *I left for my trip …*

   a. ___*yesterday*___ afternoon.

   b. _____ fall.

   c. _____ week.

   d. _____ weekend.

   e. _____ morning.

   f. two hours _____ .

   g. _____ month.

   h. three months _____ .

   i. _____ night.

   j. _____ evening.

2. *Sam is going to leave for his trip …*

   a. _____ afternoon.

   b. _____ fall.

   c. _____ week.

   d. _____ weekend.

   e. _____ morning.

   f. _____ two hours.

   g. _____ month.

   h. _____ three months.

   i. _____ night.

   j. _____ evening.

PRACTICE 12 ▸ Using *a couple of*. (Chart 10-4)
Check (✓) the expressions that can mean *a couple of*. Rewrite the expressions using ***a couple of***.

1. __✓__ two hours   ___*a couple of hours*___

2. ____ two minutes   _____

3. ____ two days   _____

4. ____ six years   _____

5. _____ ten months   _____

6. _____ two years   _____

7. _____ seven hours   _____

8. _____ one minute   _____

9. _____ two weeks   _____

PRACTICE 13 ▸ Using *a few*. (Chart 10-4)

Check (✓) the expressions that can mean *a few*. Rewrite the expressions using ***a few***.

1. __✓__ five minutes   _____*a few minutes*_____

2. _____ twelve months   _____

3. _____ four hours   _____

4. _____ three days   _____

5. _____ ten weeks   _____

6. _____ three years   _____

7. _____ one day   _____

PRACTICE 14 ▸ Using *a couple of* or *a few* with past and future. (Chart 10-4)

Make sentences using the given words.

1. I \ leave

    a. (*in a few days*) _____*I am going to leave in a few days.*_____

    b. (*a few days ago*) _____*I left a few days ago.*_____

2. Susie \ marry Paul

    a. (*a couple of months ago*) _____

    b. (*in a couple of months*) _____

3. Dr. Nelson \ retire

   a. (*a few years ago*) _____

   b. (*in a few years*) _____

4. Jack \ begin a new job

   a. (*a couple of days ago*) _____

   b. (*in a couple of days*) _____

PRACTICE 15 ▸ Using *this* with time words and *today* or *tonight*. (Chart 10-5)
Choose the meaning of each sentence: past, present, or future time.

1. Tom is going to finish school this June.	past	present	(future)
2. We took my parents to the airport this morning.	past	present	future
3. Jim is at home. He is cleaning his house this morning.	past	present	future
4. Ms. Andrew had lunch with friends today.	past	present	future
5. Our office assistant is retiring later this month.	past	present	future
6. Are you going to be home this afternoon?	past	present	future
7. I did a lot of housework today.	past	present	future
8. We heard about an interesting movie this morning.	past	present	future
9. You are going to have a good time tonight.	past	present	future
10. I had fun this evening.	past	present	future
11. What are the kids studying in school this week?	past	present	future
12. They are studying dinosaurs today.	past	present	future

dinosaurs

PRACTICE 16 ▸ Using time words. (Chart 10-5)
Read the description of Sophia's morning. Then choose all the correct time expressions.

It's 6:00 A.M. Sophia is late and needs to hurry. She is taking a shower. Then she is going to get dressed, have breakfast, and go to school.

1. Sophia woke up early	(this morning.)	(today.)	right now.
2. She is late	this morning.	today.	right now.

3. She is going to go to school   this morning.   today.   right now.

4. She is going to have breakfast   this morning.   today.   right now.

5. She is in a hurry   this morning.   today.   right now.

6. She got up before 6:00   this morning.   today.   right now.

PRACTICE 17 ▶ Using *this* with time words. (Chart 10-5)
Read the story about Sara. Then answer the questions.

Right now, I'm sitting in my kitchen. I'm thinking about going to school. This morning I woke up late. I overslept and missed my math class. I have an important chemistry test this afternoon. I have a problem. I don't want to miss it, but my chemistry teacher is also my math teacher. I'm not sure what to do. How do I explain my absence from my math class? I'm going to sit at the kitchen table and think about a solution.

1. What are two things Sara did this morning?

    a. _____*She woke up late.*_____

    b. _____

2. What are two things Sara is going to do this morning?

    a. _____

    b. _____

3. What are two things Sara is doing this morning?

    a. _____

    b. _____

PRACTICE 18 ▶ Forms of *will*. (Chart 10-6)
Complete the sentences with the correct form of ***will***.

1. We aren't late. We _____*will be*_____ there soon.

2. You aren't late. You _____ there soon.

3. They aren't late. They _____ there soon.

4. She isn't late. She _____ there soon.

5. I'm not late. I _____ there soon.

6. The students aren't late. The students _____ there soon.

7. My mother isn't late. My mother _____ there soon.

8. He isn't late. He _____ there soon.

9. Jill and I aren't late. Jill and I _____ there soon.

10. Eva and her son aren't late. Eva and her son _____ there soon.

PRACTICE 19 ▶ Using *will*. (Chart 10-6)

What will happen fifty years from now? Complete the sentences with *will* or *won't* and the verbs in parentheses.

Fifty years from now ...

1. most people (*live*) _____ to be 100.

2. people (*travel*) _____ to other planets.

3. all students (*study*) _____ online, not at school.

4. students (*study*) _____ in the classroom.

5. some people (*live*) _____ in underwater homes.

6. scientists (*discover*) _____ cures for serious diseases like cancer and AIDS.

7. there (*be*) _____ wars.

8. the world (*be*) _____ peaceful.

PRACTICE 20 ▶ Using *will*. (Chart 10-6)

Rewrite the predictions with *will*.

1. Class is going to finish a few minutes early today.

   _____*Class will finish a few minutes early today.*_____

2. You are going to need extra chairs for the party.

   _____

3. We aren't going to be on time for the movie.

   _____

4. It's going to rain tomorrow.

   _____

5. The bus isn't going to be on time today.

   _____

6. Julie will become famous one day.

   _____

7. You're going to hurt yourself on that skateboard.

   _____

PRACTICE 21 ▸ Will and be going to. (Chart 10-6)

Complete the sentences with **will** or **be going to** and the verbs in parentheses. More than one answer may be correct.

1. A: Why did you buy these vegetables?

   B: I (*make*) _____ *am going to make* _____ some soup.

2. A: Do you have any plans for the summer?

   B: Yes. We (*travel*) _____ to Vietnam.

3. A: It's really hot in here.

   B: I (*open*) _____ a window.

4. A: I would like to buy this computer.

   B: I'm sorry. I don't work in this department. I (*call*) _____
   a manager. Someone (*help*) _____ you in just a moment.

5. A: What are you going to do next weekend?

   B: The weather (*not be*) _____ very nice.
   I (*stay*) _____ home.

6. A: Hello! Welcome to Emma's. What would you like to order?

   B: I (*have*) _____ the potato soup, please.

7. A: Do you like your new job?

   B: No. I (*quit*) _____ soon.

PRACTICE 22 ▸ Questions with will. (Chart 10-7)

Make questions using the given words.

In the future

1. you \ live to be 100 years old?

   _____ *Will you live to be 100 years old?* _____

2. your friends \ live to be 100 years old?

   _____

3. your children \ live to be 100 years old?

   _____

4. we \ live on another planet?

   _____

5. my friends \ live on another planet?

_____

6. some people \ live underwater?

_____

7. I \ live underwater?

_____

8. countries \ find a solution for climate change?

_____

PRACTICE 23 ▸ Forms of *be going to* and *will*. (Chart 10-8)

Complete each sentence with the correct form of the verb.

| *BE GOING TO* + *GO* | *WILL* + *GO* |

Statement

1. I _____ *am going to go* _____ .   I _____ *will go* _____ .

2. You _____ .   You _____ .

3. The students _____ .   The students _____ .

4. Ms. Jenkins _____ .   Ms. Jenkins _____ .

5. Our friends _____ .   Our friends _____ .

Negative

6. Mr. Davis (*not*) _____ .   Mr. Davis (*not*) _____ .

7. I (*not*) _____ .   I (*not*) _____ .

8. We (*not*) _____ .   We (*not*) _____ .

Question

9. (*she, go*) _____ ?   (*she, go*) _____ ?

10. (*they, go*) _____ ?   (*they, go*) _____ ?

11. (*you, go*) _____ ?   (*you, go*) _____ ?

PRACTICE 24 ▸ Verb review: present, past, and future. (Chart 10-8)

Make questions with the given words. Use *will* for future tense.

1. you \ need \ help \ now?

     Do you need help now?

2. you \ need \ help \ tomorrow?

_____

3. you \ need \ help \ yesterday?

_____

4. Eva \ need \ help \ yesterday?

_____

5. Eva \ need \ help \ tomorrow?

_____

6. Eva \ need \ help \ now?

_____

7. the students \ need \ help \ now?

_____

8. the students \ need \ help \ tomorrow?

_____

9. the students \ need \ help \ yesterday?

_____

PRACTICE 25 ▸ Verb review: present, past, and future. (Chart 10-8)

Complete the sentences with the correct form of the verbs in parentheses. Use any appropriate verb form.

1. Right now, Noor (*eat*) _____ *is eating* _____ fish for lunch.

2. She (*eat*) _____ fish for lunch once or twice a week.

3. She also (*eat*) _____ chicken often.

4. She usually (*have*) _____ chicken for dinner.

5. Last night Noor (*cook*) _____ a spicy chicken and rice dish for her friends.

6. It (*be*) _____ delicious, and they (*love*) _____ it.

7. While she was cooking dinner, she (*drop*) _____ a pan of hot oil on the floor, but fortunately she (*be*) _____ okay. It (*burn, not*) _____ her.

8. Tomorrow Noor (*invite*) _____ her parents over for lunch.

9. (*she, cook*) _____ fish?

10. (*she, make*) _____ chicken?

11. Maybe she (*prepare, not*) _____ chicken or fish.

12. Maybe she (*surprise*) _____ her parents with a new dish.

PRACTICE 26 ▸ Verb review: *be.* (Chart 10-9)

Make sentences with the given words.

1. you \ be \ sick \ now?

   _____Are you sick now?_____

2. you \ be \ sick \ tomorrow?

   _____

3. you \ be \ sick \ yesterday?

   _____

4. Steve \ be \ sick \ yesterday?

   _____

5. Steve \ be \ sick \ tomorrow?

   _____

6. Steve \ be \ sick \ now?

   _____

7. your kids \ be \ sick \ now?

   _____

8. your kids \ be \ sick \ tomorrow?

   _____

9. your kids \ be \ sick \ yesterday?

   _____

PRACTICE 27 ▸ Verb review: *be.* (Chart 10-9)

Complete the sentences with the correct form of the verbs in parentheses. More than one answer may be correct.

1. I (*be*) _____am_____ very busy today. Right now, I (*be*) _____ in Quebec.
   Tomorrow I (*be*) _____ in New York. Yesterday I (*be*)
   _____ in Paris. I (*be*) _____ home next week.

2. A: Where (*you, be*) _____ last night? (*you, be*)
      _____ at home?

   B: No, I (*be, not*) _____. I (*be*) _____ at the library with
      my friends.

   A: I (*be*) _____ there too. Where (*you, be*) _____?

   B: We (*be*) _____ in the study area.

   A: Oh. I (*be*) _____ in the computer lab.

3. A: (*the post office, be*) _____ open now?

   B: No, it (*be, not*) _____. Today (*be*) _____ a national holiday.

   A: What about banks? (*they, be*) _____ open?

   B: No, they (*be, not*) _____. All the banks (*be*) _____
   closed.

PRACTICE 28 ▶ Simple present questions. (Charts 10-8 and 10-9)
Write **are** or **do**.

Isabella is starting a new job this morning. Her mother is asking her questions on the phone.

1. ____*Do*____ you need to get there early?

2. _____ you nervous or excited?

3. _____ you feel nervous or excited?

4. _____ you know your co-workers' names?

5. _____ you ready to begin?

6. _____ you need your ID?

7. _____ you have your phone?

8. _____ you taking the bus or subway?

9. _____ you want me to call you later?

PRACTICE 29 ▶ Simple past questions. (Charts 10-8 and 10-9)
Write **were** or **did**.

Dan had an important math test this morning. A friend is asking him about it.

1. ____*Did*____ you study for the test last night?

2. _____ you get enough sleep?

3. _____ you nervous this morning?

4. _____ you ready for the test?

5. _____ you do well?

6. _____ you make any mistakes?

7. _____ you get 100%?

8. _____ you happy when you finished?

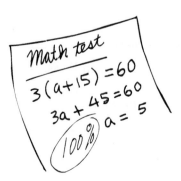

PRACTICE 30 ▶ Verb review: present, past, and future. (Charts 10-8 and 10-9)
Complete the chart with the correct forms of the verbs in bold.

EVERY DAY / NOW	YESTERDAY	TOMORROW
1. I **drink** tea every day. I _____*am drinking*_____ tea now.	I _____*drank*_____ tea yesterday.	I ___*am going to drink*___ tea tomorrow. I _____*will drink*_____ tea tomorrow.
2. We **work** every day. We _____ now.	We _____ yesterday.	We _____ tomorrow. We _____ tomorrow.
3. She **is** late every day. She _____ late now.	She _____ late yesterday.	She _____ late tomorrow. She _____ late tomorrow.
4. You _____ me every day. You _____ me now.	You **helped** me yesterday.	You _____ me tomorrow. You _____ me tomorrow.
5. She **doesn't run** every day. She _____ now.	She _____ yesterday.	She _____ tomorrow. She _____ tomorrow.
6. She _____ the dishes every day. She **isn't doing** the dishes now.	She _____ the dishes yesterday.	She _____ the dishes tomorrow. She _____ the dishes tomorrow.
7. _____ every day? **Are they exercising** now?	_____ yesterday?	_____ tomorrow? _____ tomorrow?
8. _____ on time every day? _____ on time now?	**Was he** on time yesterday?	_____ on time tomorrow? _____ on time tomorrow?
9. She **isn't** on time every day. She _____ on time now.	She _____ on time yesterday.	She _____ on time tomorrow. She _____ on time tomorrow.

PRACTICE 31 ▸ Verb review: past, present, and future. (Charts 10-8 and 10-9)
Complete the sentences with the words in parentheses. Use any appropriate verb form.

1. A: I (*lose*) _____ *lost* _____ my sunglasses yesterday.

   B: Where?

   A: I probably (*leave*) _____ them on a table at the restaurant.

2. A: What (*you, wear*) _____ to the party next weekend?

   B: I (*wear*) _____ my jeans. It (*be*) _____ a
   casual party.

3. A: Sometimes children tell little lies. You talked to Annie. (*she, tell*)
   _____ the truth, or (*she, tell*) _____ a lie?

   B: She (*tell*) _____ the truth. She's honest.

4. A: How are you getting along?

   B: Fine. I (*make*) _____ a lot of friends, and my English (*get*)
   _____ better.

5. A: What are you going to do tonight? (*you, study*) _____?

   B: No. I (*have, not*) _____ any homework.

   A: Really?

   B: Our teacher (*give*) _____ us a lot of work last week. She (*give*)
   _____ us a break this week.

6. A: Mark's wedding is next weekend. (*you, be*) _____ there?

   B: No. I have to take my dad home from the hospital on Saturday. He (*have*)
   _____ surgery in a few days.

   A: Really? That's too bad.

   B: He (*break*) _____ his leg last year, and it (*heal, not*) _____
   properly.

7. A: Good morning.

   B: Excuse me?

   A: I (*say*) _____, "Good morning."

   B: Oh! Good morning! I'm sorry. I (*understand, not*) _____ at first.

8. A: Where (*Cathy, be*) _____? I need to talk to her.

   B: She (*meet*) _____ with some students right now.

9. I almost (*have*) _____ an accident yesterday. A dog (*run*) _____ into the street in front of my car. I (*slam*) _____ on my brakes and just (*miss*) _____ the dog.

10. A: (*you, call*) _____ George tomorrow? It's his birthday.

    B: Thank you for the reminder! I always (*forget*) _____ his birthday.

PRACTICE 32 ▶ Verb review: past, present, and future. (Charts 10-8 and 10-9)
Choose the correct verbs.

Jack and the Beanstalk

A long time ago, a boy named Jack is living / lived with his mother. They are / were very
                                          1   2
poor. They didn't have / don't have money for food. His mother decided / was deciding to
                   3   4
sell their cow.

So, Jack take / took the cow to town. He meet / met a man. The man said, "I
               5   6
buy / will buy" your cow. I will give / give you magic beans. Jack took / taking the beans
    7   8   9
to his mother. She was / did very angry. She said, "You be / are a stupid boy. Now we
                        10   11
don't have / not have anything."
       12

Before he went to bed, Jack throw / threw the beans out the window. The next morning, he
                                   13
see / saw a big beanstalk outside his window. He climbed / is climbing it
   14   15
and found / find a castle. A giant's wife told him, "You need to hide. My
        16
husband eats / will eat you for breakfast." She hid Jack in the oven.
             17

The giant smelled Jack. He asked his wife, "Are you going to give /
                                                              18
Do you give me a boy for breakfast? She answered, "No, that smell
is / will be the boy from last week."
  19

After the giant fell / is going to fall asleep, Jack took some of the
                          20
giant's money and escaped.

His mother did / was very happy. She didn't want / no want Jack
                 21   22
to go back to the castle. But Jack was going / went back to the castle two
                                          23
more times. He got a hen, golden eggs, and a harp.

The giant never caught / never catch Jack. The giant
                   24
is going to run / ran after Jack, but Jack chopped down
       25
the beanstalk. Jack and his mother lives / lived happily
                                          26
ever after.

PRACTICE 33 ▸ Review. (Chapter 10)

Correct the mistakes.

     Are
1. ~~Do~~ you going to the airport today?

2. We are going travel to Europe next year.

3. Are we going to watch a movie next night?

4. My brother will helps me with the homework.

5. Vanessa got a new job two week ago.

6. When you will be home tonight?

7. I won't to go out tonight because I need to study.

8. I leaving for my vacation in three days.

PRACTICE 1 ▸ May, might, or will. (Chart 11-1)
Choose the meaning of each sentence: *sure* or *unsure*.

1. It may be stormy tomorrow.	sure	(unsure)
2. It won't be sunny.	sure	unsure
3. I won't be in class tomorrow.	sure	unsure
4. I will be absent.	sure	unsure
5. We might take a trip next week.	sure	unsure
6. Sandra might not take a vacation this year.	sure	unsure
7. We won't go camping next week.	sure	unsure
8. Eric may not be in his office.	sure	unsure
9. He might be at a meeting.	sure	unsure
10. He'll be home this evening.	sure	unsure

PRACTICE 2 ▸ May, might, or will. (Chart 11-1)
Write **may**, **might**, **will**, or **won't** and the verb in parentheses. Give your own opinion.

One hundred years from now, …

1. the earth (*be*) _____ very hot.

2. cars (*fly*) _____ .

3. people (*travel*) _____ easily
   to space.

4. all school courses (*be*) _____
   online.

5. there (*be*) _____ enough food
   and water for everyone in the world.

6. 100% of our energy for electricity (*come*) _____ from the sun.

7. everyone (*speak*) _____ the same language.

8. everyone (*live*) _____ in peace.

PRACTICE 3 ▸ *Maybe vs. may be.* (Chart 11-2)

Make sentences with the given words.

1. It \ be \ sunny tomorrow
   a. (may) _____It may be sunny tomorrow._____
   b. (maybe) _____Maybe it will be sunny tomorrow._____

2. You \ need to see \ a doctor soon
   a. (might) _____
   b. (maybe) _____

3. We \ play \ basketball after school
   a. (may) _____
   b. (might) _____

4. Our class \ go \ to a movie together
   a. (maybe) _____
   b. (may) _____

PRACTICE 4 ▸ *Maybe vs. may be.* (Chart 11-2)

Choose the correct sentences. In some cases, both sentences may be correct.

1. (a.) I may need your advice.
   (b.) Maybe I will need your advice.

2. a. The teacher may give a surprise quiz tomorrow.
   b. The teacher maybe will give a surprise quiz tomorrow.

3. a. Maybe all the students do well.
   b. Maybe all the students will do well.

4. a. Maybe traffic will be heavy later.
   b. Maybe traffic is heavy later.

5. a. You may will need more time.
   b. Maybe you will need more time.

6. a. We may delay our trip for a few days.
   b. Maybe we will delay our trip for a few days.

7. a. Maybe she'll be late.
   b. She may be late.

PRACTICE 5 ▸ *May, might,* and *maybe.* (Charts 11-1 and 11-2)

Rewrite the sentences.

Tomorrow	*MAY*	*MIGHT*
1. Maybe I will come.	*I may come.*	*I might come.*
2. Maybe they will come.		

	MIGHT	*MAY*
3. Maybe she won't study.		
4. Maybe we won't need help.		
5. Maybe I won't need help.		

	MAY	*MAYBE*
6. He might understand.		
7. You might understand.		
8. They might understand.		

PRACTICE 6 ▸ Review: *Maybe, may, might,* and *will.* (Charts 11-1 and 11-2)

Make sentences with the given words and the ideas in parentheses. Use *maybe, may, might,* or *will*.

A Winter Day

1. It \ snow \ tomorrow (*you are sure*)

   _____It will snow tomorrow._____

2. It \ snow \ next week (*you are unsure*)

   _____

3. We \ go ice skating on the lake (*you are unsure*)

   _____

4. The kids \ play in the snow (*you are sure*)

   _____

5. The snow \ melt, not \ for several days (*you are sure*)

   _____

PRACTICE 7 ▸ Review: *Maybe, may, might,* and *will.* (Charts 11-1 and 11-2)
Choose <u>all</u> the grammatically correct sentences.

1. (a.) Maybe I am going to skip class tomorrow.
   b. Maybe I skip class tomorrow.
   (c.) I might skip class tomorrow.
   (d.) Maybe I will skip class tomorrow.

2. a. It will snow in the mountains next week.
   b. It might snow in the mountains next week.
   c. Maybe it snows in the mountains next week.
   d. Maybe it will snow in the mountains next week.

3. a. We may not have a warm summer this year.
   b. We won't have a warm summer this year.
   c. Maybe we won't have a warm summer this year.
   d. Maybe we don't have a warm summer this year.

4. a. Maybe you are need extra time for the test tomorrow.
   b. You might need extra time for the test tomorrow.
   c. You may be need extra time for the test tomorrow.
   d. Maybe you will need extra time for the test tomorrow.

PRACTICE 8 ▸ *Before, after,* and *when.* (Chart 11-3)
Complete the sentences using the correct form of the verbs in parentheses. Use ***be going to***
for future.

1. Before I (*fix*) _____*fix*_____ dinner tonight, I (*get*) _*am going to get*_____ fresh
   vegetables from my garden.

2. After I (*have*) _____ dinner, I (*go*) _____ out with friends
   for dessert.

3. When I (*see*) _____ my friends, we (*make*) _____ plans for a
   bike trip this summer.

4. Before Susan (*take*) _____ the driving test next week, she (*practice*) _____
   _____ with her parents.

5. When Susan (*take*) _____ the test next week, she (*feel*) _____
   nervous.

6. After Susan (*get*) _____ her license, she (*be*) _____ a
   careful driver.

PRACTICE 9 ▸ *Before, after,* and *when.* (Chart 11-3)

Write logical sentences with the given words.

Carlos is a student. What is he going to do tomorrow?

1. make breakfast \ get up

   After _____*he gets up, he is going to make breakfast.*_____

2. eat breakfast \ go to school

   Before _____

3. go to his classroom \ get to school

   After _____

4. have lunch in the cafeteria \ talk to his friends

   When _____

5. cook dinner for his roommates \ pick up food at the grocery store

   Before _____

6. do his homework \ go to bed

   Before _____

7. fall asleep \ have good dreams

   After _____

PRACTICE 10 ▸ *Before* and *after.* (Chart 11-3)

Write "1" before the first action and "2" before the second. Then write two sentences: one with *before* and one with *after*. Use a form of *be going to* in the main clause.

1. __*1*__ I boil the water.

   __*2*__ I put in the rice.

   a. _____*Before I put in the rice, I am going to boil the water.*_____

   b. _____*After I boil the water, I am going to put in the rice.*_____

2. _____ I turn in my homework.

   _____ I check my answers.

   a. _____

   b. _____

3. _____ I wash the dishes.

   _____ I clear off the table.

   a. _____

   b. _____

4. _____ I get my umbrella.

_____ I go out in the rain.

a. _____

b. _____

5. _____ I pack my bags.

_____ I go to the airport.

a. _____

b. _____

PRACTICE 11 ▸ Clauses with *if.* (Chart 11-4)
Complete the sentences using the correct form of the verbs in parentheses.

1. If Ellen (*gets, will get*) _____*gets*_____ a scholarship, she (*goes, will go*) _____*will go*_____
   to college.

2. If she (*goes, will go*) _____ to college, she (*is going to study, studies*)
   _____ chemistry.

3. If she (*enjoys, will enjoy*) _____ chemistry, she (*takes, will take*)
   _____ pre-med courses.

4. She (*applies, will apply*) _____ to medical school if she (*is going to do, does*)
   _____ well in her pre-med* courses.

5. If she (*attends, will attend*) _____ medical school, she (*studies, is going to study*)
   _____ family medicine.

6. If she (*completes, is going to complete*) _____ her training, she (*helps, is
   going to help*) _____ people around the world.

PRACTICE 12 ▸ Clauses with *if.* (Chart 11-4)
Complete the sentences using the correct form of the verbs in parentheses.

1. If it (*be*) _____*is*_____ sunny tomorrow, Jake (*go*) _____*is going to go*_____
   _____*OR will go*_____ to the beach.

2. If it (*rain*) _____ tomorrow, I (*go, not*) _____
   to the beach.

_____

pre-med = classes that prepare a student for medical school.

3. I (*make*) _____ some soup if you (*be*) _____ hungry.

4. Your dinner (*get*) _____ cold if you (*eat, not*) _____ _____ it now.

5. We (*be*) _____ late if we (*leave, not*) _____ soon.

6. If we (*leave*) _____ right now, we (*be, not*) _____ _____ late.

7. If Lesley (*feel*) _____ sick tomorrow, she (*come, not*) _____ _____ to school.

8. She (*call*) _____ you for the homework assignments if she (*miss*) _____ class.

9. If Brian (*need*) _____ help this weekend, we (*help*) _____ _____ him.

10. We (*make*) _____ other plans if he (*need, not*) _____ _____ help next week.

PRACTICE 13 ▸ *Before, after, when,* and *if.* (Charts 11-3 and 11-4)
Complete the sentences using the correct form of the verbs in parentheses.

An Interview in Toronto

Hannah is going to travel to Toronto for a job interview with a large company. When she (*arrive*) _____*arrives*_____ in
$\frac{}{1}$
Toronto, she (*take*) _____ a taxi to the hotel.
$\frac{}{2}$
After she (*check*) _____ into the hotel, some
$\frac{}{3}$
employees from the company (*meet*) _____ her
$\frac{}{4}$
for dinner at a restaurant. The next day, Hannah will go to the company for her interview. When
she (*get*) _____ there, a manager (*interview*) _____
$\frac{}{5}$ $\frac{}{6}$
her for about an hour. After she (*finish*) _____ , the manager
$\frac{}{7}$
(*give*) _____ Hannah a tour of the company. Hannah is very excited
$\frac{}{8}$
about the job interview. If she (*get*) _____ the job, she
$\frac{}{9}$
(*move*) _____ to Toronto.
$\frac{}{10}$

PRACTICE 14 ▸ Present habits. (Chart 11-5)

Make sentences. Use the habitual present.

Part I. Match each word or phrase in Column A with a phrase in Column B. Write the letter in the blank.

COLUMN A

1. _f_ drink too much coffee

2. ____ cry

3. ____ not pay my electric bill on time

4. ____ the phone rings in the middle of the night

5. ____ get to work late

6. ____ eat a big breakfast

7. ____ not do my homework

COLUMN B

a. my eyes get red

b. stay at work late

c. not answer it

d. get low grades on the tests

e. pay a late fee

✓ f. feel shaky and nervous

g. have a lot of energy

Part II. Now, write habitual present sentences using the phrases in Part I. Begin with **If I ...** .

1. _____ If I drink too much coffee, I feel shaky and nervous. _____

2. _____

3. _____

4. _____

5. _____

6. _____

7. _____

PRACTICE 15 ▸ Present habits. (Chart 11-5)

Answer the questions. Pay special attention to punctuation.

1. How do you feel if you're late for class?

   a. If _____ I'm late for class, I feel nervous. _____

   b. _____ I feel nervous _____ if _____ I'm late for class. _____

2. How do you feel after you eat too much?

   a. After _____

   b. _____ after _____

3. What do you do if you get a headache?

   a. If _____

   b. _____ if _____

4. What do you do when your teacher talks too fast?

   a. When _____

   b. _____ when _____

PRACTICE 16 ▸ Present habits vs. future. (Chart 11-5)
Choose *present habit* or *future* for each sentence.

1. When I'm tired, I take a nap.	(present habit)	future
2. If I'm tired, I'm going to take a nap.	present habit	future
3. After the café closes, the manager will clean the kitchen.	present habit	future
4. After the café closes, the manager cleans the kitchen.	present habit	future
5. Before I go to work, I read the news.	present habit	future
6. When Nancy moves to the city, she is going to sell her car.	present habit	future
7. Tim is going to check out of his hotel room before he has breakfast.	present habit	future
8. When Tim goes to the airport, he takes a taxi.	present habit	future
9. After Tim checks out of his hotel, he will call for a taxi.	present habit	future
10. I'm going to watch a movie after I finish my homework.	present habit	future

PRACTICE 17 ▸ Present habits vs. future. (Chart 11-5)
Choose the correct verbs.

1. If it (is)/ will be noon in California, it (is)/ will be 3:00 P.M. in New York.

2. When I arrive / will arrive in New York tomorrow, it is / will be midnight.

3. If Jay takes / will take six classes next semester, he graduates / will graduate early.

4. After he graduates / will graduate, Jay works / is going to work for his father's company.

5. When it rains / will rain, I usually stay / will stay home.

6. I go / am going to go out tomorrow if it doesn't rain / won't rain.

7. I always clean / will clean my apartment before my parents visit / will visit.

8. I clean / am going to clean my apartment before my parents arrive / will arrive tomorrow.

9. We usually eat / will eat outside when the weather is / will be nice.

10. If the weather is / will be nice tomorrow, we eat / will eat outside.

PRACTICE 18 ▸ Present habits vs. future. (Chart 11-5)

Complete the sentences using the correct form of the verbs in parentheses. Use **be going to** for the future.

1. My friends and I (*like*) _____*like*_____ to go to the lake if the weather

   (*be*) _____*is*_____ warm.

2. We (*go*) _____ to the lake tomorrow if the weather

   (*be*) _____ warm.

3. Before I (*go*) _____ to class today, I (*meet*) _____

   _____ my friends for coffee.

4. Before I (*go*) _____ to my first class, I (*meet, usually*) _____

   _____ my friends in the cafeteria.

5. I (*buy*) _____ some stamps when I (*go*) _____

   to the post office this afternoon.

6. Jim (*be*) _____ often tired when he (*get*) _____

   home from work. If he (*feel*) _____ tired, he (*exercise*) _____

   _____ for thirty minutes. After he (*exercise*) _____, he

   (*begin*) _____ to feel better.

7. If I (*be*) _____ tired tonight, I (*exercise, not*) _____

   _____. I need to work late at the office tonight.

8. When Mrs. Rose (*travel*) _____ by plane, she (*bring*) _____

   _____ her own snacks.

9. When she (*travel*) _____ to New York next week, she

   (*pack*) _____ enough food for lunch and dinner.

10. Jane is usually on time for appointments. When she (*be*) _____ late

    for an appointment, she (*begin*) _____ to feel nervous.

11. Jane is late for work now. She is stuck in traffic. When she (*get*) _____

    _____ to work, she (*tell*) _____ her co-workers about the

    heavy traffic.

12. After I (*have*) _____ lunch, I usually (*take*) _____ a walk.

    I'm very busy today. I (*not, take*) _____ after I (*eat*) _____

    lunch this afternoon.

Choose the correct answers.

1. A: Is Ryan going to come with us to the soccer game this afternoon?
   B: I'm not sure. He _____ come.

   a. is going to   (b.) may   c. maybe   d. will

2. A: Are you going to be home for your vacation?
   B: No, I _____ be home. I'm going to stay with my cousins in Toronto.

   a. will   b. might   c. won't   d. don't

3. A: When _____ your parents going to be here?
   B: In a few minutes.

   a. will   b. do   c. are   d. is

4. A: Do you like all the traveling you do for your job?
   B: Yes. When I'm in a new city, I always _____ new things to see and do.

   a. discover   b. discovering   c. discovers   d. will discover

5. A: When are you going to pick up the clothes at the dry cleaners?
   B: In a little while. I'm going to stop there before I _____ the kids at school.

   a. pick up   b. will pick up   c. picked up   d. am going to pick up

6. A: Why is the dog barking?
   B: I don't know. _____ someone is outside.

   a. May   b. Is   c. Maybe   d. Did

7. A: When Chen _____ to Taiwan next month, who will he stay with?
   B: I think his sister, but I'm not completely sure.

   a. will go   b. go   c. goes   d. going

Complete each sentence with any appropriate form of the given verbs. Use *be going to* for future.

1. A: (*you, stay*) __Are you going to stay__ here during vacation next week?

   B: No. I (*take*) _____ a trip to Montreal. I (*visit*) _____

   _____ my cousins.

   A: How long (*you, be*) _____ away?

   B: About five days.

2. A: Is Carol here?

   B: No, she (*be, not*) _____. She (*leave*) _____

   a few minutes ago.

   A: (*she, be*) _____ back soon?

   B: I think so.

   A: Where (*she, go*) _____?

   B: She (*go*) _____ to the drugstore.

3. A: (*you, see*) _____ Romero tomorrow?

   B: Yes. I (*have*) _____ lunch with him.

   A: Could you give him this book? I (*borrow*) _____ it a few months

   ago and (*forget*) _____ to return it.

   B: Sure.

4. A: Why (*you, wear*) _____ a cast on your foot?

   B: I (*break*) _____ my ankle.

   A: How?

   B: I (*step*) _____ into a hole while I was running in the park.

5. A: Why (*Kevin, run*) _____?

   B: He (*be*) _____ late for work.

   A: Why (*he, be*) _____ late?

   B: He (*sleep*) _____ late this morning. He (*not, turn on*)

   _____ an alarm last night.

PRACTICE 21 ▶ Review. (Chapters 8 → 11)
Correct the mistakes.

1. I have a doctor's appointment. I ~~maybe~~ *may be* late for the meeting today.

2. Natalia mights study in Spain next year.

3. May be it will rain tomorrow.

4. I'll call you after I will get home tonight.

5. Our teacher might won't be here tomorrow.

6. Zac walks to work when the weather will be nice.

7. What will you do after you will graduate?

8. Allie will go to the game with us this weekend if she won't have homework.

PRACTICE 1 ▸ Can. (Chart 12-1)
Complete the sentences with **can** and a verb from the box.

cook	play	ride	sing	speak	swim

1. We ____can speak____ English.

2. I _____ a bike.

3. She _____.

4. They _____.

5. Joe _____ a guitar.

6. Mr. Lee _____.

PRACTICE 2 ▸ *Can* or *can't*. (Chart 12-1)

Choose the correct answers.

1. Penguins (can)/ can't swim.

2. Dogs can / can't climb trees.

3. Fish can / can't live out of water.

4. We don't need to go to the office every day. We can / can't work from home some days.

5. Maya is very sick today. She can / can't go to work.

6. I need help with this homework. I can / can't understand it.

7. The baby is three months old. He can / can't walk.

8. The kids ate all their dinner. They can / can't have ice cream for dessert now.

9. Look at that sign. You can / can't park here.

No Parking

PRACTICE 3 ▸ *Can* or *can't*. (Chart 12-1)

Make sentences about what you and other people *can* and *can't* do. Use words from the box or your own words.

do algebra	play a guitar	sail a sailboat	read Chinese
fly an airplane	repair a computer	run fast	speak two languages

1. I _____ .

2. I _____ .

3. I _____ .

4. My best friend _____ .

5. My best friend _____ .

6. My (*a person in your family*) _____ .

7. My (*a person in your family*) _____ .

8. My teacher _____ .

a sailboat

PRACTICE 4 ▸ *Can* or *can't*. (Charts 12-1 and 12-3)

Make questions and answers with the given information.

	GEORGE	MIA	PAUL	EVA
drive a car	yes	yes	no	no
play the piano	yes	yes	no	yes
repair a bike	yes	no	no	yes
swim	yes	yes	yes	yes

1. George \ repair a bike <u>*Can George repair a bike? Yes, he can.*</u>

2. George and Mia \ play the piano _____

3. Mia \ swim _____

4. Paul \ play the piano _____

5. Paul and Eva \ drive a car _____

6. Mia, George, and Paul \ swim _____

7. Eva and George \ repair a bike _____

8. Eva \ drive a car _____

PRACTICE 5 ▸ *Can* or *can't*. (Charts 12-1 and 12-3)

Read the help-wanted ad and look at John's skills. Write interview questions and answers. Use the given information and ***can*** or ***can't***.

> **Job opening at small international hotel**
> Looking for person with the following skills: good at typing, good social media skills, excellent knowledge of English, friendly manner on the phone. This person also needs to help guests with their suitcases and be available on weekends.

John can:
- ✓ type
- ✓ use social media
- ____ speak perfect English
- ✓ lift suitcases
- ____ work weekends

HOTEL MANAGER'S QUESTIONS	JOHN'S ANSWERS
1. <u>*Can you type?*</u>	<u>*Yes, I can.*</u>
2. _____	_____
3. _____	_____
4. _____	_____
5. _____	_____

PRACTICE 6 ▸ Information questions with *can.* **(Chart 12-3)**
Match the question with the correct answer.

1. What can I get you? __e__   a. The manager.
2. Where can I register for class? _____   b. After class.
3. When can we leave? _____   c. In the school administration office.
4. Who can they talk to about their problem? _____   d. At the reservation desk.
5. Where can I find the hotel manager? _____   ✓ e. Some coffee, please.

PRACTICE 7 ▸ *Know how to.* **(Chart 12-4)**
Rewrite the sentences using *know how to*.

1. Toni can make pizza.

    _____Toni knows how to make pizza._____

2. Martha can play chess.

    _____

3. Sonya and Thomas can speak Portuguese.

    _____

4. Jack can't speak Russian.

    _____

5. My brothers can't cook.

    _____

6. I can't change a flat tire.

    _____

7. We can't play musical instruments.

    _____

8. Can you type?

    _____

9. Can your children swim?

    _____

10. Can your son tie his shoes?

    _____

11. Can you edit a video?

    _____

PRACTICE 8 ▸ *Know how to.* (Chart 12-4)

Write sentences about what you and others **know how to** do or **don't know how to** do. Use the words below or your own words.

drive a stick shift car

sew clothes

knit a scarf

use chopsticks

fly a drone

climb a mountain

do advanced math

ski

1. I _____ .

2. I _____ .

3. (*name of your best friend*) _____ .

4. My best friend and I _____ .

5. (*name of a cousin*) _____ .

6. (*name of a classmate*) _____ .

7. (*name of a classmate*) _____ .

PRACTICE 9 ▸ *Could.* (Chart 12-5)

Stefan and Heidi decided to live without electricity for one month. Write what they **could** and **couldn't** do for that month.

✓ watch TV	spend time together	use electric heat
cook over a fire	use a computer	have heat from a fireplace
read books	turn on the lights	play board games

a log cabin

1. _____*They couldn't watch TV.*_____

2. _____

3. _____

4. _____

5. _____

6. _____

7. _____

8. _____

9. _____

PRACTICE 10 ▸ *Can* or *could*. (Charts 12-1 and 12-5)
Choose the correct answers.

1. Yesterday we can't /(couldn't) go to the beach. It rained all day.

2. Please turn down the music! I can't / couldn't study.

3. Could / Can you speak English a few years ago?

4. I'm a fast typist. I can / could type 90 words-per-minute on my computer.

5. Sam could / can tell time when he was four years old.

6. Could / Can you finish the math test yesterday?

7. Our neighbors can't / couldn't control their dog. She needs dog-training classes.

PRACTICE 11 ▸ *Be able to*. (Chart 12-6)
Make sentences with the present, past, and future forms of *be able to*.

	ABLE TO (PRESENT)	ABLE TO (PAST)	ABLE TO (FUTURE)
1. I can run.	*I am able to run.*	*I was able to run.*	*I will be able to run.*
2. You can draw.			
3. He can drive.			
4. She can swim.			
5. We can dance.			
6. They can type.			

PRACTICE 12 ▸ *Be able to*. (Chart 12-6)
Make sentences with the present and past forms of *be able to*.

1. When I was a newborn baby, I ____*wasn't able to*____ walk.

2. When I was a newborn baby, I _____ talk.

3. When I entered kindergarten, I _____ read and write my language.

4. A few years ago, I _____ speak a lot of English.

5. Now I _____ read and write some English.

6. I _____ understand native English speakers well now.

7. I _____ understand my English teacher all the time.

PRACTICE 13 ▸ Be able to. (Chart 12-6)
Choose the sentence that is closest in meaning to the given sentence.

1. James can run very fast.
   a. He will be able to run very fast.
   (b.) He is able to run very fast.
   c. He was able to run very fast.

2. I will be able to have dinner with you.
   a. I can have dinner with you.
   b. I could have dinner with you.
   c. I was able to have dinner with you.

3. Jean couldn't finish her science project.
   a. She isn't able to finish her science project.
   b. She wasn't able to finish her science project.
   c. She won't be able to finish her science project.

4. My roommate wasn't able to come to the party.
   a. He won't be able to come to the party.
   b. He can't come to the party.
   c. He couldn't come to the party.

5. I can't help you later.
   a. I wasn't able to help you.
   b. I couldn't help you.
   c. I won't be able to help you.

PRACTICE 14 ▸ Be able to. (Chart 12-6)
Rewrite the boldfaced verbs with the correct form of *be able to*.

An English Success Story

was able to speak

Five years ago, Chang visited Australia. He **could speak** only a little English. He had a
                                              1

difficult time when he spoke to people. People **couldn't understand** him. He **couldn't ask**
                                                        2   3

questions. He **couldn't make** friends very easily. He felt lonely.
                      4

So Chang decided to study English. He took a few English classes and practiced every day.

Now, five years later, he is traveling in Australia again. He **can understand** so much. People
                                                                      5

can have long conversations with him. He **can learn** about local customs. This time Chang is
 6   7

having a great trip. Learning English makes a big difference.

PRACTICE 15 ▸ Can, can't, be able to, and know how to.
(Charts 12-1 and 12-4 → 12-6)
Choose all the grammatically correct verbs.

1. Alex _____ to program computers.
   a. can
   (b.) is able
   c. are able
   d. know how
   (e.) knows how

2. Mr. and Mrs. Cox _____ fix their car.
   a. can
   b. know how to
   c. knows how to
   d. isn't able to
   e. aren't able to

3. Jerry is _____ speak several languages.
   a. able to
   b. not able to
   c. can't
   d. know how to
   e. knows how to

4. Two of my friends don't _____ swim.
   a. can't
   b. aren't able to
   c. knows how to
   d. able to
   e. know how to

5. Ellen _____ create movies on a computer.
   a. knows how to
   b. doesn't know how to
   c. can
   d. able to
   e. can't

PRACTICE 16 ▸ Very or too. (Chart 12-7)
Write *very* or *too*.

1. This leather coat is _____ *too* _____ expensive. I can't buy it.

2. The tea is _____ hot, but I can drink it.

3. The shoe store is _____ big. There's a good selection.

4. My daughter can't drive. She's _____ young.

5. The neighbors are _____ noisy. I want them to move.

6. These pants are _____ short. I'm not going to buy them.

7. My teacher talks _____ fast. It's good practice for me.

8. This car is _____ small. It won't use a lot of gas.

9. The Arctic Circle is _____ cold. I don't want to travel there.

10. We had a great time at the zoo. The weather was _____ nice.

PRACTICE 17 ▸ *Very or too.* (Chart 12-7)

Choose the best answer.

1. Do you like this book?
   (a.) Yes, it's very interesting.   b. Yes, it's too interesting.

2. I can't watch this movie.
   a. It's too violent.   b. It's very violent.

3. You had no mistakes on your math test.
   a. Your knowledge of math is too good.   b. Your knowledge of math is very good.

4. We can do these math problems.
   a. They're too easy.   b. They're very easy.

5. This dress is too tight.
   a. I can't wear it.   b. I can wear it.

6. This puzzle looks very tricky.
   a. Let's see if we can figure it out.   b. It will be impossible to do.

7. Thomas is too angry.
   a. I feel comfortable around him.   b. I feel uncomfortable around him.

8. Let's buy this mattress.
   a. It's very comfortable.   b. It's too comfortable.

PRACTICE 18 ▸ *Very or too.* (Chart 12-7)

Write answers to the questions.

1. What school subjects are very hard for you?

   _____

2. What school subjects are too hard for you?

   _____

3. What foods do you think are very spicy?

   _____

4. What foods are too spicy for you?

   _____

5. What cities are too hot for you?

   _____

6. What cities are too cold for you?

   _____

PRACTICE 19 ▸ Asking for Permission. (Chart 12-8)

Make polite questions. Use the modals in parentheses and *please*.

Requests

1. Your co-workers are sitting at a table in the cafeteria. There is an empty seat. You want to sit there.

   (May) _____ *May I please sit here? / May I sit here, please?* _____

2. Your phone battery is almost dead. You want to borrow your friend's charger.

   (Can) _____

3. You have an appointment. You need to leave work a few minutes early.

   (May) _____

4. You are going to a movie with some friends. You don't want to drive. You would like to ride in your friend's car.

   (Could) _____

5. You didn't finish your homework on time. You want to turn it in a day late.

   (May) _____

6. Your friends are playing a card game. You want to join them.

   (Could) _____

7. You are watching TV with your roommate. You want to change the channel.

   (Can) _____

PRACTICE 20 ▸ Review. (Chapter 12)

Choose the correct answers.

1. _____ play a musical instrument?
   a. Do you can   b. Can you   c. Do you be able to   d. Can you to

2. I _____ my homework. I was too tired.
   a. couldn't to finish   b. could finish   c. couldn't finish   d. couldn't finished

3. I don't know how _____ to the Palace Hotel from here.
   a. do I get   b. get   c. getting   d. to get

4. Gina _____ understand the speaker at the lecture last night.
   a. couldn't   b. doesn't able to   c. won't be able to   d. can't

5. My uncle can't _____ English.
   a. to speak   b. speaking   c. speaks   d. speak

6. The driving test was _____ . I was so happy to pass it.
   a. very hard   b. too difficult   c. very easy   d. too fun

7. Sorry, I _____ to get movie tickets. They were sold out.
   a. can't   b. didn't   c. couldn't   d. wasn't able

PRACTICE 21 ▶ Review. (Chapter 12)
Correct the mistakes.

        can't
1. Sara ~~doesn't can~~ come to class today.

2. I can to speak Chinese.

3. They will can meet us after class.

4. Pedro couldn't spoke English before he moved here.

5. When I was a child, I can walked to school.

6. Chris knows how program a videogame.

7. My brother not know how to drive.

8. Where I can buy fresh vegetables?

9. I need to do my homework now. I not able to finish it last night.

10. This food is too spicy. I can eat it.

11. May I borrowing your pen?

12. Can I to park in this parking lot?

CHAPTER 13

Modals, Part 2: Advice, Necessity, Requests, Suggestions

PRACTICE 1 ▶ Should. (Chart 13-1)
Complete the sentences with **should** and a verb from the box.

call	leave	✓ see	study	take	wear

1. Mrs. Wang is sick. She _____*should see*_____ a doctor.

2. The baby is sleepy. He _____ a nap.

3. We have a test tomorrow. We _____ a lot tonight.

4. I am going to be late for work. I _____ now.

5. Michael and Leo need to go to the airport. They _____ a taxi.

6. It's cold outside. You _____ a jacket.

PRACTICE 2 ▶ Should. (Chart 13-1)
Write **should** or **shouldn't**.

Sami wants to be on his high school soccer team.

1. He _____*should*_____ practice kicking a ball with his friends.

2. He _____ exercise a lot.

3. He _____ smoke cigarettes.

4. He _____ stop doing homework so he has more time for soccer.

5. He _____ practice running fast.

6. He _____ watch famous soccer games.

7. He _____ eat a lot of snack foods.

PRACTICE 3 ▶ Should. (Chart 13-1)
Make sentences with **should** or **shouldn't**.

Rose gets failing grades in school. She wants to get better grades.

1. She doesn't do her homework.

   She should do her homework.

2. She copies her roommate's homework.

    She shouldn't copy her roommate's homework.

3. She doesn't study for her tests.

    _____

4. She stays up late.

    _____

5. She daydreams in class.

    _____

6. She is absent from class a lot.

    _____

7. She doesn't take notes during lectures.

    _____

8. She doesn't take her notebooks to school.

    _____

PRACTICE 4 ▶ *Should.* (Chart 13-1)
Give advice with *should* or *shouldn't*.

1. Sara's bedroom is very messy. She can't find her clothes.

    Sara ___*should clean her room.*___

2. The Browns play loud music at night. It wakes up the neighbors.

    The neighbors _____

3. Janet is a dance teacher. She has a backache.

    Janet _____

4. Bill has a sore tooth. It began to hurt four weeks ago.

    Bill _____

5. Ronnie isn't careful with his money. He spends too much and he's always broke.★

    Ronnie _____

6. Mr. and Mrs. Tanner are traveling to South America soon. They don't have visas.

    They _____

★ *be broke* = have no money.

PRACTICE 5 ▸ Have to and has to. (Chart 13-2)
Write **have to** or **has to** + **leave**.

1. I _____*have to leave*_____ soon.

2. We _____ soon.

3. They _____ soon.

4. You _____ soon.

5. He _____ soon.

6. She _____ soon.

7. My parents (*not*) _____ soon.

8. I (*not*) _____ soon.

9. Mark (*not*) _____ soon.

10. Mark and I (*not*) _____ soon.

11. A: _____ Kate _____ work tomorrow?
    B: Yes, she does.

12. A: What time _____ you _____ leave today?
    B: Around noon.

PRACTICE 6 ▸ Have to and has to. (Chart 13-2)
Write **has to** or **doesn't have to**.

Roger wants to be a pediatrician (children's doctor). What qualities does he have to have?

1. He _____*has to*_____ be smart.

2. He _____*doesn't have to*_____ be good-looking.

3. He _____ be patient.

4. He _____ speak several languages fluently.

5. He _____ be athletic.

6. He _____ like children.

7. He _____ like working with sick people.

PRACTICE 7 ▸ Have to and has to. (Chart 13-2)
Write **have to/has to** or **don't have to/doesn't have to**.

1. We _____*have to*_____ leave now. Our class starts soon.

2. We _____ hurry. We're almost there.

3. A good teacher _____ begin on time.

4. The students _____ arrive on time. Late students get lower grades.

5. Students _____ arrive before 8:00. The school isn't open.

6. I _____ study hard. I want to go to medical school.

7. Jane _____ take a lot of science classes. She wants to be an artist.

8. Teachers _____ correct a lot of homework. They collect it every day.

9. My teacher _____ correct a lot of papers. She has 50 students.

10. My friend's teacher has five students. She _____ correct a lot of papers.

PRACTICE 8 ▸ *Had to* or *didn't have to*. (Chart 13-2)
Read the information about Mr. Napoli. Then write ***had to*** or ***didn't have to***.

Mr. Napoli is retired now. For thirty years, he owned a successful bakery. His bakery opened at 5:00 A.M. and closed at 7:00 P.M. What did he have to do? What didn't he have to do?

1. He _____*had to*_____ work hard.

2. He _____ get up early.

3. His home was above the bakery. He _____ take the bus to work.

4. He _____ be friendly to his customers.

5. His wife took their children to school. He _____ take them.

6. He _____ work long hours.

7. His workers did the cleaning. He _____ clean up at night.

8. He _____ begin baking before 5:00 A.M.

PRACTICE 9 ▶ Had to or *didn't have to.* (Chart 13-2)

What chores did Nina have to do last week? Write **had to** or ***didn't have to***.

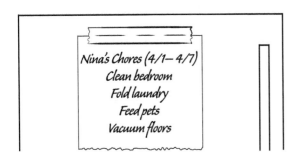

Nina's Chores (4/1– 4/7)
Clean bedroom
Fold laundry
Feed pets
Vacuum floors

1. She _____*had to*_____ clean her bedroom.

2. She _____ cook dinner for her family.

3. She _____ empty the garbage.

4. She _____ fold the laundry.

5. She _____ wash her clothes.

6. She _____ feed the pets.

7. She _____ sweep the floors.

8. She _____ vacuum the floors.

PRACTICE 10 ▶ *Should, have to,* and *don't have to.* (Charts 13-1 and 13-2)

Write ***should, have to***, or ***don't have to***.

High school students in my country …

1. _____ work hard.

2. _____ go to school on Saturdays.

3. _____ stand up when the teacher comes in the room.

4. _____ clean the classroom after class.

5. _____ do homework every day.

6. _____ take extra classes after school or in the evening.

7. _____ memorize a lot of information.

8. _____ work together in small groups.

9. _____ be polite to other students.

10. _____ bring textbooks to class.

11. _____ wear uniforms to school.

PRACTICE 11 ▸ Must or must not. (Chart 13-3)
Write **must** or **must not**.

Beth is going to have surgery. What is her doctor going to tell her after the surgery?

1. She _____*must*_____ take her medicine.

2. She _____ go to work the next day.

3. She _____ rest.

4. She _____ lift heavy objects for several weeks.

5. She _____ call her doctor if she gets a fever.

PRACTICE 12 ▸ Must or must not. (Chart 13-3)
Write **must** or **must not**.

Swimming Pool Rules

1. Swimmers _____*must*_____ take a shower before entering the pool.

2. Parents _____ watch their children.

3. Guests _____ run around the pool.

4. Guests _____ bring food or drinks to the pool area.

5. Swimmers _____ dive in the pool.

6. Children _____ obey their parents.

PRACTICE 13 ▸ Must or should. (Charts 13-1 and 13-3)
Write **must** or **should**.

1. You _____*should*_____ make your bed every day. Your bedroom looks nicer when you make it.

2. You _____ take vitamins every day. They may help you stay healthy.

3. You _____ obey the speed limit. If you drive too fast, you will get a ticket.

4. If you want to go to a top university, you _____ have good grades.

5. You _____ watch old movies if you want to relax.

6. You _____ rest when you are tired.

7. You _____ stop in traffic when the light is red.

8. You _____ have a passport when you travel to another country.

PRACTICE 14 ▸ Polite requests with modals. (Chart 13-4)

Choose the correct answers.

1. A: (May)/ Would I help you?
   B: Yes. I'm looking for the restrooms.

2. A: May / Could you please open the door?
   B: Yes, of course.

3. A: Would / Can I borrow a pen?
   B: Sure.

4. A: Can / May you help carry these boxes?
   B: I'd be happy to.

5. A: May / Would you please pass the salt and pepper?
   B: Sure.

6. A: Hello. Would / Could I please speak with Michael?
   B: I'm sorry. He isn't in the office today. Would / May you like to leave a message?

PRACTICE 15 ▸ Polite requests with modals. (Chart 13-4)

Make polite questions. Use *May I/Could I/Can I please* or *Could you/Would you please*.

1. You are at a restaurant. Your coffee is cold. You want hot coffee.

   _____*May / Could / Can I please have some hot coffee?*_____

2. You didn't hear your teacher's question. You want him/her to repeat it.

   _____*Could / Would / Can you please repeat the question?*_____

3. You are a parent. You want your teenager to clean his bedroom.

   _____

4. You are a teenager. You want your parent to give you some money for a movie.

   _____

5. You are taking a test. You want to sharpen your pencil.

   _____

6. You are stuck in traffic with your friend. You want to borrow her cell phone.

   _____

7. You are at a park with your friends. You want someone to take a picture of all of you.
   You ask a person nearby.

   _____

8. You are studying at home. You want your roommate to turn down the TV.

   _____

PRACTICE 16 ▸ Modal auxiliaries. (Chart 13-5)

Add *to* where necessary. If *to* is not necessary, write Ø (nothing).

1. The sky is dark. It is going ___*to*___ rain.

2. Would you please _____ speak more slowly?

3. You should _____ meet John. He's very interesting.

4. Do we have _____ take a test tomorrow?

5. Will you _____ join us for lunch?

6. Robert might not _____ work tomorrow. He doesn't feel well.

7. I'm not able _____ help you right now.

8. The neighbors shouldn't _____ have loud parties late at night.

9. We weren't able _____ get any email messages yesterday.

10. Monica can't _____ talk much because she has a bad cough.

PRACTICE 17 ▸ Modal auxiliaries and similar expressions. (Chart 13-6)

Choose the sentence that is closest in meaning.

1. We must leave.
   a. We should leave.
   b. We have to leave.
   c. We may leave.

2. I wasn't able to come.
   a. I couldn't come.
   b. I didn't have to come.
   c. I shouldn't come.

3. Mrs. Jones will pick us up tomorrow.
   a. Mrs. Jones may pick us up.
   b. Mrs. Jones is going to pick us up.
   c. Mrs. Jones could pick us up.

4. I won't be able to meet with you tomorrow.
   a. I don't want to meet with you.
   b. I don't have to meet with you.
   c. I can't meet with you.

5. Would you close the door, please?
   a. Should you close the door?
   b. Must you close the door?
   c. Could you close the door?

6. You should take a break.
    a. You have to take a break.
    b. You might take a break.
    c. It's a good idea for you to take a break.

7. Tom didn't have to work yesterday.
    a. Tom didn't need to work.
    b. Tom couldn't work.
    c. Tom didn't want to work.

8. It might be stormy tomorrow.
    a. It must be stormy.
    b. It may be stormy.
    c. It will be stormy.

PRACTICE 18 ▶ Let's. (Chart 13-7)
Write a response with *Let's*.

1. A: The sun is shining. It's going to be a warm day.
    B: ___*Let's go to the park.*___

2. A: We worked hard today.
    B: _____

3. A: Sandra's birthday is this weekend.
    B: _____

4. A: Breakfast is ready.
    B: _____

5. A: Mario's Pizzeria is having a special tonight: free pizza for kids.
    B: _____

PRACTICE 19 ▶ Review. (Chapter 13)
Choose the correct answers.

1. It's very late and I have to get up early. I _____ go to bed.
    a. can   b. should   c. had to

2. We _____ up late last night. We had a lot of homework.
    a. have to stay   b. had to stayed   c. had to stay

3. It's a beautiful day. Let's _____ to the beach.
    a. going   b. to go   c. go

4. Please be quiet. I _____ the speaker very well.
    a. can't hear   b. am not hearing   c. couldn't hear

5. It's hot in here. _____ the window, please?
   a. You will open   b. Could you open   c. Should you open

6. Excuse me. _____ me lift this box?
   a. Would you help   b. Would you to help   c. Would you helping

7. _____ leave now? We're having so much fun.
   a. Do we has to   b. Are we have to   c. Do we have to

8. Mia _____ pay for her groceries. She lost her wallet in the store.
   a. wasn't able   b. couldn't   c. can't to

9. The kids are excited. It _____ snow tonight or tomorrow.
   a. can   b. must   c. might

10. You _____ take this medicine. You are very sick and you need it to get better.
    a. must   b. could   c. might

PRACTICE 20 ▶ Review. (Chapter 13)
Choose all the correct answers.

1. _____ help me carry this box?
   (a.) Would you   b. Do you   (c.) Could you   d. Let's

2. Mario has a toothache. He _____ to call the dentist.
   a. has   b. should   c. needs   d. must

3. I want to watch a movie, but I _____ finish my homework first.
   a. should   b. have to   c. had to   d. must

4. When I was young, I _____ bend over and put my hands flat on the floor.
   a. am able   b. could   c. have   d. was able to

5. But now it's too hard, and I _____ .
   a. can't   b. couldn't   c. am not able to   d. could

6. It's really nice outside. _____ take a walk.
   a. We had to   b. Let's   c. Would we   d. We should

7. _____ you please pass the salt?
   a. May   b. Would   c. Could   d. Can

8. A: Would you help me with the dishes?
   B: _____
   a. No problem.   b. I'd be happy to.   c. I'd be glad.   d. Yes, of course.

Correct the mistakes.

1. It's cold outside. You should ~~to~~ wear a jacket.

2. Where should we having lunch this afternoon?

3. Alex has to works tomorrow.

4. I was sick yesterday. I had to went to the doctor.

5. You must wearing a seatbelt when you drive.

6. Today is a holiday. We not have to go to school.

7. What time you have to work tomorrow?

8. May you help me with this homework?

9. Could you please to turn off the light?

10. The weather is beautiful. Let eat outside.

CHAPTER 14
Nouns and Modifiers

PRACTICE 1 ▸ Nouns and adjectives. (Chart 14-1)

Are the words in the box usually adjectives or nouns? Write each word in the correct column.

✓ tall	pens	boat	true
pretty	sad	store	happy
✓ clothes	hot	horse	truth

ADJECTIVES	NOUNS
tall	*clothes*
_____	_____
_____	_____
_____	_____
_____	_____
_____	_____

PRACTICE 2 ▸ Nouns and adjectives. (Chart 14-1)

Write all the words from the box that can go before each noun. You may use a word more than once.

airplane	concert	grammar	movie
delicious	flower	great	rose
chicken	friendly	math	vegetable

1. _____ soup

2. _____ garden

3. _____ teacher

4. _____ tickets

a rose

PRACTICE 3 ▸ Nouns and adjectives. (Chart 14-1)

How is the underlined word used? Choose *adjective* or *noun*.

1. The <u>camera</u> store has photography classes.   (adjective)   noun

2. Do you have a digital <u>camera</u>?   adjective   noun

3. What are you going to order for <u>lunch</u>?   adjective   noun

4. Nancy's Café has a delicious <u>lunch</u> menu.   adjective   noun

5. This movie has a lot of good <u>action</u>.   adjective   noun

6. I like to watch <u>action</u> movies.   adjective   noun

7. The <u>dog</u> is hungry.   adjective   noun

8. We need to get some <u>dog</u> food.   adjective   noun

9. The <u>pet</u> store is having a sale.   adjective   noun

10. Do you have a <u>pet</u>?   adjective   noun

PRACTICE 4 ▸ Nouns and adjectives. (Chart 14-1)

Complete the sentences. Use the information in the first part of the sentence. Use **noun + noun**.

1. A house for a dog is a ___*dog house*___.

2. Articles in a magazines are _____.

3. A card for business is a _____.

4. An appointment with a dentist is a _____.

5. Sauce for spaghetti is _____.

6. A key for a house is a _____.

7. Chargers for phones are _____.

8. A carton for milk is a _____.

9. Stores with groceries are _____.

10. A curtain for a shower is a _____.

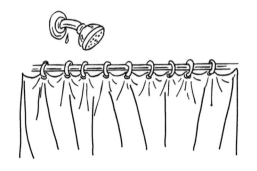

PRACTICE 5 ▸ Nouns and adjectives. (Chart 14-1)

Use the words to make common **adjective + noun** or **noun + noun** phrases.

1. **birthday**

   a. present   _birthday present_

   b. happy   _happy birthday_

   c. cake   _birthday cake_

2. **kitchen**

   a. messy _____

   b. cabinets _____

   c. counter _____

3. **bus**

   a. city _____

   b. schedule _____

   c. route _____

4. **airplane**

   a. noise _____

   b. small _____

   c. ticket _____

5. **apartment**

   a. manager _____

   b. new _____

   c. building _____

6. **phone**

   a. number _____

   b. smart _____

   c. call _____

7. **patient**

   a. hospital _____

   b. sick _____

   c. information _____

PRACTICE 6 ▸ Word order of adjectives. (Chart 14-2)

Put the adjectives in the correct category.

big	green	nice	short	tiny
British	Japanese	old	silk	wood
✓ delicious	metal	pretty	small	yellow
easy	modern	purple	Spanish	young
glass	new	red	Thai	

OPINION	SIZE	AGE	COLOR	NATIONALITY	MATERIAL
delicious					

PRACTICE 7 ▸ Word order of adjectives. (Chart 14-2)

Choose the correct answers.

1. We work in _____ office building.
   a. a large old   b. an old large

2. I spoke with a _____ man at the park today.
   a. Greek friendly   b. friendly Greek

3. I need some _____ socks.
   a. brown comfortable   b. comfortable brown

4. My sister makes _____ soup.
   a. vegetable delicious   b. delicious vegetable

5. The children found _____ box at the beach.
   a. an old metal   b. a metal old

6. My family loves _____ food.
   a. spicy Indian   b. Indian spicy

7. Robert gave his girlfriend _____ ring.
   a. an antique beautiful   b. a beautiful antique

8. We shared our _____ online.
   a. favorite pictures   b. pictures favorite

9. There is a _____ soccer field near our house.
   a. wonderful big grassy* b. grassy big wonderful

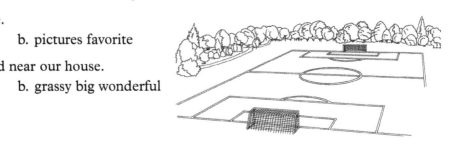

•*grassy* = covered with grass.

PRACTICE 8 ▸ Word order of adjectives. (Chart 14-2)
Write the words in the correct order.

1. house
   brick
   small

   a ____*small brick house*____

2. spicy
   food
   Mexican

   some _____

3. man
   young
   kind

   a _____

4. dirty
   shoes
   brown

   two _____

5. videogame
   new
   fun

   a _____

6. old
   paintings
   interesting

   some _____

7. glass
   tall
   building

   a _____

8. yellow
   flowers
   little

   some _____

9. middle-aged
   woman
   short

   a _____

10. silk
    dress
    Chinese

    a _____

PRACTICE 9 ▸ Linking verbs + adjectives. (Chart 14-3)
Check (✓) the sentences that have a linking verb. Underline the linking verb.

1. __✓__ After it rains, the air <u>smells</u> very fresh.

2. ____ Your vacation plans sound interesting.

3. ____ The kids are playing happily in the backyard.

4. ____ They like to run and climb trees.

5. ____ Does the vegetable soup taste good?

6. ____ The roses smell wonderful.

7. _____ They look beautiful too.

8. _____ Jack looked for some flowers for his wife.

9. _____ Cindy went to bed early because she felt sick.

10. _____ Emily seems sad. Do you know why?

PRACTICE 10 ▸ Linking verbs + adjectives. (Chart 14-3)
Complete each sentence with an appropriate adjective.

1. There's a new movie about space at the theater. I really want to go. It sounds
   _____ *interesting* _____.

2. Carl woke up at 3:00 A.M. and never went back to sleep. He looked _____
   this morning.

3. Mmm. What are you baking? The kitchen smells _____.

4. I got 100% on all my tests. I feel _____.

5. Whew! Do you smell that smell? I think it's a skunk. It smells _____.

a skunk

6. I'm sorry, this chicken tastes _____. I can't eat it.

7. The Smiths are having a beach party this weekend. It sounds _____. Do you
   want to go?

8. A few hours after dinner, Ellen and Bill got sick. They felt _____ for the rest of
   the evening.

9. I don't know how to do this math homework. It's very _____.

10. We have new neighbors. I want to meet them soon. They look _____.

PRACTICE 11 ▸ Adverbs. (Chart 14-4)
Write the adverb forms for the given adjectives.

1. quiet _____ *quietly* _____
2. clear _____
3. neat _____
4. correct _____
5. hard _____
6. good _____
7. early _____

8. careful _____
9. quick _____
10. slow _____
11. late _____
12. honest _____
13. fast _____
14. easy _____

PRACTICE 12 ▸ Adverbs. (Chart 14-4)

Complete each sentence with the adverb form of the given adjective.

1. *clear*   Our teacher explains everything _____*clearly*_____.

2. *easy*   This is a simple car repair. I can do it _____.

3. *late*   Spiro came to class _____.

4. *safe*   The plane arrived at the airport _____.

5. *fast*   Mike talks too _____. I can't understand him.

6. *hard*   Ms. Chan is a hard worker. She worked _____ all her life.

7. *good*   I didn't understand my manager's instructions very _____.

8. *honest*   Answer the questions _____ at your job interview.

9. *soft*   When the students became loud, the teacher spoke _____.

10. *quick*   We cleaned the house _____ before our guests arrived.

PRACTICE 13 ▸ Linking verbs, adjectives, and adverbs. (Charts 14-3 and 14-4)

Complete the sentences with the adjective or adverb form of the given word. Remember, adjectives, not adverbs, follow linking verbs.

1. *nervous*   Bill looked _____*nervous*_____.

    He began his speech _____*nervously*_____.

    He spoke _____*nervously*_____ into the microphone.

2. *beautiful*   Rita dressed _____ for the party.

    She looked _____.

    She wears _____ clothes.

3. *good*   The flowers smell _____.

    They grow _____ in this sunny garden.

4. *good*   Does the food taste _____?

    Robert is a _____ cook.

5. *interesting*   Your idea for the project sounds _____.

    The project looks _____.

6. *hard*   We studied _____ for the test.

    This test looks _____.

    The test has some _____ questions.

7. *fast*   Tom drives _____.

    He speaks _____ too.

PRACTICE 14 ▸ Adjectives and adverbs. (Charts 14-3 and 14-4)

Complete each sentence with the adjective or adverb form of the given word.

1. *clear*   The teacher speaks _____*clearly*_____. She gives _____*clear*_____ examples.

2. *correct*   You answered the question _____. That is the _____ answer.

3. *late*   I paid my phone bill _____. I don't like to make _____ payments.

4. *beautiful* Look at the _____ pictures. The artist draws _____.

5. *honest*   Michael is an _____ child. He never lies. He answers questions _____.

6. *handsome*   Anton looked _____ on his wedding day. He is a _____ man.

7. *good*   Mmm. The food smells _____. I'm glad my roommate is a _____ cook.

8. *easy*   Isabelle writes _____ in English. Writing is an _____ subject for her.

9. *good*   The students swam _____. The team had a _____ competition.

10. *quick*   I need these copies _____. Is your copy machine _____?

11. *sweet*   Candy tastes very _____. I love _____ snacks.

12. *careless* John is a _____ driver. Why does he drive so _____?

PRACTICE 15 ▸ Adjective and adverb review. (Charts 14-3 and 14-4)

Complete each sentence with the correct form of the given adjective or adverb.

1. *slow*   This is a _____*slow*_____ bus. I'm afraid we'll be late.

2. *slow*   There's a lot of traffic. The bus driver has to drive _____.

3. *hard*   The whole class studied _____ for the test.

4. *hard*   The teacher always gives _____ exams.

5. *clear*   The sky looks very _____ today.

6. *early*   The birds woke me up _____ this morning.

7. *fluent*   Jane speaks _____ French, but she can't speak English

_____ .

8. *neat*   Your homework looks very _____ .

9. *careful*   It's clear that you do your work _____ .

10. *good*   The teacher said our group gave a _____ presentation.

11. *good*   She said we worked together _____ .

PRACTICE 16 ▶ *All of, most of, some of,* and *almost all of.* (Chart 14-5)
Match the picture with the sentence.

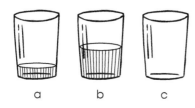

1. Meg drank most of the milk. Now the glass looks like __a__ .

2. Meg drank all of the milk. Now the glass looks like _____ .

3. Meg drank some of the milk. Now the glass looks like _____ or _____ .

4. Meg drank almost all of the milk. Now the glass looks like _____ .

PRACTICE 17 ▶ Understanding quantity expressions. (Charts 14-5 and 14-6)
Choose the percentage that is closest in meaning to the quantity expression.

1. Almost all of the students are coming to the picnic.   (95%)   75%   100%

2. Most of the staff is coming to the picnic.   90%   100%   50%

3. All of the food for the picnic is ready.   90%   100%   95%

4. Some of the dishes are very spicy.   100%   60%   0%

5. Half of the class is bringing a friend.   50%   60%   40%

6. A lot of people in my class ride bikes to school.   75%   10%   0%

7. Some of the people in my class have motorcycles.   0%   99%   30%

8. Most of the teachers take the bus to school.   85%   50%   20%

9. All of the bus drivers are careful.   97%   90%   100%

10. Almost all of the drivers are friendly.   97%   100%   60%

PRACTICE 18 ▸ Subject-verb agreement with quantity words. (Chart 14-6)
Choose the correct answers.

1. All of your English homework (is)/ are correct.

2. All of your sentences is / are correct.

3. Some of your math homework is / are correct.

4. Almost all of your science homework is / are correct.

5. All of your facts is / are correct.

6. Most of my classes is / are hard.

7. Almost all of my classes is / are interesting.

8. Almost all of the students is / are here today.

9. Half of your homework is / are due.

10. Half of your assignments is / are due.

PRACTICE 19 ▸ Subject-verb agreement with quantity words. (Chart 14-6)
Write *is* or *are*.

1. All of the work ____is____ correct.

2. All of the answers _____ correct.

3. All of the information _____ correct.

4. All of the facts _____ correct.

5. Some of your homework _____ incorrect.

6. Some of the students _____ ready.

7. Almost all of the children _____ tired.

8. A lot of the students _____ tired.

9. Half of the vocabulary _____ new for me.

10. Half of the words _____ new for me.

11. Most of the food _____ spicy.

12. Some of the food _____ cold.

13. All of the apples _____ from our apple tree.

14. Almost all of the fruit _____ ripe.

15. Most of the vegetables _____ fresh.

PRACTICE 20 ▸ Review: expressions of quantity. (Charts 14-5 and 14-6)
Choose the correct sentence in each group.

1. a. Some of the book are hard.
   b. Some of book is hard.
   c. Some of the book is hard.

2. a. Some of the money is missing.
   b. Some of money is missing.
   c. Some of the money are missing.

3. a. All of students have books.
   b. All of the students have books.
   c. All of the students has books.

4. a. Most of the chairs is empty.
   b. Most of the chairs are empty.
   c. Most of chairs are empty.

5. a. Almost all of people are late.
   b. Almost all of the people are late.
   c. Almost all of the people is late.

6. a. Half of the students is from Asia.
   b. Half of the students are from Asia.
   c. Half of the students is from Asia.

7. a. Half of the hotel rooms are ready.
   b. Half of hotel rooms are ready.
   c. Half of the hotel rooms is ready.

PRACTICE 21 ▸ Subject-verb agreement with *every* and *all*. (Chart 14-7)
Choose the correct answer for each sentence.

1. All of the _____ are ready to graduate.
   a. student   b. students

2. Every _____ in this room works hard.
   a. person   b. people

3. All of the _____ in the store are for sale.
   a. shirt   b. shirts

4. Are all of the _____ on sale too?
   a. sweater   b. sweaters

5. Every _____ at this party likes to dance.
   a. teenager   b. teenagers

6. Do all _____ like to dance?
   a. teenager   b. teenagers

7. Every _____ in the world wants loving parents.
   a. child   b. children

8. Do all _____ worry about their children?
   a. parent   b. parents

PRACTICE 22 ▸ Subject-verb agreement with *every* and *all*. (Chart 14-7)
Choose the correct answers.

1. All of the teachers _____ tests every week.
   a. gives   b. give

2. Everyone at this school _____ hard.
   a. studies   b. study

3. _____ all of the students in your class participate in discussions?
   a. Does   b. Do

4. _____ everyone in your class participate in discussions?
   a. Does   b. Do

5. Not everybody in the class _____ to give their opinion.
   a. likes   b. like

6. All of the people in line _____ concert tickets.
   a. is buying   b. are buying

7. Everything in these rooms _____ from South America.
   a. is   b. are

8. Every child at the party _____ a present to take home.
   a. get   b. gets

9. _____ everything look okay?
   a. Does   b. Do

10. Everything _____ okay.
   a. looks   b. look

PRACTICE 23 ▸ Subject-verb agreement with *every* and *all*. (Chart 14-7)
Check (✓) the incorrect sentences and correct them.

1. _✓_ Every ~~of the~~ teachers is on time.

2. _____ Every students is on time too.

3. _____ Everything in this room is very clean.

4. _____ Everything in the kitchen sink are dirty.

5. _____ Where does all of your friends live?

6. _____ Where was everyone when I called last night?

7. _____ Everybody in my family like dessert after dinner.

8. _____ Do everyone in your family likes dessert?

9. _____ Was everybody from your office at the wedding?

10. _____ Was all of the people at the wedding your friends?

11. _____ There are ten families in my apartment building. Everyone are friendly.

12. _____ Everything is okay.

PRACTICE 24 ▸ Indefinite pronouns. (Chart 14-8)

Write *something*, *someone*, *somebody*, *anything*, *anyone*, or *anybody*.

STATEMENT	NEGATIVE
1. He ate _something_ .	He didn't eat _anything_ .
2. She met _____/_____ .	She didn't meet _____/_____ .

QUESTION

3. Did he eat _____/_____?

4. Did she meet _____/_____/_____/_____?

STATEMENT	NEGATIVE
5. They bought _____ .	They didn't buy _____ .
6. They spoke to _____/_____ .	They didn't speak to _____/_____ .

QUESTION

7. Did they buy _____/_____?

8. Did they speak to _____/_____/_____/_____?

PRACTICE 25 ▸ Indefinite pronouns. (Chart 14-8)

Choose all of the correct answers.

1. Did you talk to _____ at the pharmacy?
   a. somebody
   b. anything
   c. someone
   d. anyone
   e. anybody
   f. something

2. Did you see _____ outside?
   a. somebody
   b. anything
   c. someone
   d. anyone
   e. anybody
   f. something

3. I dropped off _____ at the airport.
   a. somebody
   b. anything
   c. someone
   d. anyone
   e. anybody
   f. something

4. Did you buy _____ at the mall?
   a. somebody
   b. anything
   c. someone
   d. anyone
   e. anybody
   f. something

PRACTICE 26 ▸ Indefinite pronouns. (Chart 14-8)

Write *something, someone, somebody, anything, anyone,* or *anybody*. Use any word that fits.

1. I didn't buy ___*anything*___ on sale at the grocery store.

2. Did you talk to _____ at the grocery store?

3. I bought _____ for you at the mall.

4. I met _____ from high school at the train station.

5. Did you learn _____ at school today?

6. Did you know _____ at the party?

7. Did the doctor give you _____ for your headaches?

8. I need to talk to _____ about my work schedule.

9. A lot of people are absent. _____ got a cold, and now half of the class is sick.

10. I heard a loud noise. Maybe _____ is in the garage.

PRACTICE 27 ▸ Review. (Chapter 14)

Correct the mistakes.

1. We made potatoes soup for dinner.

2. I can't find my keys car.

3. Chris drives a black small car.

4. We watched an Italian interesting film last weekend.

5. Those flowers look beautifully.

6. Sara always drives careful.

7. The weather is clearly today.

8. I finished almost all of homework this afternoon.

9. All of my friend are here today.

10. Everyone in my class are very nice.

11. Every computers in this store is expensive.

12. You dropped anything. I think it was a pen.

CHAPTER 15

Making Comparisons

PRACTICE 1 ▶ Comparative form. (Chart 15-1)
Write the comparative form for each adjective.

1. young   _younger than_

2. wide   _____

3. cheap   _____

4. dark   _____

5. smart   _____

6. old   _____

7. happy   _____

8. important   _____

9. difficult   _____

10. expensive   _____

11. easy   _____

12. funny   _____

13. good   _____

14. far   _____

15. fat   _____

16. hot   _____

17. thin   _____

18. bad   _____

19. pretty   _____

20. famous   _____

PRACTICE 2 ▸ Comparatives. (Chart 15-1)

Complete the sentences. Write the comparative form of the given words.

1. *warm*   The weather today is ___*warmer than*___ it was yesterday.

2. *funny*   This story is _____ that story.

3. *interesting*   This book is _____ that book.

4. *smart*   Joe is _____ his brother.

5. *wide*   A highway is _____ an alley.

6. *large*   Your apartment is _____ mine.

7. *dark*   Ravi's hair is _____ Olaf's.

8. *good*   My roommate's cooking is _____ mine.

9. *bad*   My cooking is _____ my roommate's.

10. *confusing*   Your homework is _____ my homework.

11. *far*   My house is _____ from downtown _____ your house is.

12. *easy*   My English class is _____ my history class.

13. *young*   A baby is _____ a teenager.

14. *expensive*   A car is _____ than a bike.

PRACTICE 3 ▸ Comparatives. (Chart 15-1)

Compare the three places. Make comparative sentences with the given words. Give your own opinion.

the country   the city   the suburbs

Life in the ...

1. *quiet*   *Life in the country is quieter than life in the city.*

2. *expensive*   _____

3. *relaxing*   _____

4. *busy*   _____

5. *convenient*   _____

6. *beautiful* _____

7. *cheap* _____

8. *nice* _____

9. *safe* _____

10. *good* _____

PRACTICE 4 ▶ Comparatives. (Chart 15-1)

Compare the two culture classes. Use the given words. Give your own opinion.

STUDENT RATING	
Culture 101 A	★★★★★
Culture 101 B	★★

CULTURE COURSES		
CLASSES	101 A	101 B
Teaching style	discussions / games / movies	lecture
Student rating★	5/5	2/5
Homework	3 times/week	every day
Tests	3/term	every week
Average student grade	90%	75%

1. *interesting*   _*101 A is more interesting than 101 B.*_ _____

2. *boring* _____

3. *hard* _____

4. *easy* _____

5. *popular* _____

6. *difficult* _____

7. *enjoyable* _____

8. *fun* _____

★*rating* = 5 = (excellent); 1 = (bad).

PRACTICE 5 ▸ Comparative and superlative forms. (Charts 15-1 and 15-2)
Write both the comparative form and superlative form of the given words.

	COMPARATIVE	SUPERLATIVE
1. expensive	*more expensive than*	*the most expensive*
2. lazy		
3. clean		
4. old		
5. young		
6. new		
7. beautiful		
8. exciting		
9. nice		
10. quiet		
11. bad		
12. fat		
13. thin		
14. hot		
15. good		
16. cheap		
17. far		
18. funny		

PRACTICE 6 ▸ Superlatives. (Chart 15-2)
Complete the sentences. Use superlatives. Give your opinion.

1. *hard subject in high school*

   The ___*hardest subject in high school is calculus.*___

2. *beautiful city in the world*

   The _____

3. *interesting show on TV*

   The _____

4. *boring sport to watch*

   The _____

5. *easy language to learn*

The _____

6. *talented movie star*

The _____

7. *relaxing place to go for vacation*

The _____

8. *good place to live*

The _____

PRACTICE 7 ▸ Superlatives. (Chart 15-2)

Compare the three places to eat. Make superlative sentences with the given words.
Give your opinion.

a fast-food restaurant

a fancy restaurant

a coffee shop

1. expensive _____*A fancy restaurant is the most expensive.*_____

2. convenient _____

3. relaxing _____

4. busy _____

5. nice _____

6. interesting _____

7. popular _____

8. quiet _____

9. cheap _____

10. useful _____

PRACTICE 8 ▶ Review: comparatives and superlatives. (Charts 15-1 and 15-2)
Make sentences with comparatives and superlatives. Use the given information.

Fluffy	Rex	Polly
9 lbs / 4 kilos	70 lbs / 32 kilos	2.2 lbs /1 kilo
likes to sleep all day	likes to run and play	likes to sing and look around
gray and white fur	brown fur	green and yellow feathers
2 years old	7 years old	10 years old

1. lazy   *Fluffy is lazier than Rex.*
               Fluffy is the laziest.

2. active _____

_____

3. young _____

_____

4. heavy _____

_____

5. colorful _____

_____

6. big _____

_____

7. old _____

_____

8. small _____

_____

9. light* _____

_____

_____
light = opposite of heavy.

PRACTICE 9 ▸ *One of* + superlative + plural noun. (Chart 15-3)

Complete the sentences with the correct form of the given adjective and noun.

1. hot \ month   August is one of _____ *the hottest months* _____ in my hometown.

2. fast \ car   A Ferrari is one of _____ in the world.

3. happy \ family   Sam and Mia have one of _____
                      in our neighborhood.

4. funny \ child   Ricky is one of _____ in his school.

5. good \ manager   Louisa Hoff is one of _____ in our office.

6. tall \ woman   Donna is one of _____ in our class.

7. old \ man   Ken is one of _____ in our class.

8. interesting \ professor Daniel is one of _____
                      in our college.

9. scary \ animal   A tiger is one of _____ in the world.

10. easy \ language   Is English one of _____ to learn?

PRACTICE 10 ▸ *One of* + superlative + plural noun. (Chart 15-3)

Make sentences with **one of** + **superlative**. Use the given adjectives and the activities from the box. Give your opinion.

biking
gymnastics
running
skateboarding
tennis
volleyball
weightlifting
✓ walking
yoga

1. easy   _____ *Walking is one of the easiest activities.* _____

2. dangerous   _____

3. expensive   _____

4. safe   _____

5. difficult   _____

6. interesting   _____

7. healthy   _____

8. good for children _____

PRACTICE 11 ▸ *One of* + superlative. (Chart 15-3)
Make sentences with ***one of* + superlative**. Use the given words. Give your opinion.

1. small \ country

   <u>   Liechtenstein is one of the smallest countries   </u> in the world.

2. big \ city

   _____ in this country.

3. hard \ language

   _____ to learn.

4. interesting \ place

   _____ in my hometown.

5. pretty \ place

   _____ to visit.

6. expensive \ city

   _____ to live in.

7. important \ person

   _____ in the world.

PRACTICE 12 ▸ Review: comparatives, superlatives, and *one of*.
(Charts 15-1 → 15-3)
Complete the sentences with the correct form of the given words.

1. big   Asia is _____ <u>the biggest</u> _____ continent in the world.

2. big   North America is _____ South America.

3. hot \ place The Sahara Desert is one of _____ in
                the world.

4. cold \ place The Arctic Circle is one of _____.

5. long   The Nile is _____ the Amazon.

6. large   Is Canada _____ Russia?

7. large   Russia is _____ country in the world.

8. scary   Is a snake _____ a spider?

9. scary   What do you think is _____ animal in
                the world?

10. dangerous \ animal The hippopotamus is one of _____ in
                        the world.

11. expensive \ city   One of _____ in the world is Tokyo.

12. expensive   Is Tokyo _____ London?

13. long   The femur (thigh bone) is _____ bone in our body.

14. small   _____ bone in our body is in the ear.

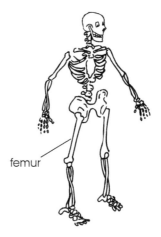

femur

PRACTICE 13 ▸ Comparisons with adverbs. (Charts 14-4 and 15-4)
Write the correct forms of the given adjectives.

ADJECTIVE	ADVERB	COMPARATIVE	SUPERLATIVE
1. quick	*quickly*	*more quickly*	*the most quickly*
2. clear			
3. slow			
4. beautiful			
5. neat			
6. careful			
7. fluent			
8. good			
9. hard			
10. early			
11. late			
12. fast			

PRACTICE 14 ▶ Adverbs: comparatives and superlatives. (Chart 15-4)
Write the correct comparative or superlative form of the given adverbs.

1. beautifully   The art students draw ____*more beautifully than*____ their instructor.

2. carefully   Rob drives _____ his brother.

3. quickly   Ted finished the test _____ of all.

4. hard   Who works _____ in your class?

5. late   The bride arrived at her wedding _____ the guests.

6. early   The groom arrived _____ of all.

7. good   Tina can swim _____ Tom.

8. quickly   Ana learns math _____ her classmates.

9. slowly   My grandfather walks _____ my grandmother.

10. fluently   Ben speaks English _____ of all the students.

11. fast   Ben learns languages _____ his classmates.

12. fast   Sam can run _____ of all his teammates.

PRACTICE 15 ▶ Adjectives and adverbs: comparatives and superlatives.
(Charts 15-1 → 15-4)
Write the correct adjective or adverb form of the given words.

1. dangerous   a. A motorcycle is ____*more dangerous than*____ a bike.

   b. Tom drives _____ Fred.

   c. Steven drives _____ of all.

2. clear   a. Pedro speaks _____ Ernesto.

   b. Our math teacher is _____ our history teacher.

   c. Our math teacher speaks _____ of all.

3. hard   a. Nina's job is _____ Ivan's job.

   b. Nina works _____ Ivan.

   c. Nina works _____ of all.

4. good   a. Leah can play the guitar _____ I can.

          b. She can play the guitar _____ of all.

          c. I like the guitar _____ the piano.

5. fast   a. Haley runs _____ her teammates.

          b. Haley is _____ I am.

          c. Haley is _____ runner on her team.

6. neat   a. Daniel's handwriting looks _____ mine.

          b. Daniel writes _____ his classmates.

          c. Daniel has _____ handwriting.

PRACTICE 16 ▸ *The same (as), similar (to), and different (from).* (Chart 15-5)
Write *to, as, from,* or *Ø*.

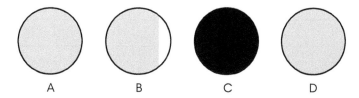

1. A and D are the same ___Ø___ .

2. A is the same _____ D.

3. A and C are different _____ .

4. A and B are similar _____ .

5. A is different _____ C.

6. A is similar _____ B.

7. B and D are similar _____ .

8. C and D are different _____ .

PRACTICE 17 ▸ *The same (as), similar (to), and different (from).* (Chart 15-5)
Write *the same (as)*, *similar (to)*, or *different (from)*.

 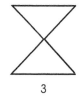

1   2   3   4

1. 1 and 2 are ___similar___ .

2. 1 is ___similar to___ 2.

3. 2 and 4 are _____ .

4. 2 and 3 are _____ .

5. 2 is _____ 3.

6. 4 is _____ 2.

7. 1 and 3 are _____ .

8. 3 is _____ 4.

9. 4 is _____ 1.

10. 1 and 4 are _____ .

PRACTICE 18 ▶ *The same* (as), *similar* (to), and *different* (from). (Chart 15-5)
Make sentences. Use the given words.

1. English \ Japanese
   a. (*different*) ___English and Japanese are different.___
   b. (*different from*) ___English is different from Japanese.___

2. trains \ buses
   a. (*similar*) _____
   b. (*similar to*) _____

3. your grammar book \ my grammar book
   a. (*the same as*) _____
   b. (*the same*) _____

4. cats \ dogs
   a. (*different*) _____
   b. (*different from*) _____

PRACTICE 19 ▶ *Like* and *alike*. (Chart 15-6)
Write ***like*** or ***alike***.

1. A pen is ___like___ a pencil.

2. Fingers and toes are _____.

3. Hands and feet are _____.

4. Highways and freeways are _____.

5. A freeway is _____ a highway.

6. The Pacific Ocean and Atlantic Ocean are _____.

7. A mouse is _____ a rat.

8. A mouse isn't _____ a lion.

9. Are people around the world _____?

10. Are lakes and rivers _____ oceans?

11. French and Italian are _____ because they are both Romance languages.

12. French is _____ Italian. They both come from Latin.

PRACTICE 20 ▸ Like and alike. (Chart 15-6)
Complete the sentences with **like** or **alike** and a word from the box. Then explain why they are alike.

dark chocolate	knives	newspapers	Thailand
✓ doctors	milkshakes	physics	

1. *like*   Nurses ___*are like doctors. They help people.*_____

2. *alike*   White chocolate _____

3. *like*   Magazines _____

4. *alike*   Scissors _____

5. *alike*   Malaysia _____

6. *like*   Ice-cream cones _____

7. *alike*   Chemistry _____

PRACTICE 21 ▸ *The same as, similar* (to), *different* (from), *like*, and *alike*.
(Charts 15-5 and 15-6)
Choose all the completions that are grammatically correct and make sense.

1. Chapter 1 and Chapter 15 of this book are _____.
   a. different
   b. different from
   c. similar to
   d. like
   e. not the same

2. The color red is _____ the color orange.
   a. alike
   b. similar to
   c. similar
   d. like
   e. the same as

3. Lemons and oranges taste _____.
   a. the same
   b. different
   c. different from
   d. alike
   e. similar

Part I. Read the story.

A Career Change

Martina is in college, but she is older than the other students. In fact, she is the oldest student in the class. This is her second time in college. The first time she went to college, she studied accounting. Now she is back in school because she wants to change careers.

She is interested in two fields: medicine and firefighting. Martina likes to help people. Her mother was a nurse, and Martina learned a lot about taking care of people from her mother. Her brother is a firefighter, and she loves to hear stories about his work. She is thinking about three different careers: emergency room doctor, paramedic, or firefighter.

Martina wants an exciting job because she gets bored easily. She likes adventure and physical work. Firefighters have physically hard jobs. The work is also very dangerous. Martina likes the idea of going into burning buildings to rescue people. Of the three jobs, Martina thinks firefighting will be the most exciting.

Paramedic and emergency room work are similar. Both paramedics and doctors treat people in emergency situations. But Martina will need to spend more time in school if she wants to be a doctor. If she becomes a paramedic, she can finish her studies more quickly.

The cost of education is important to her. The training for a doctor is the most expensive of the three careers. She will need scholarships or loans to pay for her education. Right now she has enough money for paramedic or firefighter training. But she knows she will earn more money later as a doctor. She's not sure which job is the best for her. She knows she wants to help people, and she wants to do something exciting, so she is sure that she will choose one of these careers.

Part II. Check (✓) the true statements, according to the information in the story.

1. _____ The training for a paramedic is more expensive than the training for a doctor.

2. _____ Martina can become a paramedic more quickly than she can become a doctor.

3. _____ Firefighter training is cheaper than training for a doctor.

4. _____ An emergency room doctor works harder than a paramedic.

5. _____ The most exciting job for Martina will be firefighting.

6. _____ Doctors and paramedics do exactly the same work.

PRACTICE 23 ▶ Using *but.* (Chart 15-7)

Complete each sentence with the opposite adjective.

1. A sports car is fast, but a bike is _____*slow*_____.

2. The sun is hot, but the moon is _____.

3. Mr. Benton is an easy teacher, but Mrs. Benton is a _____ teacher.

4. Building a paper airplane is simple, but building a real airplane is _____.

5. A giraffe has a long neck, but a rabbit has a _____ neck.

6. Real diamonds are expensive, but fake diamonds are _____.

7. A hard pillow is uncomfortable, but a soft pillow is _____.

8. Yellow is a bright color, but gray is a _____ color.

9. Feathers are light, but rocks are _____.

10. The wheel is an old invention, but the car is a _____ invention.

PRACTICE 24 ▸ Verbs after *but*. (Chart 15-8)
Complete each sentence with an appropriate verb: affirmative or negative.

1. Fried foods are greasy, but boiled foods _____*aren't*_____.

2. Cars can't fly, but planes _____.

3. Kids often don't like vegetables, but adults generally _____.

4. Warm baths feel relaxing, but cold baths _____.

5. A warm bath feels relaxing, but a cold bath _____.

6. The students were in class yesterday, but their teacher _____.

7. Susan won't be at the party, but her husband _____.

8. I don't like fish, but my husband _____.

9. Ralph studied hard, but Daniel _____.

10. Newborn babies sleep most of the day, but adults usually _____.

11. Billy isn't a hard worker, but his brother _____.

12. A few students in the class can understand the math problems, but I _____.

13. Dr. Jones will work this weekend, but his partner _____.

14. The English books aren't in the bookstore, but the science books _____.

15. Mark wasn't on time for class, but Gary _____.

16. Mark didn't arrive on time, but Gary _____.

17. Electric cars are quiet, but diesel cars _____.

PRACTICE 25 ▸ Verbs after *but*. (Chart 15-8)
Complete the sentences with your own words.

1. Birds have wings, but _____*cows don't*_____.

2. Dogs bark, but _____.

3. Fish can breathe underwater, but _____.

4. Skunks don't smell good, but _____.

5. The weather in the desert is hot, but _____.

6. Tight shoes aren't comfortable, but _____.

7. Honey is sweet, but _____.

8. It wasn't cold yesterday, but _____.

9. I will be here tomorrow, but _____.

10. I didn't go out last night, but _____.

PRACTICE 26 ▶ Review. (Chapter 15)
Choose the correct answers.

1. Fingers and toes are _____.
   a. similar   b. like   c. the same   d. different from

2. The weather in Canada is _____ the weather in Mexico.
   a. coolest   b. cooler than   c. the coolest   d. more cool than

3. What is your _____ color?
   a. more favorite   b. the most favorite c. favorite   d. more favorite than

4. Kids are _____ adults.
   a. different from   b. different as   c. different   d. different to

5. We live _____ from town than you do.
   a. far   b. more far   c. farthest   d. farther

6. Is happiness _____ money?
   a. importanter than b. more important than c. important   d. more important

7. The weather is cold today, but yesterday it _____.
   a. isn't   b. doesn't   c. wasn't   d. didn't

8. I have _____ you.
   a. a same shirt   b. same shirt   c. the same shirt as d. same shirt as

9. The Atlantic Ocean isn't _____ ocean in the world.
   a. a biggest   b. the biggest   c. a big   d. bigger than

10. Alison and Jeff don't study in the library, but Kathy _____.
    a. does   b. doesn't   c. isn't   d. is

11. I thought the math test was hard, but my friends thought it was _____.
    a. easy   b. difficult   c. easier   d. hardest

12. I thought it was one of _____ of the year.
    a. the hard test   b. a hard tests   c. a hard test   d. the hardest tests

PRACTICE 27 ▸ Review. (Chapter 15)

Correct the mistakes.

1. My new apartment is ~~big~~ *bigger* than my old apartment.

2. The weather today is more bad than it was yesterday.

3. This class is easyer than our math class.

4. You were very sick yesterday. Do you feel more good today?

5. Chicago is one of the biggest city in the United States.

6. What is coldest month of the year?

7. You type more quick than I do.

8. Jackson works more hardly than his brother.

9. Make sure all your passwords are not same. They need to be different from.

10. Frozen yogurt is similar with ice cream.

11. William and his twin brother look like.

12. Helen can't speak Chinese, but her parents speak.

Appendix

Appendix 1

Irregular Verbs

SIMPLE FORM	SIMPLE PAST	SIMPLE FORM	SIMPLE PAST
be	was, were	lose	lost
become	became	make	made
begin	began	meet	met
break	broke	pay	paid
bring	brought	put	put
build	built	read	read
buy	bought	ride	rode
catch	caught	ring	rang
choose	chose	run	ran
come	came	say	said
cost	cost	see	saw
cut	cut	sell	sold
do	did	send	sent
drink	drank	shut	shut
drive	drove	sing	sang
eat	ate	sit	sat
fall	fell	sleep	slept
feel	felt	speak	spoke
fight	fought	spend	spent
find	found	stand	stood
fly	flew	steal	stole
forget	forgot	swim	swam
get	got	take	took
give	gave	teach	taught
go	went	tell	told
grow	grew	think	thought
have	had	throw	threw
hear	heard	understand	understood
hide	hid	wake	woke
hit	hit	wear	wore
hurt	hurt	win	won
know	knew	write	wrote
leave	left		

English Handwriting

PRINTING			CURSIVE		
Aa	Jj	Ss	Aa	Jj	Ss
Bb	Kk	Tt	Bb	Kk	Tt
Cc	Ll	Uu	Cc	Ll	Uu
Dd	Mm	Vv	Dd	Mm	Vv
Ee	Nn	Ww	Ee	Nn	Ww
Ff	Oo	Xx	Ff	Oo	Xx
Gg	Pp	Yy	Gg	Pp	Yy
Hh	Qq	Zz	Hh	Qq	Zz
Ii	Rr		Ii	Rr	

Vowels = *a, e, i, o, u*
Consonants = *b, c, d, f, g, h, j, k, l, m, n, p, q, r, s, t, v, w, x, y, z*[*]

---

[*]The letter *z* is pronounced "zee" in American English and "zed" in British English.

Numbers

CARDINAL NUMBERS		ORDINAL NUMBERS	
1	one	1st	first
2	two	2nd	second
3	three	3rd	third
4	four	4th	fourth
5	five	5th	fifth
6	six	6th	sixth
7	seven	7th	seventh
8	eight	8th	eighth
9	nine	9th	ninth
10	ten	10th	tenth
11	eleven	11th	eleventh
12	twelve	12th	twelfth
13	thirteen	13th	thirteenth
14	fourteen	14th	fourteenth
15	fifteen	15th	fifteenth
16	sixteen	16th	sixteenth
17	seventeen	17th	seventeenth
18	eighteen	18th	eighteenth
19	nineteen	19th	nineteenth
20	twenty	20th	twentieth
21	twenty-one	21st	twenty-first
22	twenty-two	22nd	twenty-second
23	twenty-three	23rd	twenty-third
24	twenty-four	24th	twenty-fourth
25	twenty-five	25th	twenty-fifth
26	twenty-six	26th	twenty-sixth
27	twenty-seven	27th	twenty-seventh
28	twenty-eight	28th	twenty-eighth
29	twenty-nine	29th	twenty-ninth
30	thirty	30th	thirtieth
40	forty	40th	fortieth
50	fifty	50th	fiftieth
60	sixty	60th	sixtieth
70	seventy	70th	seventieth
80	eighty	80th	eightieth
90	ninety	90th	ninetieth
100	one hundred	100th	one hundredth
200	two hundred	200th	two hundredth
1,000	one thousand	1,000th	one thousandth
10,000	ten thousand	10,000th	ten thousandth
100,000	one hundred thousand	100,000th	one hundred thousandth
1,000,000	one million	1,000,000th	one millionth

Days/Months/Seasons

DAYS	ABBREVIATION	MONTHS	ABBREVIATION	SEASONS*
Monday	Mon.	January	Jan.	winter
Tuesday	Tues.	February	Feb.	spring
Wednesday	Wed.	March	Mar.	summer
Thursday	Thurs.	April	Apr.	fall or autumn
Friday	Fri.	May	May	
Saturday	Sat.	June	Jun.	
Sunday	Sun.	July	Jul.	
		August	Aug.	
		September	Sept.	
		October	Oct.	
		November	Nov.	
		December	Dec.	

*Seasons of the year are only capitalized when they begin a sentence.

Writing Dates

MONTH/DAY/YEAR

10/31/1985	=	October 31, 1985
4/15/98	=	April 15, 1998
5/5/00	=	May 5, 2000
12/01/10	=	December 1, 2010
7/4/1921	=	July 4, 1921
7/4/21	=	July 4, 2021

Saying Dates

USUAL WRITTEN FORM	USUAL SPOKEN FORM
January 1	January first / the first of January
March 2	March second / the second of March
May 3	May third / the third of May
June 4	June fourth / the fourth of June
August 5	August fifth / the fifth of August
October 10	October tenth / the tenth of October
November 27	November twenty-seventh / the twenty-seventh of November

Two-Syllable Verbs: Spelling of *-ED* and *-ING*

	VERB	SPEAKING STRESS	Some verbs have two syllables. In (a): *visit* has two syllables: *vis* + *it*. In the word *visit*, the stress is on the first syllable. In (b): the stress is on the second syllable in the word *admit*.
(a)	visit	**VIS** • it	
(b)	admit	ad • **MIT**	

	VERB	STRESS	*-ED* FORM	*-ING* FORM	For two-syllable verbs that end in a vowel and a consonant:
(c)	visit	**VIS** • it	visited	visiting	• The consonant is not doubled if the stress is on the first syllable, as in (c) and (d).
(d)	open	**O** • pen	opened	opening	
(e)	admit	ad • **MIT**	admitted	admitting	• The consonant is doubled if the stress is on the second syllable, as in (e) and (f).
(f)	occur	oc • **CUR**	occurred	occurring	

COMMON VERBS

Stress on first syllable:

VERB	STRESS	*-ED* FORM	*-ING* FORM
answer	**AN** • swer	answered	answering
happen	**HAP** • pen	happened	happening
listen	**LIS** • ten	listened	listening
offer	**OF** • fer	offered	offering
enter	**EN** • ter	entered	entering

Stress on second syllable:

VERB	STRESS	*-ED* FORM	*-ING* FORM
prefer	pre • **FER**	preferred	preferring
permit	per • **MIT**	permitted	permitting
refer	re • **FER**	referred	referring
begin	be • **GIN**	(no *-ed* form)	beginning

Ways of Saying the Time

9:00   It's nine o'clock.
       It's nine.

9:05   It's nine-oh-five.
       It's five (minutes) after nine.
       It's five (minutes) past nine.

9:10   It's nine-ten.
       It's ten (minutes) after nine.
       It's ten (minutes) past nine.

9:15   It's nine-fifteen.
       It's a quarter after nine.
       It's a quarter past nine.

9:30   It's nine-thirty.
       It's half past nine.

9:45   It's nine-forty-five.
       It's a quarter to ten.
       It's a quarter of ten.

9:50   It's nine-fifty.
       It's ten (minutes) to ten.
       It's ten (minutes) of ten.

12:00   It's noon.
       It's midnight.

A.M. = morning: It's 9:00 A.M.
P.M. = afternoon/evening/night: It's 9:00 P.M.

Basic Capitalization Rules

	Use a capital letter for:
(a) Joan and I are friends.	the pronoun "I"
(b) They are late.	the first word of a sentence
(c) Sam Bond and Tom Adams are here.	names of people
(d) Mrs. Peterson Professor Jones Dr. Costa	titles of people*
(e) Monday, Tuesday, Wednesday	the days of the week
(f) April, May, June	the months of the year
(g) New Year's Day	holidays
(h) Los Angeles Florida, Ontario Germany Lake Baikal Amazon River Pacific Ocean Mount Everest Broadway, Fifth Avenue	names of places: cities, states and provinces, countries, lakes, rivers, oceans, mountains, streets
(i) German, Chinese, Swedish	languages and nationalities
(j) Pirates of the Caribbean Romeo and Juliet	the first word of a title, for example, in a book or movie. Capitalize the other words, but not: articles (*the, a, an*), short prepositions (*with, in, at, etc.*), and these words: *and, but, or*.
(k) Buddhism, Christianity, Hinduism, Islam, Judaism	religions

*<i>Mrs.</i> = woman: married   <i>Miss</i> = woman: unmarried
 Ms. = woman: married or unmarried   Mr. = man: married or unmarried

Index

Be + there (*there is*):
in *how many* questions (*how many are there?*), 107
in *yes/no* questions (*is there?*), 106–107
But, 234–236
verbs after, 235–236

C

Can, 185–188
contraction of negative of (*can't*), 186–187, 192
vs. *could*, 190
in expressions of ability, 185–192
in expressions of permission, 194
information questions with, 188
vs. *know how to*, 188–189, 192
in polite requests, 202
Capitalization, of sentences, 17, 143
Cardinal numbers, 240
Clauses:
if-, 178–179
time (SEE Time clauses)
Commas, with time clauses, 146–147
Comparatives (*more/-er*), 221–224
adjectives as, 221–224, 230–231
adverbs as, 229–231
review of, 226, 228–229
vs. superlatives, 224
Comparisons:
with comparatives (SEE Comparatives)
like, alike, 232–233
with superlatives (SEE Superlatives)
the same (*as*), *similar* (*to*), *different* (*from*), 231–233
Contractions of verbs:
with *not*:
can't, 186–187, 192
couldn't, 189–190
isn't, aren't, 7–9
shouldn't, 196–197
wasn't, weren't, 115–116
won't, 163
with pronouns and *am, is, are* (*she's*), 6–8
Could, 189–190
vs. *can*, 190
in expressions of ability, 189–190
in expressions of permission, 194
negative of (*couldn't*), 189–190
in polite requests, 202
Count/noncount nouns, 88–90
a/an with, 91–93, 95, 97–98, 100–101
any with, 99–101
many/much and *a few/a little* with, 95–96
measurements with (*a cup of coffee*), 94–95
no article with, for making generalizations, 97–98
some with, 92–93, 95, 99
the with, 97–98
(A) couple of, 159–161

D

Dates:
it for talking about, 102–103
written vs. spoken form of, 241
Days of the week, 241
Different from, 231–233
Does, do, did, 34
negative of (*I don't*):
with *have to*, 198–200
in imperative sentences, 64–65
in simple past, 126–127
in simple present, 36–39, 58
in questions:
in simple past (*did you?*), 127–129, 168
in simple present (*do you?*), 39–43, 46, 58, 127, 168
with *what*, 44–46
with *where*, 44–46
with *why*, 137–138

E

-Ed (*asked, played*):
in simple past (SEE Simple past)
spelling of, 120–121, 133, 242
-Er/more (SEE Comparatives)
-Es/-s (SEE *-S/-es*)
-Est/most (SEE Superlatives)
Every, 217–218

F

(A) few, 96, 160–161
Frequency:
adverbs of (*always, sometimes*), 27–31
position of, 30–31
expressions of (*a lot, every day*), 29–30
From:
in *different from*, 231–233
in *from … to*, to express time, 103–104
Future time:
be going to for, 154–157, 165, 176–178
*if-*clauses for, 178–179
in a couple of/in a few for, 159–161
may or *might* for, 173, 175–176
vs. present habits, 181–182
present progressive for, 157–158
review of, 165–166, 169–171
time clauses for, 176–178
will for, 162–165, 173, 175–176

G

Generalizations, 97–98
Go, 34

H

Habits, present, time clauses and *if-*clauses for, 180–182
Handwriting, printing vs. cursive, 239

review of, 24, 49
in simple past (*did you?*), 168
in simple present (*do you?*), 168
about time, 102–103, 105
about weather, 104–105
yes/no (SEE *Yes/no* questions)

R

Rarely, 27–30

S

-S/-es:
with count/noncount nouns (*books*), 89, 96
with plural nouns (*cats, dishes*), 4, 69
with simple present verbs (*eats*), 31–33, 48
spelling with, 31–33, 69
Same, 231–233
Seasons, 241
See, 61–63
Seldom, 27–31
Sentences:
capitalization of, 17, 143
complete vs. incomplete, 74, 143
imperative, 64–65
objects of, 72–74
pronouns as, 74–78
review of, 11
subjects of, 72–73
pronouns as, 74–78
Short answers to *yes/no* questions, 16–18, 24, 41–42
Should, 196–197
in expressions of advice, 196–197
vs. *must*, 201
negative of, 196–197
Similar, 231–233
Simple past:
be in (*was/were*), 114–118
negative of (*was/were not*), 115–116
in questions (*were you?*), 116–118, 168
do in (*did*):
negative of (*did/did not*), 126–127
in questions (*did you?*), 127–129, 168
irregular verbs in, 123–125, 129–133, 151–153, 238
vs. past progressive, 149–151
regular verbs in, 118–119, 122
review of, 133–135, 165–166, 169–171
spelling of, 120–121, 133
what questions in, 138–139
where/why/when/what time questions in, 136–138, 141–143
who questions in, 139–141
yes/no questions in, 116–118, 127–129
Simple present, 26–27, 34–35
be in questions in (*are you?*), 42–43, 168
do in:
negative of (*I don't*), 36–39, 58
in questions (*do you?*), 39–43, 46, 58, 127, 168

frequency adverbs in, 27–31
information questions in, 44–47
irregular verbs in, 34–35, 129–131
negatives in (*does/do not*), 36–39, 58
vs. present progressive, 58–60
review of, 48–50, 134–135, 165–166, 169–171
-s/-es with, 31–33, 48
spelling of, 33
yes/no questions in, 39–43, 46, 47, 58, 127
Singular and plural:
nouns (*pen, pens*), 4, 68–70 (SEE ALSO Count/noncount nouns)
with *be* (*is a country*), 4–6
irregular (*tomatoes, fish, men*), 70, 90–91
possessive (*student's, students'*), 80–81
pronouns, *be* after (*I am/we are*), 1–3, 5
Some:
vs. *a/an*, 92–93, 95
with count/noncount nouns, 92–93, 95, 99
review of, 95
in *some of*, 215–217
Somebody, 219–220
Someone, 219–220
Something, 219–220
Sometimes, 28–31
Spelling:
-ed, 120–121, 133, 242
-ing, 53, 242
-s/-es, 31–33, 69
-y, 32–33
Subject pronouns (*I, she, they*), 74–78
Subjects of sentences, 72–73
pronouns as, 74–78
Subject–verb agreement, in expressions of quantity, 216–218
Superlatives (*-est/most*), 224–225
adjectives as, 224–225, 230–231
adverbs as, 230–231
with *one of* and plural noun, 227–229
review of, 226, 228–229

T

Temperature, 104
Tenses (SEE *individual tenses*)
That, 13–15
in *think that*, 63–64
The:
with count/noncount nouns, 97–98
with *same*, 231–233
There + be (*there is*), 105–107
in *how many* questions (*how many are there?*), 107
in *yes/no* questions (*is there?*), 106–107
These, 14–15
Think about, 63–64
Think that, 63–64
This, 13–15
with time words, 161–162
Those, 14–15

Answer Key

CHAPTER 1: USING *BE*

PRACTICE 1, p. 1
2. She is absent.
3. It is a country.
4. He is sick.
5. She is also sick.
6. He is ready.
7. It is cold.
8. She is here.

PRACTICE 2, p. 1
2. am
3. are
4. is
5. is
6. is
7. is
8. are
9. is
10. is

PRACTICE 3, p. 1
2. they
3. you
4. they
5. we

PRACTICE 4, p. 2
3. A
4. B
5. A
6. A, B
7. B

PRACTICE 5, p. 2
are, are   is, are   is, are   is

PRACTICE 6, p. 2
3. She
4. He
5. She
6. They
7. We
8. We
9. She
10. You
11. They
12. They
13. She
14. He
15. We

PRACTICE 7, p. 3
2. a
3. a
4. an
5. a
6. an
7. an
8. a
9. a
10. an

PRACTICE 8, p. 3
2. a, yes
3. a, no
4. an, yes
5. a, no
6. a, no
7. a, yes
8. an, yes

PRACTICE 9, p. 4
2. dogs
3. languages
4. animals
5. countries
6. peanuts
7. berries

PRACTICE 10, p. 4
3. Ø ... Ø
4. s ... s
5. Ø ... Ø
6. s ... s
7. Ø ... Ø
8. s ... s ... s

PRACTICE 11, p. 4
2. are
3. are
4. is
5. is
6. are
7. is
8. are
9. is
10. are

PRACTICE 12, p. 5
2. I am a student.
3. You are a student.
4. You are students.
5. They are students.
6. He is a student.
7. We are students.
8. Carlos and you are students.
9. He and I are students.
10. Mia and I are students.

PRACTICE 13, p. 5
3. An elephant is an animal.
4. China is a country.
5. Africa is a continent.
6. Asia and Africa are continents.
7. Russian and Spanish are languages.
8. Arabic is a language.
9. Lima is a city.
10. Lima and Beijing are cities.
11. A carrot is a vegetable.
12. Carrots are vegetables.

PRACTICE 14, p. 6
3. is a language
4. are languages
5. are countries
6. is a country
7. is an island
8. are islands
9. is a vegetable
10. are vegetables
11. is a city
12. are cities

PRACTICE 15, p. 6
2. you're
3. he's
4. we're
5. it's
6. they're
7. she's

PRACTICE 16, p. 6
2. You're busy.
3. They're students.
4. It's cold.
5. She's here.
6. He's absent.
7. We're tired.
8. I'm a student.

PRACTICE 17, p. 7
2. are not
3. is not
4. is not
5. is not
6. is not
7. are not
8. are not
9. are not
10. are not
11. is not
12. are not

PRACTICE 18, p. 7

2. is not; isn't, She's not
3. am not; I'm not
4. is not; isn't, He's not
5. is not; isn't
6. is not; isn't, It's not
7. are not; aren't, We're not
8. are not; aren't, You're not
9. are not; aren't, They're not

PRACTICE 19, p. 7

2. isn't   4. is   6. aren't   8. is
3. are   5. isn't   7. isn't

PRACTICE 20, p. 8

2. aren't … 're animals   5. aren't … 're snacks
3. isn't … 's a continent   6. 'm not … 'm a student
4. isn't … 's a language

PRACTICE 21, p. 8

2. isn't   6. isn't … is OR is … isn't
3. are   7. aren't … are
4. aren't   8. are … aren't
5. is … isn't

PRACTICE 22, p. 8

2. Bananas aren't orange. They're yellow.
3. The sun isn't cold. It's hot.
4. A car isn't cheap. It's expensive.
5. Africa isn't small. It's big.
6. The exercise isn't hard. It's easy.
7. Babies aren't old. They're young.

PRACTICE 23, p. 9

2. at, at the library   6. under, under my desk
3. from, from Kuwait   7. on, on your street
4. on, on my desk   8. in, in my backpack
5. next to, next to the bank

PRACTICE 24, p. 9

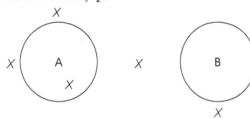

PRACTICE 25, p. 10

3. The students are downtown.
4. The students are on the bus.
5. The teacher is here.
6. The teacher is in the room.
7. Sam is at work.
8. Sam is inside.

PRACTICE 26, p. 10

Nouns: country, parents, sister, teacher
Adjectives: cold, happy, hungry, small
Prepositions: between, next to, on, under

PRACTICE 27, p. 11

Sample answers:
2. Anna is my friend. (noun)
   Anna is at school. (place)
   Anna is hungry. (adjective)
3. France is beautiful. (adjective)
   France is in Europe. (place)
   France is a country. (noun)
4. *Basic English Grammar Workbook* is on my desk. (place)
   Basic English Grammar Workbook is red. (adjective)
   Basic English Grammar Workbook is a book. (noun)

PRACTICE 28, p. 11

2. Canada is in North America.
3. France is next to Germany.
4. Apples and oranges aren't vegetables.
5. Airplanes are fast.
6. Vegetables are healthy.
7. Nora is a doctor.
8. Ben and Sofia are police officers.

PRACTICE 29, p. 12

2. are   4. is   6. are
3. is   5. are   7. are

PRACTICE 30, p. 12

2. is   4. am   6. is   8. is
3. is   5. is   7. is   9. am

PRACTICE 31, p. 12

2. Hawaii is **an** island.
3. Peas and carrots are **vegetables**.
4. The weather **is** warm today.
5. Kate and Leah **are** late.
6. Michael **is** at the library.
7. She is **not** a teacher.
8. Sam is **here**.

CHAPTER 2: USING *BE* AND *HAVE*

PRACTICE 1, p. 13

2. This   4. That   6. This   8. This
3. This   5. That   7. That

PRACTICE 2, p. 14

2. These   3. Those   4. These   5. Those

PRACTICE 3, p. 14

2. Those   4. Those   6. These
3. This   5. That   7. This

PRACTICE 4, p. 14

2. These … Those   5. This … That
3. This … That   6. These … Those
4. These … That   7. This … Those

PRACTICE 5, p. 15

2. c   5. a   8. c
3. b   6. c   9. b
4. b   7. c   10. c

PRACTICE 6, p. 15

2. Is he a student?
3. Are they students?
4. Is she from Vietnam?
5. Are you ready?
6. Are we ready?
7. Is it ready?
8. Am I ready?

PRACTICE 7, p. 16

2. Are bananas healthy?
3. Is Taka a nurse?
4. Are the kids at school?
5. Are you ready for the test?
6. Is Liz at school?
7. Are you tired?

PRACTICE 8, p. 16

2. they are
3. they are
4. he is
5. they are
6. it is
7. she is
8. I am
9. we are
10. you are

PRACTICE 9, p. 17

2. Is ... is
3. Is ... isn't
4. Is ... is
5. Is ... isn't
6. Are ... aren't
7. Are ... are
8. Are ... are
9. Are ... am
10. Are ... are

PRACTICE 10, p. 17

2. Are they students? Yes, they are.
3. Is the library open today? Yes, it is.
4. Are those books expensive? No, they aren't.

PRACTICE 11, p. 18

1. A: Are you
2. A: Are you
   B: aren't ... 're
   B: he isn't ... 's

PRACTICE 12, p. 18

2. b
3. a
4. b
5. a
6. b

PRACTICE 13, p. 18

2. Where are ... Are
3. Where is ... Where is
4. Is ... Where is
5. Where are ... Is ... Where is

PRACTICE 14, p. 19

2. Is the teacher in the classroom?
3. Where are Pablo and Dina?
4. Are Pablo and Dina at home?
5. Is the train station nearby?
6. Where is the store?
7. Are you outside?
8. Where are you?

PRACTICE 15, p. 20

2. have
3. has
4. has
5. have
6. have
7. has
8. has
9. have
10. have

PRACTICE 16, p. 20

2. has
3. have
4. have ... has
5. has ... has
6. have ... have
7. has
8. have
9. has ... has
10. has
11. have

PRACTICE 17, p. 21

2. has
3. have
4. has
5. has
6. is

PRACTICE 18, p. 21

1. c. is
   d. is
   e. has
   f. is
   g. is
   h. has
   i. has
2. a. is
   b. has
   c. is
   d. has
   e. has
   f. is
   g. is
   h. is
   i. has

PRACTICE 19, p. 21

2. Your
3. My
4. Our
5. Your
6. Their
7. Their
8. His
9. Her
10. Their
11. Our
12. Our

PRACTICE 20, p. 22

2. Her
3. His
4. Her
5. His
6. Their

b. Ellen
c. Tim
d. Amy

PRACTICE 21, p. 22

2. has ... His
3. has ... Her
4. have ... Your
5. have ... Their
6. have ... Our
7. have ... Their
8. have ... My
9. have ... Their
10. has ... His

PRACTICE 22, p. 23

2. a
3. b
4. a
5. a
6. b

PRACTICE 23, p. 23

2. Who is that?
3. What is this?
4. Who are they?
5. Who is he?
6. What are those?

PRACTICE 24, p. 24

2. This is Donna.
3. Yes, it is.
4. Yes, she is.
5. No, it isn't.
6. Yes, he is.
7. It's in Canada.
8. Yes, I am.
9. This is a ruler.

PRACTICE 25, p. 24

2. is
3. has
4. is
5. is
6. is
7. is
8. has
9. is
10. is
11. is
12. am
13. am
14. have
15. are

PRACTICE 26, p. 25

2. His 4. their 6. Their
3. His 5. her

PRACTICE 27, p. 25

2. **This** phone is expensive.
3. Where **is** my car?
4. Zac **is** twenty years old.
5. Sofia **is** sick. She **has** a cold.
6. What is **your** phone number?
7. A: Where **are** Jeff and Kevin?
   B: They **are** at school.
8. B: Yes, **she is**.
9. A: **What** are those?
10. A: Where **is** your roommate from?
    B: **He's** from Mexico.

CHAPTER 3: USING THE SIMPLE PRESENT

PRACTICE 1, p. 26

2. wake up 6. wakes up 10. wakes up
3. wake up 7. wakes up 11. wakes up
4. wakes up 8. wakes up 12. wakes up
5. wake up 9. wake up

PRACTICE 2, p. 26

Underline: teaches, leaves, catches, comes, takes, begin, teaches, stays, drives, gets

PRACTICE 3, p. 26

2. get 5. leave 8. work 11. take
3. makes 6. drive 9. arrive
4. cooks 7. listen 10. come

PRACTICE 4, p. 27

2. wake 5. leaves 8. falls 11. see
3. eat 6. take 9. eat 12. have
4. eats 7. cooks 10. fall

PRACTICE 5, p. 27

2. I rarely eat breakfast.
3. The students seldom buy their lunch at school.
4. They usually bring lunch from home.
5. My husband and I often go out to a restaurant for dinner.
6. My husband sometimes drinks coffee with dinner.
7. We never have dessert.

PRACTICE 6, p. 28

2. Roger rarely gets up late. / Roger seldom gets up late.
3. Mr. and Mrs. Phillips usually go to the movies on weekends.
4. I often clean my apartment.
5. My roommate never cleans our apartment.
6. The students always do their homework.
7. The teacher sometimes corrects papers on weekends.

PRACTICE 7, p. 28

Answers will vary.

PRACTICE 8, p. 29

Answers will vary.

PRACTICE 9, p. 29

2. I pay my phone bill once a month.
3. I exercise once a day.
4. I visit my cousins twice a year.
5. Dr. Williams checks her email three times a day.
6. The Browns take a vacation once a year.
7. Cyndi works from home once a week.
8. Sam buys vegetables at the farmers' market twice a week.

PRACTICE 10, p. 30

2. often ... Ø 9. never ... Ø
3. Ø ... sometimes 10. Ø ... always
4. Ø ... rarely 11. always ... Ø
5. rarely ... Ø 12. Ø ... never
6. Ø ... usually 13. seldom ... Ø
7. usually ... Ø 14. usually ... Ø
8. never ... Ø 15. sometimes ... Ø

PRACTICE 11, p. 30

2. The students often help the teacher.
3. The classroom is always clean.
4. The parents usually visit the class.
5. The parents sometimes help the students with their work.
6. The parents are always helpful.
7. The classroom is seldom quiet.

PRACTICE 12, p. 31

-s: eats, listens, talks, sleeps
-es: fixes, finishes, kisses, wishes

PRACTICE 13, p. 32

2. teaches 6. miss 10. washes 14. begins
3. fix 7. brush 11. cooks 15. come
4. fixes 8. brushes 12. reads 16. comes
5. misses 9. wash 13. watches

PRACTICE 14, p. 32

2. study 4. study 6. studies 8. studies
3. studies 5. study 7. study

PRACTICE 15, p. 33

-ies: copies, flies, tries, studies, worries
-s: employs, enjoys, pays, plays, stays

PRACTICE 16, p. 33

2. brushes 5. carries 8. pays 11. washes
3. closes 6. catches 9. studies 12. finishes
4. flies 7. fixes 10. plays

PRACTICE 17, p. 34

1. b. does homework at 10:00.
   c. goes to work at 11:00.
2. a. has class at 10:00
   b. does homework at 11:00.
   c. goes to work at 2:00.
3. a. do homework at 9:00.
   b. have class at 11:00.
   c. go to work at 1:00.

PRACTICE 18, p. 34

2. catches
3. gets
4. works
5. fixes
6. come
7. finishes
8. often meets
9. helps
10. usually have
11. goes
12. has
13. is often
14. enjoys

PRACTICE 19, p. 35

Answers will vary.

PRACTICE 20, p. 35

2. to watch
3. to play
4. to talk to
5. to do
6. to wash
7. to buy
8. to marry
9. to take
10. to eat
11. to listen to

PRACTICE 21, p. 36

2. You need to call your parents.
3. We want to watch a movie.
4. I would like to eat outside.
5. Andre wants to study French.
6. He would like to travel to Africa.
7. Ava wants to go to the park.
8. She likes to play basketball.

PRACTICE 22, p. 36

2. don't have   don't eat   are not
3. doesn't have   doesn't eat   isn't
4. doesn't have   doesn't eat   isn't
5. doesn't have   doesn't eat   isn't
6. don't have   don't eat   aren't
7. don't have   don't eat   aren't

PRACTICE 23, p. 37

2. You don't need more time.
3. They don't eat breakfast.
4. Yoshi doesn't like bananas.
5. Susan doesn't do her homework.
6. We don't save our money.
7. The printer doesn't work.
8. The coffee isn't good.
9. Mr. and Mrs. Costa don't drive to work.
10. They aren't here today.

PRACTICE 24, p. 37

3. doesn't have
4. don't fly
5. grow
6. doesn't walk
7. cries
8. don't have
9. helps
10. doesn't fix
11. fixes
12. isn't
13. rains
14. doesn't rain

PRACTICE 25, p. 38

Part I.
2. Mark watches TV.
3. Tom walks to school.
4. Tom, Janet, and Mark study grammar.
5. Janet goes shopping.

Part II.
7. Tom and Janet don't watch TV.
8. Mark doesn't skip lunch.
9. Janet doesn't eat dinner at home.
10. Tom and Mark don't eat dinner out.

PRACTICE 26, p. 38

2. knows … doesn't know
3. want … don't want
4. isn't … doesn't want
5. doesn't drink … drinks
6. am not … don't have
7. doesn't belong … belongs
8. don't live … have
9. is … isn't … don't need
10. is … don't have
11. doesn't eat … isn't
12. doesn't read … watches

PRACTICE 27, p. 39

2. Do they study?
3. Does he know?
4. Does the doctor know?
5. Do we know?
6. Do I understand?
7. Do you understand?
8. Does the manager understand?
9. Does your roommate work?
10. Does the car work?
11. Does it work?
12. Does she care?

PRACTICE 28, p. 40

1. b. Does he swim?
   c. Does he play soccer?
2. a. Does she run?
   b. Does she play soccer?
   c. Does she swim?
3. a. Does he play soccer?
   b. Does he swim?
   c. Does he run?
4. a. Do they play soccer?
   b. Do they run?
   c. Do they swim?

PRACTICE 29, p. 41

2. a
3. b
4. b
5. a
6. b
7. a
8. b

PRACTICE 30, p. 41

2. Does he fix … he doesn't
3. Do you cook … I don't
4. Do you teach … we don't
5. Do you clean … we don't
6. Do they play … they don't
7. Does she write … she doesn't
8. Do you work … I don't
9. Do they build … they don't
10. Does he study … he doesn't

PRACTICE 31, p. 42

2. Is
3. Does
4. Do
5. Is
6. Do
7. Do
8. Do
9. Do
10. Are

PRACTICE 32, p. 42

Conversation 2:
A: Do
B: do ... 's

Conversation 3:
A: Are
B: am
A: Do
A: Do
B: don't

Conversation 4:
A: Do
A: Are
A: are
B: 're

Conversation 5:
A: Is
B: isn't
A: is
A: Is
B: isn't
A: is

Conversation 6:
A: are ... Do
B: Are
A: aren't
B: Are
B: 're

PRACTICE 33, p. 44

2. Where   4. What   6. What   8. What
3. What   5. Where   7. Where

PRACTICE 34, p. 44

2. What does the teacher want?
3. Where does Dr. Varma stay?
4. Where do you catch the bus?
5. What does Lillian need?
6. What do the children want?
7. Where do the construction workers eat lunch?
8. Where are Victoria and Franco?
9. What does Mark bring his wife every week?
10. What do you need?

PRACTICE 35, p. 45

2. What does he fix?
3. Where does he go after work?
4. What does he coach?
5. Where does he eat dinner?
6. Where does he go on weekends?
7. What does he ride?

PRACTICE 36, p. 45

3. When   5. Where   7. What   9. When
4. What   6. When   8. What   10. Where

PRACTICE 37, p. 46

2. Do you get up early?
3. When does the bus come?
4. Does the bus come on time?
5. Where do you work?
6. When do you start work?
7. When do you leave work?
8. Do you like your job?
9. Is it interesting work?
10. Are you a doctor?

PRACTICE 38, p. 47

2. What does he teach?
   Biology and chemistry.
3. Where does he teach chemistry?
   In the chemistry lab.
4. When is he in the chemistry lab?
   At 12:00.

5. Where does he teach biology?
   In the biology lab.
6. Is he in his office every day?
   No, he isn't.
7. Is he in his office at 1:00 on Monday?
   Yes, he is.
8. Does he teach at 8:00?
   No, he doesn't.
9. When does he teach?
   At 9:00, 10:00, and 12:00.

PRACTICE 39, p. 48

2. Ø   6. Ø   10. Ø   14. s
3. Ø   7. s   11. s   15. s
4. Ø   8. s   12. Ø   16. Ø
5. Ø   9. Ø   13. s

PRACTICE 40, p. 48

3. studies   7. costs   11. has
4. don't have   8. know   12. look, am not
5. doesn't clean 9. don't want
6. tastes   10. doesn't have

PRACTICE 41, p. 49

2. Where is Jane?
3. Are Suzie and Jack home?
4. Where are Suzie and Jack?
5. When is dinner?
6. What does Jane have for dinner?

PRACTICE 42, p. 49

2. b   5. c   8. b
3. a   6. c   9. b
4. c   7. a   10. c

PRACTICE 43, p. 50

2. Martin **is usually** late for class.
3. **Does** Ivan speak Russian?
4. What time **do** you have class?
5. Where **does** Isabel **live**?
6. Kevin and Jeff often **eat** lunch together.
7. Diana **is** not at home today.
8. Does your apartment **have** a pool?
9. I need **to** do my homework.
10. **Does** your roommate work on weekends?

CHAPTER 4: USING THE PRESENT PROGRESSIVE AND THE IMPERATIVE

PRACTICE 1, p. 51

Answers will vary.

PRACTICE 2, p. 51

2. is   5. is   8. is
3. am   6. are   9. are
4. is   7. are   10. are

PRACTICE 3, p. 52

2. is parking   5. is talking   8. are eating
3. is waiting   6. are standing   9. are watching
4. is entering   7. are carrying   10. are reading

PRACTICE 4, p. 52

2. are studying
3. is raining
4. are watching
5. am talking
6. is washing
7. is sleeping
8. are playing

PRACTICE 5, p. 53

2. winning
3. joining
4. signing
5. flying
6. paying
7. studying
8. getting
9. waiting
10. writing

PRACTICE 6, p. 53

2. coming
3. looking
4. taking
5. smiling
6. swimming
7. helping
8. clapping
9. keeping
10. camping

PRACTICE 7, p. 54

2. are sitting
3. are talking
4. is doing
5. is reading
6. are kicking
7. is coming
8. are going

PRACTICE 8, p. 54

2. 'm not drinking
3. aren't eating
4. isn't watching
5. isn't wearing
6. aren't playing
7. aren't buying
8. aren't working

PRACTICE 9, p. 54

Part I.
Check: look at his computer, talk on the phone
Possible sentences: He is looking at his computer. He is talking on the phone. He isn't riding a horse. He isn't buying food for dinner.

Part II.
Check: talk to patients, work with doctors, give medicine to patients
Possible sentences: They are talking to patients. They are working with doctors. They are giving medicine to patients. They aren't washing cars. They aren't watching movies.

Part III.
Answers will vary.

PRACTICE 10, p. 55

Possible answers:
2. am writing / am not writing
3. am listening / am not listening
4. am traveling / am not traveling
5. is sitting / isn't sitting
6. is singing / isn't singing
7. is ringing / isn't ringing
8. is making / isn't making

PRACTICE 11, p. 56

2. Are you working?
3. Are they leaving?
4. Is she staying home?
5. Are we going to school?
6. Is the computer working?
7. Is it working?
8. Am I driving?
9. Is your friend coming?
10. Are the students laughing?

11. Is Mr. Kim sleeping?
12. Is Monica dreaming?

PRACTICE 12, p. 56

2. A: Is he running
   B: he isn't ... is driving
3. A: Are they studying
   B: they aren't ... are swimming
4. A: Is she teaching
   B: she isn't ... is shopping
5. A: Is she fishing
   B: she isn't ... is sleeping
6. A: Are they working
   B: they aren't ... are playing
7. A: Are you washing dishes
   B: I'm not ... am reading a book

PRACTICE 13, p. 57

2. are working
3. is working
4. are working
5. is working
7. are not working
8. is not working
9. are not working
10. is not working
12. Is ... working
13. Are ... working
14. Are ... working
15. Is ... working

PRACTICE 14, p. 58

2. work
3. works
4. work
5. works
7. do not work
8. does not work
9. do not work
10. does not work
12. Does ... work
13. Do ... work
14. Do ... work
15. Does ... work

PRACTICE 15, p. 58

2. now
3. every day
4. every day
5. now
6. now
7. every day
8. now
9. now
10. every day

PRACTICE 16, p. 59

2, 6, 8, 9

PRACTICE 17, p. 59

2. am looking
3. are fishing
4. are sitting
5. are playing
6. are swimming
7. is jumping
8. swim
9. walk
10. go
11. am working
12. work
13. teach
14. am teaching

PRACTICE 18, p. 60

1. isn't talking
2. rains ... isn't raining ... is shining ... Does it rain
3. are sitting ... help ... is helping
4. cooks ... is cooking ... Is he cooking ... never eats ...
   Do you eat ... Are you

PRACTICE 19, p. 60

2. Are
3. Is
4. Are
5. Do
6. Is
7. Does
8. Do
9. Does
10. Do
11. Does
12. Do
13. Are
14. Do

PRACTICE 20, p. 61

2. smell
3. is crying ... wants
4. tastes ... like
5. are running ... likes ... hates

PRACTICE 21, p. 61

1. B: think
2. A: does Jan want
   B: needs ... wants
3. A: loves
   B: don't believe ... loves
4. A: Do you hear
   B: hear ... don't see

PRACTICE 22, p. 61

2. a	4. b	6. a	8. a
3. b	5. a	7. b	9. a

PRACTICE 23, p. 62

2. is playing
3. is also listening
4. looking
5. is wearing
6. is talking
7. is telling
8. is not listening
9. doesn't hear
10. is listening

PRACTICE 24, p. 62

2. hear
3. hear
4. listen to
5. A: look at
   B: look at ... watch
6. A: Do you see
   B: see

PRACTICE 25, p. 63

Answers will vary.

PRACTICE 26, p. 63

2. a	3. b	4. b	5. a

PRACTICE 27, p. 63

1. B: am thinking about
   A: think that
2. A: think that
   B: do not think that ... think that
3. A: am thinking about
   B: Are ... thinking about
   A: think that
   B: think that

PRACTICE 28, p. 64

Underline: use, write, don't write, open, don't talk, don't forget, write

PRACTICE 29, p. 64

2. Stop.
3. Don't run.
4. Don't bring pets inside.
5. Download the file.
6. Send the message.
7. Recycle your trash.
8. Please be quiet.
9. Connect to Bluetooth.
10. Don't eat here.

11. Fasten your seatbelt.
12. Throw away your trash.

PRACTICE 30, p. 65

1. rings ... doesn't answer ... don't want ... believe
2. flies ... is flying
3. A: Are you waiting
   B: am
   A: does the bus stop
   A: Is it usually
   B: rarely comes
4. A: does your teacher usually do
   B: think ... corrects ... has
   A: is she doing
   B: is talking
5. A: Do you know
   B: think ... is
   B: know

PRACTICE 31, p. 66

2. is looking at
3. is working
4. is studying
5. listening to
6. hears
7. isn't listening to
8. is thinking about
9. is playing
10. is sleeping
11. is learning
12. likes
13. thinks
14. understands
15. is
16. doesn't like
17. is cooking
18. cooks
19. is cutting
20. is standing
21. is taking off
22. is wearing
23. usually exercises
24. is thinking about
25. is
26. smells
27. wants
28. to watch

PRACTICE 32, p. 67

2. I **don't need** an umbrella. It isn't **raining** today.
3. What **are you doing** right now?
4. The soup **tastes** wonderful.
5. John is **thinking** about his next vacation.
6. Why are you **standing**? **Please have** a seat.
7. What's that noise? **Do you hear** it?
8. What **do you think** about this homework? I **think** that it is easy.

CHAPTER 5: NOUNS AND PRONOUNS

PRACTICE 1, p. 68

Check: 5, 6, 7, 8, 9

PRACTICE 2, p. 68

2. tomatoes	5. babies	8. wife
3. zoos	6. keys	9. dishes
4. pen	7. city	10. thieves

PRACTICE 3, p. 69

-s: girls, keys, shoes, trays
-ies: babies, cities, countries, ladies, parties
-ves: knives, lives, thieves, wives
-es: brushes, glasses, sandwiches, taxes, tomatoes

PRACTICE 4, p. 69

2. keys	7. boxes	12. textbooks
3. classes	8. clocks	13. lives
4. thieves	9. parties	14. leaves
5. tests	10. cats	
6. Babies	11. sandwiches	

PRACTICE 5, p. 70

2. men	4. fish	6. mice	8. sheep
3. children	5. feet	7. women	

PRACTICE 6, p. 70

2. bright – adjective
3. rooms – noun, large – adjective, tall – adjective, ceilings – noun
4. building – noun, Japanese – adjective, restaurant – noun
5. food – noun, other – adjective, countries – noun
6. Mexican – adjective, food – noun, spicy – adjective, delicious – adjective
7. wonderful – adjective, café – noun, our – adjective, neighborhood – noun
8. café – noun, good – adjective, coffee – noun
9. Henry – noun, large – adjective, company – noun
10. job – noun, interesting – adjective
11. difficult – adjective, test – noun, today – noun
12. students – noun, nervous – adjective, test – noun

PRACTICE 7, p. 71

Nouns: *Adjectives:*
chair   easy
food   fresh
job   nervous
leg   poor
rain   quiet
tree   wet

PRACTICE 8, p. 71

Sample answers:

2. old	5. old	8. short
3. hard	6. exciting	9. difficult
4. ugly	7. slow	10. quiet

PRACTICE 9, p. 71

2. Australia	10. Korea
3. Canada	11. Malaysia
4. China	12. Mexico
5. Egypt	13. Russia
6. India	14. Saudi Arabia
7. Indonesia	15. (*Answers will vary.*)
8. Italy	16. (*Answers will vary.*)
9. Japan	

PRACTICE 10, p. 72

2. Snow
3. The sun
4. Some people
5. Some teenagers
6. The kids and their parents

PRACTICE 11, p. 72

2. subject: I, verb: drink, object: tea
3. subject: Kylie, verb: is working, no object
4. subject: She, verb: has, object: a job
5. subject: Zac and Brandon, verb: are running, no object
6. subject: They, verb: are playing, object: soccer

PRACTICE 12, p. 73

2. c. soccer		5. b. lunch
3. b. eggs		6. a. English
	c. eggs	d. English
4. a. bones		7. no direct objects
	b. furniture	8. b. Maria

PRACTICE 13, p. 74

Check: 3, 4, 5, 6, 8

Possible answers:

3. My father is in the library.
4. He is a teacher.
5. My mother is a professor.
6. She is an excellent professor.
8. The university has many interesting and useful classes.

PRACTICE 14, p. 74

2. He ... her		6. They ... him
3. She ... them		7. They ... her
4. He ... them		8. They ... them
5. They ... them		9. They ... them

PRACTICE 15, p. 75

2. her	6. us	10. he★	14. you
3. them	7. him★	11. they	
4. him	8. her★	12. he	
5. me	9. she	13. you	

★Some people say *it* for animals.

PRACTICE 16, p. 75

2. a	3. b	4. b	5. a

PRACTICE 17, p. 76

2. it	4. him	6. it	8. her
3. them	5. them	7. it	9. him

PRACTICE 18, p. 76

2. B: They ... them ... They ... it
3. A: her
   B: She ... her
4. B: I ... me
   A: he

PRACTICE 19, p. 77

3. Her ... her	7. Her ... her★
4. His ... him	8. His ... him★
5. Our ... us	9. Its ... it
6. Their ... them	

★Some people say *it* for animals.

PRACTICE 20, p. 77
2. me   4. it   6. Our ... our
3. him ... his   5. you   7. their

PRACTICE 21, p. 78
1. His ... him
2. their ... They ... them ... their
3. She ... Her ... her
4. their ... Their ... their
5. I ... our ... our ... us

PRACTICE 22, p. 78
2. with   3. for   4. between   5. near

PRACTICE 23, p. 79
2. us   5. you ... me   8. her
3. me   6. it
4. them   7. him

PRACTICE 24, p. 79
2. hers   5. yours   9. his   12. our
3. ours   6. theirs   10. their
4. mine   8. my   11. your

PRACTICE 25, p. 79
1. B: yours ... mine   4. B: our
   A: mine   B: Ours
   B: your   5. A: Their
2. A: her   B: theirs ... Our
   B: hers ... her
3. A: your
   B: mine
   A: his

PRACTICE 26, p. 80
2. car ... Bill   5. truck ... parents
3. desk ... teacher   6. offices ... professors
4. schedules ... students

PRACTICE 27, p. 80
2. more than one   5. one
3. more than one   6. more than one
4. one   7. one

PRACTICE 28, p. 81
2. Dan's   5. Dr. Smith's   8. mother's
3. teacher's   6. pets'
4. sister's   7. neighbors'

PRACTICE 29, p. 81
3. Ø   5. Ø   7. 's
4. 's   6. Ø

PRACTICE 30, p. 82
2. Jane's   4. Ruff's   6. Belle's   8. Jane's
3. Mike's   5. Marie's   7. John's

PRACTICE 31, p. 82
2. possessive   5. possessive   8. possessive
3. is   6. is
4. is   7. is

PRACTICE 32, p. 83
2. Whose glasses are these?   6. Whose shirt is this?
3. Whose toy is this?   7. Whose phone is this?
4. Whose keys are these?   8. Whose pens are these?
5. Whose shoes are these?

PRACTICE 33, p. 83
2. Whose children are those?
3. Who is next?
4. Whose shoes are in the middle of the floor?
5. Who is absent today?
6. Whose package is this?

PRACTICE 34, p. 83
2. a   4. b   6. b
3. a   5. a   7. b

PRACTICE 35, p. 84
2. Whose   5. Whose   8. Who's
3. Who's   6. Whose   9. Who's
4. Who's   7. Whose   10. Whose

PRACTICE 36, p. 84
2. one   6. more than one
3. more than one   7. one
4. one   8. one
5. more than one   9. more than one

PRACTICE 37, p. 85
3. girls' bikes   8. women's books
4. girl's bike   9. people's ideas
5. children's toys   10. person's ideas
6. students' passwords   11. men's coats
7. woman's books   12. man's coats

PRACTICE 38, p. 85
Check: 2, 3, 6, 7, 8
2. students'   6. people's   8. husband
3. friends   7. Women's

PRACTICE 39, p. 85
2. b   5. d   8. b   11. d
3. b   6. d   9. c   12. a
4. a   7. c   10. a

PRACTICE 40, p. 86
2. a   5. b   8. a   11. a
3. b   6. d   9. c   12. d
4. b   7. b   10. c

PRACTICE 41, p. 87
2. The bab**ies** are sleeping.
3. **He and I** are **good** friends.
4. Would you like to join **us**?
5. Jenny lives near my husband and **me**.
6. Is this **your** book? It isn't **mine**.
7. The **teachers'** office is in Room 119. **Their** office is large.
8. Luca**'s** brother**s** live in Italy.
9. **Whose** keys are these? They aren't **my** keys.
10. A pediatrician is a children**'s** doctor.

CHAPTER 6: COUNT AND NONCOUNT NOUNS

PRACTICE 1, p. 88
2. noncount   5. noncount   8. noncount
3. count   6. count   9. count
4. noncount   7. count   10. noncount

PRACTICE 2, p. 88
2. C   6. NC   10. C   14. C
3. C   7. NC   11. NC   15. NC
4. NC   8. C   12. C   16. NC
5. C   9. NC   13. NC

PRACTICE 3, p. 89
2. i   5. f   8. h   11. l
3. c   6. j   9. g   12. e
4. b   7. a   10. k

PRACTICE 4, p. 89
1. Ø, s, s   3. Ø, Ø, Ø
2. Ø, Ø, s, s   4. Ø, Ø, s, s

PRACTICE 5, p. 89
2. a, one   7. a lot of
3. five, a lot of   8. a lot of
4. a lot of   9. a, one
5. five, a lot of   10. a lot of
6. a lot of

PRACTICE 6, p. 90
2. a lot of, ten, twenty   6. a lot of
3. a lot of   7. a, one
4. a lot of   8. a lot of, ten, twenty
5. a, one

PRACTICE 7, p. 90
2. horses   7. traffic   12. tomatoes
3. cities   8. children   13. weather
4. countries   9. furniture   14. work
5. Monkeys   10. feet   15. men
6. help   11. fruit

PRACTICE 8, p. 91
2. an   5. an   8. a
3. an   6. an   9. a
4. a   7. an   10. an

PRACTICE 9, p. 91
2. a   5. a   8. a ... a
3. an ... an 6. an ... an 9. an
4. A   7. a   10. an ... a

PRACTICE 10, p. 92
a: cousin, dog, house, letter, suggestion, university
an: elevator, hour, idea, umbrella
some: advice, furniture, mail, umbrellas

PRACTICE 11, p. 92
3. a, singular   7. some, singular
4. some, plural   8. some, singular
5. an, singular   9. a, singular
6. some, plural   10. some, singular

PRACTICE 12, p. 93
2. some   5. an   8. some
3. Some   6. Some   9. some
4. a   7. a   10. an

PRACTICE 13, p. 93
2. b   4. a, c   6. b
3. a, b 5. b

PRACTICE 14, p. 94
2. a tube of toothpaste   6. a jar of pickles
3. a bar of soap   7. a box of candy
4. a bunch of bananas   8. a bottle of olive oil
5. a carton of milk   9. a can of corn

PRACTICE 15, p. 94
2. paper
3. lettuce
4. bread, cheese, paper, lettuce
5. bread
6. bananas
7. cereal, ice cream, rice
8. oil, water
9. honey, pickles
10. toothpaste

PRACTICE 16, p. 95
1. b. some   2 b. a
   c. some   c. some
   d. a   d. a
   e. an   e. a
   f. a   f. some
   g. some   g. some
   h. some   h. some

PRACTICE 17, p. 95
2. many   5. much   8. much   11. much
3. much   6. much   9. many   12. many
4. many   7. much   10. many

PRACTICE 18, p. 96
2. a few   5. a little   8. a few
3. a few   6. a few   9. a little
4. a little 7. a few   10. a few

PRACTICE 19, p. 96
3. a few, s
4. a few, s
5. much, Ø, a little, Ø
6. many, s
7. a few, s, many, s

PRACTICE 20, p. 96

2. How much cheese do we need?
3. How many eggs do we need?
4. How much flour do we need?
5. How much fruit do we need?
6. How many potatoes do we need?

PRACTICE 21, p. 97

2. the ... the   4. The ... the   6. The
3. The   5. The ... Ø

PRACTICE 22, p. 97

1. the
2. The
3. a ... The ... the
4. a ... a ... a ... The ... the
5. a ... The
6. a ... The
7. a ... a
8. a ... The ... the

PRACTICE 23, p. 97

2. specific   5. specific   8. specific
3. general   6. specific
4. general   7. general

PRACTICE 24, p. 98

2. The   9. The ... the
3. Ø   10. Ø ... Ø
4. a   11. Ø ... Ø ... a
5. an   12. the
6. Ø [Oranges]   13. Ø
7. an   14. a
8. Ø   15. The

PRACTICE 25, p. 98

2. b   4. a   6. a   8. b
3. b   5. b   7. a

PRACTICE 26, p. 99

2. any   7. some
3. some   8. some
4. any   9. some OR any
5. some OR any   10. Some
6. any

PRACTICE 27, p. 99

1. *some* + nouns (*Answers will vary.*)
2. *any* + nouns (*Answers will vary.*)
Add *-s / -es*: avocados, eggs, potatoes, bananas, grapes, vegetables

PRACTICE 28, p. 100

2. any   5. any   8. any   11. any
3. any   6. a   9. any
4. a   7. a   10. an

PRACTICE 29, p. 100

4. any   8. any   12. any   16. a
5. any   9. a   13. a
6. any   10. any   14. any
7. a   11. a   15. any

PRACTICE 30, p. 101

2. ~~some~~, ~~a~~, ~~two~~
3. ~~an~~, a
4. a, ~~an~~, ~~any~~

PRACTICE 31, p. 101

2. Does this town have **much traffics** at 5:00 P.M.?
3. Are you **a** hungry? Do you want some food?
4. My children come home every day with a lot of homework**s**.
5. Michael is a vegetarian. He doesn't eat **meat** or **fish**.
6. My eggs and coffee don't taste very good. **The** eggs are very salty, and **the** coffee is weak.
7. Claire is looking for **a** new job. She has a **few** interviews this week.
8. I wear dresses for work and ~~the~~ jeans at home.
9. I'm going to **the** bank. I need **a** money.
10. We need to get **some** furniture. Do you know **a** good furniture store?

CHAPTER 7: MORE ABOUT THE PRESENT TENSE

PRACTICE 1, p. 102

2. What time is it?   5. What's the date?
3. What month is it?   6. What time is it?
4. What year is it?   7. What's the date?

PRACTICE 2, p. 102

2. b   3. b   4. a   5. b

PRACTICE 3, p. 103

1. b. at   4. a. in
2. a. at   b. on
   b. in   c. in
   c. on   d. at ... in
3. a. in   e. on
   b. at   f. in
   c. from ... to
   d. on
   e. on

PRACTICE 4, p. 103

2. at   6. at
3. from ... to   7. in
4. on   8. on
5. in   9. from ... to

PRACTICE 5, p. 104

2. What's the temperature in Sydney today?
3. How's the weather / What's the weather like in Cairo?
4. How's the weather / What's the weather like in Moscow?
6. no
7. no
8. yes

PRACTICE 6, p. 104

1. like   4. the weather
2. How's   5. it's
3. temperature

PRACTICE 7, p. 105
2. a   4. a   6. b
3. b   5. a   7. a

PRACTICE 8, p. 105
1. is, yes   5. are, yes   9. is, yes
2. are, yes   6. is, no   10. are, no
3. is, yes   7. is, no
4. are, no   8. is, no

PRACTICE 9, p. 106
2. There is a couch.   6. There are two plants.
3. There is one table.   7. There is a TV.
4. There are four pillows.   8. There are some curtains.
5. There is one lamp.

PRACTICE 10, p. 106
1. Are … are   4. Are … are
2. Are … aren't   5. Is … is
3. Is … isn't   6. Is … isn't

PRACTICE 11, p. 107
2. Is there a bus station?
3. Are there good restaurants?
4. Is there an art museum?
5. Are there nice parks?
6. Is there a zoo?
7. Are there movie theaters?
8. Is there a library?

PRACTICE 12, p. 107
2. lakes   5. minutes   8. airplanes
3. cars   6. seconds
4. words   7. stars

PRACTICE 13, p. 107
2. How many days are there
3. How many colors are there
4. How many meters are there
5. How many letters are there
6. How many main languages are there

PRACTICE 14, p. 108
2. in   4. at   6. in   8. at
3. on   5. on   7. on

PRACTICE 15, p. 108
2. at   5. in   8. in
3. at   6. at   9. in
4. in   7. at   10. in

PRACTICE 16, p. 108
1. in   5. at   9. on … at
2. in   6. at … at   10. on … in
3. in … in   7. in
4. at   8. on

PRACTICE 17, p. 109
2. at   4. at … in   6. at … at
3. in … at   5. in   7. in

PRACTICE 18, p. 109
1. on   4. between   7. on top of
2. next to   5. near
3. in   6. below

PRACTICE 19, p. 110
2. in front of   6. over / above
3. behind   7. under / beneath
4. next to / beside   8. between
5. on / on top of

PRACTICE 20, p. 110
2. between, in the middle of
3. on, on top of
4. above, behind, near
5. below, in front of, near, under
6. next to, near

PRACTICE 21, p. 111
2. would like   6. would like   10. would like
3. would like   7. would like   11. would like
4. would like   8. would like   12. would like
5. would like   9. would like

PRACTICE 22, p. 111
2. like   4. wants   6. want
3. likes   5. like

PRACTICE 23, p. 111
1. does   4. wouldn't
2. would   5. like
3. doesn't   6. like … would like

PRACTICE 24, p. 112
1. doesn't have   7. is riding
2. is   8. listen
3. takes   9. are not listening
4. rides   10. are talking
5. has   11. is
6. is   12. are

PRACTICE 25, p. 112
2. a   5. d   8. c   11. b
3. a   6. d   9. b   12. d
4. c   7. a   10. b   13. b

PRACTICE 26, p. 113
2. What time **is it**?
3. Carolina was born **on** January 1, 2020.
4. I have class **from** 9:00 to 10:00.
5. Terry works **in** the afternoon.
6. My family always travels **in** June.
7. How**'s** the weather in London?
8. What's the weather **like** today?
9. There **is** a lot of traffic today.
10. **Are** there good restaurants in your city?
11. How many chapters **are** there in this book?
12. Julia lives **at** 107 Maple Street.
13. Chris is not **at** home right now.
14. He'd **like** to watch a movie.

CHAPTER 8: EXPRESSING PAST TIME, PART 1

PRACTICE 1, p. 114
2. were
3. was
4. were
5. was
6. was
7. were
8. were
9. was
10. were

PRACTICE 2, p. 114
2. were
3. was
4. was
5. was
6. was
7. was
8. were
9. was
10. were

PRACTICE 3, p. 115
2. weren't
3. weren't
4. weren't
5. wasn't
6. wasn't
7. wasn't
8. weren't
9. wasn't
10. weren't
11. weren't
12. wasn't

PRACTICE 4, p. 115
2. wasn't
3. weren't
4. weren't
5. wasn't
6. weren't
7. wasn't
8. wasn't
9. weren't
10. wasn't

PRACTICE 5, p. 116
2. Ricardo wasn't at work / at school / out-of-town. He was on vacation.
3. Loria wasn't at work / at school / on vacation. She was out-of-town.
4. Lori and Eva weren't at work / at school / on vacation. They were out-of-town.

PRACTICE 6, p. 116
2. I was / wasn't happy.
3. I was / wasn't quiet.
4. I was / wasn't active.
5. I was / wasn't serious.
6. I was / wasn't noisy.

PRACTICE 7, p. 116
2. Was
3. Was
4. Were
5. Were
6. Was
7. Was
8. Was
9. Were
10. Were

PRACTICE 8, p. 117
2. A: Was Ellen at the library?
   B: No, she wasn't.
   A: Where was she?
   B: She was at the mall.
3. A: Were you at a party?
   B: No, I wasn't.
   A: Where were you?
   B: I was at home.
4. A: Was Thomas at the airport?
   B: No, he wasn't.
   A: Where was he?
   B: He was at the train station.
5. A: Were your kids at school?
   B: No, they weren't.
   A: Where were they?
   B: They were at the zoo.

6. A: Were you and Liz at the park?
   B: No, we weren't.
   A: Where were you?
   B: We were at the library.

PRACTICE 9, p. 118
2. Were
3. Were
4. Was
5. Was
6. Was
7. Were
8. Were

PRACTICE 10, p. 118
2. studied
3. walked
4. worked
5. smiled
6. smiled
7. talked
8. helped
9. helped
10. listened
11. listened

PRACTICE 11, p. 119
2. exercised at a gym.
3. cooked breakfast.
4. texted a friend.
5. watched TV.

PRACTICE 12, p. 119
2. learned
3. tasted
4. waited
5. stopped
6. carried
7. rubbed
8. stayed ... cried
9. failed
10. smiled

PRACTICE 13, p. 120
1. liked
2. closed
3. shaved
4. loved
5. hated
6. exercised
7. planned
8. dropped
9. clapped
10. joined
11. shouted
12. waited
13. pointed
14. touched
15. jumped
16. married
17. tried
18. hurried
19. replied
20. dried
21. stayed
22. enjoyed

PRACTICE 14, p. 121
2. rained
3. helped
4. planned
5. dreamed
6. erased
7. closed
8. yawned
9. studied
10. worried
11. dropped

PRACTICE 15, p. 122
2. finished
3. watched
4. erased
5. laughed
6. asked
7. helped
8. snowed
9. arrived
10. played
11. enjoyed
12. closed
13. rained
14. stayed
15. worked
16. visited
17. cooked
18. invited
19. wanted
20. washed

PRACTICE 16, p. 123
2. yesterday
3. last
4. last
5. last
6. last
7. yesterday
8. ago
9. ago
10. ago
11. yesterday
12. last

PRACTICE 17, p. 123
2. Bonnie walked to the park yesterday afternoon.
3. Tom worked last week.
4. Sam graduated from high school five years ago.
5. Jan worked 12 hours last Thursday.
6. Martin stayed with his parents last January.
7. We streamed a movie last night.

PRACTICE 18, p. 123

1. did	3. had	5. hid	7. paid
2. did	4. had	6. made	8. heard

PRACTICE 19, p. 124

2. sang	5. rang	8. ran
3. gave	6. began	9. came
4. drank	7. saw	10. sat

PRACTICE 20, p. 124

2. won	4. chose	6. rode	8. spoke
3. forgot	5. wrote	7. wore	9. woke

PRACTICE 21, p. 125

The final sound changes to *d*: did, had, heard, hid, made
Vowels change to *a*: ate, began, drank, gave, ran, saw, sat
Vowels change to *o*: broke, chose, got, rode, spoke, sold, woke, wrote
The vowel changes to *oo*: stood, understood, took

PRACTICE 22, p. 125

2. do	8. see	14. hear
3. pay	9. come	15. ride
4. have	10. forget	16. drive
5. make	11. sit	17. speak
6. swim	12. ring	18. understand
7. begin	13. run	

PRACTICE 23, p. 126

2. didn't do	8. didn't play
3. didn't clean	9. didn't speak
4. didn't wake	10. didn't forget
5. didn't watch	11. didn't go
6. didn't eat	12. didn't take
7. didn't drink	

PRACTICE 24, p. 126

2. I drove to school this morning. / I didn't drive to school this morning.
3. I wrote a long email last night. / I didn't write a long email last night.
4. I walked to school yesterday. / I didn't walk to school yesterday.
5. I got groceries last week. / I didn't get groceries last week.
6. I went on vacation last month. / I didn't go on vacation last month.
7. I did housework last weekend. / I didn't do housework last weekend.
8. I worked outside yesterday. / I didn't work outside yesterday.
9. I paid some bills yesterday. / I didn't pay bills yesterday.
10. I stopped at a café yesterday afternoon. / I didn't stop at a café yesterday afternoon.

PRACTICE 25, p. 127

3. Does she play	7. Does she work
4. Did she play	8. Did she work
5. Does he walk	9. Do you like
6. Did he walk	10. Did you like

PRACTICE 26, p. 128

2. Was	4. Did	6. Did	8. Did
3. Did	5. Were	7. Was	9. Were

PRACTICE 27, p. 128

2 a. Do they understand? They don't understand.
  b. Did they understand? They didn't understand.
3 a. Does she drive? She doesn't drive.
  b. Did she drive? She didn't drive.
4 a. Does he work? He doesn't work.
  b. Did he work? He didn't work.
5 a. Does the baby cry? The baby doesn't cry.
  b. Did the baby cry? The baby didn't cry.
6 a. Are we sick? We aren't sick.
  b. Were we sick? We weren't sick.

PRACTICE 28, p. 129

2. Is it cold today? No, it isn't.
3. Do you come to class every day? Yes, I do.
4. Was Roberto absent yesterday? Yes, he was.
5. Did Roberto stay home yesterday? Yes, he did.
6. Does Phillip change his passwords often? No, he doesn't.
7. Is Mohammed in class today? No, he isn't.
8. Was he here yesterday? Yes, he was.
9. Did he come to class the day before yesterday? Yes, he did.
10. Does he usually come to class every day? Yes, he does.

PRACTICE 29, p. 129

2. shut	4. hurt	6. hit
3. read	5. put	7. cost

PRACTICE 30, p. 130

2. fall	4. meet	6. lose	8. build
3. spend	5. sleep	7. leave	

PRACTICE 31, p. 130

2. hurt	5. slept	8. left
3. cost	6. read	9. lost
4. fell	7. put	10. built

PRACTICE 32, p. 131

2. know	4. fly	6. buy	8. teach
3. throw	5. grow	7. catch	9. bring

PRACTICE 33, p. 131

2. grew	6. flew
3. threw … caught	7. thought
4. taught	8. bought
5. found	

PRACTICE 34, p. 132

2. shut … broke	5. paid … cost	8. hurt
3. came	6. had	
4. forgot	7. hit	

PRACTICE 35, p. 132

2. heard	5. met	8. spoke
3. woke	6. left … went	9. hurt
4. took	7. rang	10. felt

PRACTICE 36, p. 133

3. kissed	8. added	13. played
4. planned	9. pointed	14. touched
5. joined	10. patted	15. ended
6. hoped	11. shouted	16. danced
7. dropped	12. replied	

PRACTICE 37, p. 133

2. went … bought
3. caught … rode … got off … was
4. ate … drank … didn't eat
5. asked … thought … answered
6. wanted … stayed … studied
7. didn't pass … failed
8. drove … slept … swam … went … caught … cooked … was … enjoyed

PRACTICE 38, p. 134

2. is walking	7. didn't see
3. Does Tom walk	8. Did you see
4. Do you walk	9. didn't walk … took
5. walked	10. didn't walk
6. saw	

PRACTICE 39, p. 134

1. fell
2. isn't standing … is sitting
3. isn't … was
4. isn't raining … stopped
5. wrote … didn't spend
6. were … started … didn't arrive
7. asked … didn't answer
8. went … bought … didn't buy
9. lost … found
10. didn't go … didn't feel … stayed … is

PRACTICE 40, p. 135

2. Did you call me **yesterday** morning?
3. I **paid** my rent a few days ago.
4. Sebastian **hurt** his hand. He **cut** it on a piece of glass.
5. Nicole **didn't drive** to work yesterday.
6. Did you **go** on vacation last week?
7. Ryan was **not** at home last night.
8. The test **was** difficult. I didn't **know** the answers.
9. **Were** you ready for the test yesterday?
10. I texted you an hour **ago**. Did you **get** my message?

CHAPTER 9: EXPRESSING PAST TIME, PART 2

PRACTICE 1, p. 136

2. A: When did he leave?
   B: He left on March 22nd.
3. A: Why did he go there?
   B: He visited family.
4. A: Where did Serena go?
   B: She went to the Canary Islands.
5. A: What time did she leave?
   B: She left at 6 A.M.
6. A: Why did she go there?
   B: She went for vacation.

PRACTICE 2, p. 137

2. f	4. c	6. a
3. e	5. d	

PRACTICE 3, p. 137

2. What time did you leave the library?
3. Why did you leave?
4. Where did you and your friends go yesterday afternoon?
5. When did Sandra get back from Brazil?
6. Why was Bobby in bed?
7. Why was he sick?
8. Where did you buy your sandals?

PRACTICE 4, p. 137

2. Why didn't you ask the teacher?
3. Why didn't you bring it?
4. Why didn't you tell me the truth?
5. Why didn't you go to her party?
6. Why didn't you clean the kitchen?

PRACTICE 5, p. 138

3. What did you study?
4. Did you study math?
5. What are they looking at?
6. Are they looking at pictures?
7. What did David talk about?
8. Did David talk about his country?
9. What are you thinking about?
10. Are you thinking about your homework?
11. What did you dream about last night?
12. Did you dream about English grammar last night?
13. What are you afraid of?
14. Are you afraid of spiders?

PRACTICE 6, p. 139

2. a. Lea
   b. the nurse check
3. a. Felix help
   b. the new assistant
4. a. the advanced students … Professor Jones
   b. Professor Jones teach … The advanced students
5. a. the police catch … The criminal
   b. the criminal … The police
6. a. the manager … Oliver
   b. Oliver speak to … The manager

PRACTICE 7, p. 140

2. a. Who did the doctor examine?
   b. Who examined the patient?
3. a. Who called the supervisor?
   b. Who did Miriam call?
4. a. Who surprised the teacher?
   b. Who did the students surprise?
5. a. Who did Andrew and Catherine wait for?
   b. Who waited for Mrs. Allen?

PRACTICE 8, p. 140

3. Who had a graduation party?
4. Who did Professor Brown invite?
5. Who had a New Year's party?
6. Who did Dr. Martin invite?

PRACTICE 9, p. 141
2. Who did you talk to?
3. Who did you visit?
4. Who answered the phone?
5. Who taught the English class?
6. Who helped you?
7. Who did you help?
8. Who carried your suitcases?
9. Who called?

PRACTICE 10, p. 141
2. Who went with you?
3. Why did you go there?
4. Who did you meet?
5. What did you have for lunch?
6. What time did you go?
7. When did you get back?

PRACTICE 11, p. 142
2. When did Simone go to a meeting?
3. Who went to a meeting?
4. Who did you see?
5. Where did you see Ali?
6. When did you see Ali? / What time did you see Ali?
7. What is the teacher talking about?
8. Why did the kids play in the pool?
9. Who called?
10. When did they call?
11. Who did you talk to?
12. Where were you last night?
13. What does *ancient* mean?
14. Where do you live?
15. What do you have in your thermos?

PRACTICE 12, p. 143
Incomplete sentence: after they left, after several minutes, before school starts, after we finish dinner
Complete sentence: They left. Before school starts, I help the teacher. We ate at a restaurant. We were at home.

PRACTICE 13, p. 143
2. 2, 1
   After I looked in the freezer, I closed the freezer door.
   OR
   I closed the freezer door after I looked in the freezer.
3. 1, 2
   After we ate dinner, we washed the dishes. OR
   We washed the dishes after we ate dinner.
4. 2, 1
   After I put on my exercise clothes, I exercised. OR
   I exercised after I put on my exercise clothes.
5. 1, 2
   After the alarm rang at the fire station, the firefighters got in their truck. OR
   The firefighters got in their truck after the alarm rang at the fire station.

PRACTICE 14, p. 144
2. 2, 1   3. 2, 1   4. 1, 2
   b, c   a, d   b, c

PRACTICE 15, p. 145
2. After he packed his bags, he left.
   He left after he packed his bags.
   Before he left, he packed his bags.
   He packed his bags before he left.
3. She sat down before she ordered some food.
   Before she ordered some food, she sat down.
   She ordered some food after she sat down.
   After she sat down, she ordered some food.

PRACTICE 16, p. 146
2. When did the movie start?
   When the movie started,
3. When you were in high school,
   When were you in high school?
4. When it snowed,
   When did it snow?
5. When was Dave sick?
   When Dave was sick,

PRACTICE 17, p. 146
3. ?
4. , we felt sad.
5. ?
6. ?
7. , I woke up.
9. , everyone clapped.
10. ?

PRACTICE 18, p. 147
2. a. When did the dog get sick?
   b. When the dog got sick, I called the vet.
3. a. When did the electricity go out?
   b. When the electricity went out, we used flashlights.
4. a. When did my parents visit?
   b. When my parents visited, we had a great time.

PRACTICE 19, p. 147
3. are sitting
4. were sitting
5. is sitting
6. was sitting
7. are sitting
8. were sitting
9. is sitting
10. was sitting
11. are sitting
12. were sitting

PRACTICE 20, p. 148
2. were studying.
3. was studying.
4. was studying.
5. were studying.
6. were studying.
7. were not studying. / weren't studying.
8. were not studying. / weren't studying.
9. was not studying. / wasn't studying.
10. were not studying. / weren't studying.
11. were not studying. / weren't studying.
12. was not studying. / wasn't studying.

PRACTICE 21, p. 148

2. a. Another student interrupted us while I was talking to the teacher.
   b. While I was talking to the teacher, another student interrupted us.
3. a. A police officer stopped me for speeding while I was driving to work.
   b. While I was driving to work, a police officer stopped me for speeding.
4. a. A dead tree fell over while we were walking in the forest.
   b. While we were walking in the forest, a dead tree fell over.
5. a. My dog began to bark at a squirrel while I was talking to my neighbor.
   b. While I was talking to my neighbor, my dog began to bark at a squirrel.

PRACTICE 22, p. 149

2. called … was taking
3. was eating … remembered
4. began … became
5. was driving … saw
6. was exercising … came
7. texted … was talking … told
8. heard … stopped

PRACTICE 23, p. 150

2. he interrupted her.
3. he continued to talk.
4. he began to tell her about his health.
5. she stood up.
6. he was talking to another passenger.

PRACTICE 24, p. 150

2. rang
3. didn't answer
4. wanted
5. noticed
6. was slowing
7. drove
8. saw

PRACTICE 25, p. 151

2. were sitting
3. came
4. screamed
5. saw
6. did your cousin do
7. yelled
8. Did your husband do
9. ran
10. was running
11. ran
12. dropped
13. yelled
14. went

PRACTICE 26, p. 151

2. She caught a cold yesterday.
3. She found it under her bed.
4. He lost his wallet.
5. He ate too much for lunch.
6. It sold in three days.
7. She had a job interview after class.
8. She finished after midnight.
9. Sam picked it up for her.
10. I took a taxi.
11. Some students came to class without their homework.
12. I grew up there.

PRACTICE 27, p. 152

2. broke
3. told
4. spent
5. made
6. put
7. cost
8. knew
9. met
10. fell
11. lost
12. took

PRACTICE 28, p. 152

2. sang
3. flew
4. left
5. won
6. understood
7. built
8. ate
9. fought
10. cut

PRACTICE 29, p. 153

2. What time **did** you **come** home last night?
3. What did you **buy** at the store?
4. Why **did the teacher** leave early yesterday?
5. Where did Claire **work** last year?
6. When you texted me, I was **sitting** in class.
7. I forgot to lock the door when I **left** this morning.
8. Vanessa called me while she **was** waiting for the bus.
9. I fell asleep before the movie **ended**.
10. I was washing dishes when I **broke** a plate.

CHAPTER 10: EXPRESSING FUTURE TIME, PART 1

PRACTICE 1, p. 154

2. are going to
3. is going to
4. are going to
5. are going to
6. are going to
7. is going to
8. are going to
9. is going to
10. are going to

PRACTICE 2, p. 154

1. B: am going to be
2. A: Is Albert going to fix
   B: am going to call
3. A: Are you going to apply
   B: am going to complete
4. A: Are Ed and Nancy going to join
   B: are going to meet

PRACTICE 3, p. 155

is going to have a quick breakfast of toast and coffee. She is going to catch the 5:45 train to work. At 6:30, she is going to have a weekly meeting with her employees. For the rest of the morning, she is going to be at her desk. She is going to answer phone calls and emails. She is going to answer a lot of questions. She is going to have a big lunch at 11:00. In the afternoon, she is going to visit job sites. She is going to meet with builders and architects. She is going to finish by 7:00 and be home by 8:00.

PRACTICE 4, p. 155

2. am going to eat a big lunch.
3. is going to take some medicine.
4. are going to call the neighbors.
5. is going to rain this afternoon.
6. are going to move to a big house.
7. is going to check the lost-and-found.
8. am going to take it back to the store.

PRACTICE 5, p. 156

Sample answers:
2. I am going to take some medicine.
3. I am going to see a dentist.
4. I am going to run to class.
5. I am going to go to bed.
6. I am going to call the police.

PRACTICE 6, p. 156

2. You are not going to eat. Are you going to eat?
3. He is not going to eat. Is he going to eat?
4. She is not going to eat. Is she going to eat?
5. We are not going to eat. Are we going to eat?
6. They are not going to eat. Are they going to eat?
7. My friend is not going to eat. Is my friend going to eat?
8. The students are not going to eat. Are the students going to eat?

PRACTICE 7, p. 157

1. B: are going to go
   A: Are you going to stay
   B: are going to come
2. A: is Sally going to work
   B: is not going to work, is going to take
3. A: Are the students going to have
   B: are going to have
4. A: Are Joan and Bob going to move
   B: is going to start
   A: Are they going to look for
   B: are not going to look for, are going to rent

PRACTICE 8, p. 157

2. F
3. P
4. F
5. P
6. F
7. A: P
   B: P
8. P
9. F

PRACTICE 9, p. 158

2. They are taking their teenage grandchildren with them.
3. They are staying in parks and campgrounds.
4. They are leaving from Vancouver in June.
5. They are arriving in Montreal in August.
6. Mr. and Mrs. Johnson are driving back home.
7. Their grandchildren are flying home.
8. Their parents are meeting them at the airport.

PRACTICE 10, p. 158

2. ago
3. ago
4. last
5. next
6. in
7. yesterday
8. tomorrow
9. in
10. yesterday
11. last
12. tomorrow
13. ago
14. next

PRACTICE 11, p. 159

1. b. last
   c. last
   d. last
   e. yesterday
   f. ago
   g. last
   h. ago
   i. last
   j. yesterday
2. a. tomorrow
   b. next
   c. next
   d. next
   e. tomorrow
   f. in
   g. next
   h. in
   i. tomorrow
   j. tomorrow

PRACTICE 12, p. 159

2. a couple of minutes
3. a couple of days
6. a couple of years
9. a couple of weeks

PRACTICE 13, p. 160

3. a few hours
4. a few days
6. a few years

PRACTICE 14, p. 160

2. a. Susie married Paul a couple of months ago.
   b. Susie is going to marry Paul in a couple of months.
3. a. Dr. Nelson retired a few years ago.
   b. Dr. Nelson is going to retire in a few years.
4. a. Jack began a new job a couple of days ago.
   b. Jack is going to begin a new job in a couple of days.

PRACTICE 15, p. 161

2. past
3. present
4. past
5. future
6. future
7. past
8. past
9. future
10. past
11. present
12. present

PRACTICE 16, p. 161

2. this morning, today, right now
3. this morning, today, right now
4. this morning, today, right now
5. this morning, today, right now
6. this morning, today

PRACTICE 17, p. 162

1. b. She overslept and missed her math class.
2. a. She is going to explain her absence to her math teacher.
   b. She is going to sit at the kitchen table and think about a solution.
3. a. She is sitting in her kitchen.
   b. She is thinking about going to school.

PRACTICE 18, p. 162

2. will be
3. will be
4. will be
5. will be
6. will be
7. will be
8. will be
9. will be
10. will be

PRACTICE 19, p. 163

1. will live / won't live
2. will travel / won't travel
3. will study / won't study
4. will study / won't study
5. will live / won't live
6. will discover / won't discover
7. will be / won't be
8. will be / won't be

PRACTICE 20, p. 163

2. You will need extra chairs for the party.
3. We won't be on time for the movie.
4. It will rain tomorrow.
5. The bus won't be on time today.
6. Julie will be famous one day.
7. You will hurt yourself on that skateboard.

PRACTICE 21, p. 164

2. are going to travel
3. will open
4. will call ... will help
5. is not going to be / won't be ... will stay
6. am going to have / will have
7. am going to quit

PRACTICE 22, p. 164

2. Will your friends live to be 100 years old?
3. Will your children live to be 100 years old?
4. Will we live on another planet?
5. Will my friends live on another planet?
6. Will some people live underwater?
7. Will I live underwater?
8. Will countries find a solution for climate change?

PRACTICE 23, p. 165

2. are going to go, will go
3. are going to go, will go
4. is going to go, will go
5. are going to go, will go
6. is not going to go, will not go
7. am not going to go, will not go
8. are not going to go, will not go
9. Is she going to go? Will she go?
10. Are they going to go? Will they go?
11. Are you going to go? Will you go?

PRACTICE 24, p. 165

2. Will you need help tomorrow?
3. Did you need help yesterday?
4. Did Eva need help yesterday?
5. Will Eva need help tomorrow?
6. Does Eva need help now?
7. Do the students need help now?
8. Will the students need help tomorrow?
9. Did the students need help yesterday?

PRACTICE 25, p. 166

2. eats
3. eats
4. has
5. cooked
6. was ... loved
7. dropped ... was ... didn't burn
8. is going to invite
9. Is she going to cook / Will she cook
10. Is she going to make / Will she make
11. isn't going to prepare / won't prepare
12. is going to surprise / will surprise

PRACTICE 26, p. 167

2. Will you be sick tomorrow? / Are you going to be sick tomorrow?
3. Were you sick yesterday?
4. Was Steve sick yesterday?
5. Will Steve be sick tomorrow? / Is Steve going to be sick tomorrow?
6. Is Steve sick now?
7. Are your kids sick now?
8. Will your kids be sick tomorrow? / Are your kids going to be sick tomorrow?
9. Were your kids sick yesterday?

PRACTICE 27, p. 167

1. am ... am going to be / will be ... was ... am going to be
2. A: were you ... Were you
   B: wasn't ... was
   A: was ... were you
   B: were
   A: was
3. A: Is the post office
   B: isn't ... is
   A: Are they going to be / Will they be...
   B: aren't / won't ... are going to be / will be

PRACTICE 28, p. 168

2. Are	4. Do	6. Do	8. Are
3. Do	5. Are	7. Do	9. Do

PRACTICE 29, p. 168

2. Did	4. Were	6. Did	8. Were
3. Were	5. Did	7. Did	

PRACTICE 30, p. 169

2. are working, worked, are going to work, will work
3. is, was, is going to be, will be
4. help, are helping, are going to help, will help
5. isn't running, didn't run, isn't going to run, won't run
6. does, did, is going to do, will do
7. Do they exercise, Did they exercise, Are they going to exercise, Will they exercise
8. Is he, Is he, Is he going to be, Will he be
9. isn't, wasn't, isn't going to be, won't be

PRACTICE 31, p. 170

1. A: left
2. A: are you going to wear
   B: am going to wear … is going to be
3. A: Did she tell … did she tell
   B: told
4. B: am making … is getting
5. A: Are you going to study
   B: don't have
   B: gave … is giving
6. A: Are you going to be
   B: is going to have
   B: broke … didn't heal
7. A: said
   B: didn't understand
8. A: is Cathy?
   B: is meeting
9. had … ran … slammed … missed
10. A: Are you going to call
    B: forget

PRACTICE 32, p. 171

1. lived	14. saw
2. were	15. climbed
3. didn't have	16. found
4. decided	17. will eat
5. took	18. Are you going to give
6. met	19. is
7. will buy	20. fell
8. will give	21. was
9. took	22. didn't want
10. was	23. went
11. are	24. never caught
12. don't have	25. ran
13. threw	26. lived

PRACTICE 33, p. 172

2. We are going **to** travel to Europe next year.
3. Are we going to watch a movie **tomorrow** night?
4. My brother will **help** me with the homework.
5. Vanessa got a new job two **weeks** ago.
6. When **will you** be home tonight?
7. I **won't go** out tonight because I need to study.
8. I **am leaving** / **am going to leave** for my vacation in three days.

CHAPTER 11: EXPRESSING FUTURE TIME, PART 2

PRACTICE 1, p. 173

2. sure	5. unsure	8. unsure
3. sure	6. unsure	9. unsure
4. sure	7. sure	10. sure

PRACTICE 2, p. 173

Answers will vary.

PRACTICE 3, p. 174

2. a. You might need to see a doctor soon.
   b. Maybe you will need to see a doctor soon.
3. a. We may play basketball after school.
   b. We might play basketball after school.
4. a. Maybe our class will go to a movie together.
   b. Our class may go to a movie together.

PRACTICE 4, p. 174

2. a	4. a	6. a, b
3. b	5. b	7. a, b

PRACTICE 5, p. 175

2. They may come. They might come.
3. She might not study. She may not study.
4. We might not need help. We may not need help.
5. I might not need help. I may not need help.
6. He may understand. Maybe he will understand.
7. You may understand. Maybe you will understand.
8. They may understand. Maybe they will understand.

PRACTICE 6, p. 175

Possible answers:

2. It may / might snow next week. OR Maybe it will snow next week.
3. We may / might go ice skating on the lake. OR Maybe we will go ice skating on the lake.
4. The kids will play in the snow.
5. The snow won't / will not melt for several days.

PRACTICE 7, p. 176

2. a, b, d	3. a, b, c	4. b, d

PRACTICE 8, p. 176

2. have, am going to go
3. see, are going to make
4. takes, is going to practice
5. takes, is going to feel
6. gets, is going to be

PRACTICE 9, p. 177

2. he goes to school, he is going to eat breakfast.
3. he gets to school, he is going to go to his classroom.
4. he has lunch in the cafeteria, he is going to talk to his friends.
5. he cooks dinner for his roommates, he is going to pick up food at the grocery store.
6. he goes to bed, he is going to do his homework.
7. he falls asleep, he is going to have good dreams.

PRACTICE 10, p. 177

2. 2, 1
   a. Before I turn in my homework, I'm going to check my answers. OR I'm going to check my answers before I turn in my homework.
   b. After I check my answers, I'm going to turn in my homework. OR I'm going to turn in my homework after I check my answers.
3. 2, 1
   a. Before I wash the dishes, I'm going to clear off the table. OR I'm going to clear off the table before I wash the dishes.
   b. After I clear off the table, I'm going to wash the dishes. OR I'm going to wash the dishes after I clear off the table.
4. 1, 2
   a. Before I go out in the rain, I'm going to get my umbrella. OR I'm going to get my umbrella before I go out in the rain.
   b. After I get my umbrella, I'm going to go out in the rain. OR I'm going to go out in the rain after I get my umbrella.
5. 1, 2
   a. Before I go to the airport, I'm going to pack my bags. OR I'm going to pack my bags before I go to the airport.
   b. After I pack my bags, I'm going to go to the airport. OR I'm going to go to the airport after I pack my bags.

PRACTICE 11, p. 178

2. goes, is going to study
3. enjoys, will take
4. will apply, does
5. attends, is going to study
6. completes, is going to help

PRACTICE 12, p. 178

2. rains ... won't go / am not going to go
3. will make / am going to make ... are
4. will get / is going to get ... don't eat
5. will be / are going to be ... don't leave
6. leave ... won't be / aren't going to be
7. feels ... won't come / isn't going to come
8. will call / is going to call ... misses
9. needs ... will help / are going to help
10. will make / are going to make ... doesn't need

PRACTICE 13, p. 179

2. will take / is going to take
3. checks
4. will meet / are going to meet
5. gets
6. will interview / is going to interview
7. finishes
8. will give / is going to give
9. gets
10. will move / is going to move

PRACTICE 14, p. 180

Part 1

2. a	4. c	6. g
3. e	5. b	7. d

Part II

2. If I cry, my eyes get red.
3. If I don't pay my electric bill, I pay a late fee.
4. If the phone rings in the middle of the night, I don't answer it.
5. If I get to work late, I stay at work late.
6. If I eat a big breakfast, I have a lot of energy.
7. If I don't do my homework, I get low grades on the tests.

PRACTICE 15, p. 180

Answers will vary.

PRACTICE 16, p. 181

2. future	7. future
3. future	8. present habit
4. present habit	9. future
5. present habit	10. future
6. future	

PRACTICE 17, p. 181

2. arrive ... will be
3. takes ... will graduate
4. graduates ... is going to work
5. rains ... stay
6. am going to go ... doesn't rain
7. clean ... visit
8. am going to clean ... arrive
9. eat ... is
10. is ... will eat

PRACTICE 18, p. 182

2. are going to go ... is
3. go ... am going to meet
4. go ... usually meet
5. am going to buy ... go
6. is ... gets ... feels ... exercises ... exercises ... begins
7. am ... am not going to exercise
8. travels ... brings
9. travels ... is going to pack
10. is ... begins
11. gets ... is going to tell
12. have ... take ... am not going to take ... eat

PRACTICE 19, p. 183

2. c	4. a	6. c
3. c	5. a	7. c

PRACTICE 20, p. 183

1. B: am going to take ... am going to visit
   A: are you going to be
2. B: isn't ... left
   A: Is she going to be
   A: did she go
   B: went
3. A: Are you going to see
   B: am going to have
   A: borrowed ... forgot
4. A: are you wearing
   B: broke
   A: stepped

4. A: is Kevin running
   B: is
   A: is he
   B: slept … didn't turn on

PRACTICE 21, p. 184

2. Natalia **might** study in Spain next year.
3. **Maybe** it will rain tomorrow.
4. I'll call you after I **get** home tonight.
5. Our teacher might **not** be here tomorrow. / Our teacher **won't** be here tomorrow.
6. Zac walks to work when the weather **is** nice.
7. What will you do after you **graduate**?
8. Allie will go to the game with us this weekend if she **doesn't** have homework.

CHAPTER 12: MODALS, PART 1: EXPRESSING ABILITY AND PERMISSION

PRACTICE 1, p. 185

2. can ride	4. can sing	6. can cook
3. can swim	5. can play	

PRACTICE 2, p. 186

2. can't	5. can't	8. can
3. can't	6. can't	9. can't
4. can	7. can't	

PRACTICE 3, p. 186

Answers will vary.

PRACTICE 4, p. 187

2. Can George and Mia play the piano? Yes, they can.
3. Can Mia swim? Yes, she can.
4. Can Paul play the piano? No, he can't.
5. Can Paul and Eva drive a car? No, they can't.
6. Can Mia, George, and Paul swim? Yes, they can.
7. Can Eva and George repair a bike? Yes, they can.
8. Can Eva drive a car? No, she can't.

PRACTICE 5, p. 187

2. Can you use social media? Yes, I can.
3. Can you speak perfect English? No, I can't.
4. Can you lift suitcases? Yes, I can.
5. Can you work weekends? No, I can't.

PRACTICE 6, p. 188

2. c	3. b	4. a	5. d

PRACTICE 7, p. 188

2. Martha knows how to play chess.
3. Sonya and Thomas know how to speak Portuguese.
4. Jack doesn't know how to speak Russian.
5. My brothers don't know how to cook.
6. I don't know how to change a flat tire.
7. We don't know how to play musical instruments.
8. Do you know how to type?
9. Do your children know how to swim?
10. Does your son know how to tie his shoes?
11. Do you know how to edit a video?

PRACTICE 8, p. 189

Answers will vary.

PRACTICE 9, p. 189

2. They could spend time together.
3. They couldn't use electric heat.
4. They could cook over a fire.
5. They couldn't use a computer.
6. They could have heat from a fireplace.
7. They could read books.
8. They couldn't turn on the lights.
9. They could play board games.

PRACTICE 10, p. 190

2. can't	4. can	6. Could
3. Could	5. could	7. can't

PRACTICE 11, p. 190

2. You are able to draw. You were able to draw. You will be able to draw.
3. He is able to drive. He was able to drive. He will be able to drive.
4. She is able to swim. She was able to swim. She will be able to swim.
5. We are able to dance. We were able to dance. We will be able to dance.
6. They are able to type. They were able to type. They will be able to type.

PRACTICE 12, p. 190

2. wasn't able to	5. am able to
3. wasn't able to	6. am (not) able to
4. wasn't able to	7. am (not) able to

PRACTICE 13, p. 191

2. a	3. b	4. c	5. c

PRACTICE 14, p. 191

2. weren't able to understand
3. wasn't able to ask
4. wasn't able to make
5. is able to understand
6. are able to have
7. is able to learn

PRACTICE 15, p. 192

2. a, b, e	4. e
3. a, b	5. a, b, c, e

PRACTICE 16, p. 192

2. very	5. too	8. very
3. very	6. too	9. too
4. too	7. very	10. very

PRACTICE 17, p. 193

2. a	4. b	6. a	8. a
3. b	5. a	7. b	

PRACTICE 18, p. 193

Answers will vary.

PRACTICE 19, p. 194

2. Can I please borrow your phone charger? / Can I borrow your phone charger, please?
3. May I please leave work a few minutes early? / May I leave work a few minutes early, please?
4. Could I please ride with you? / Could I ride with you, please?
5. May I please turn in my homework a day late? / May I turn in my homework a day late, please?
6. Could I please join your game? / Could I join your game, please?
7. Can I please change the channel? / Can I change the channel, please?

PRACTICE 20, p. 194

2. c   4. a   6. a
3. d   5. d   7. d

PRACTICE 21, p. 195

2. I **can speak** Chinese.
3. They **can** meet us after class. / They **will** meet us after class.
4. Pedro couldn't **speak** English before he moved here.
5. When I was a child, I **could walk** to school.
6. Chris knows how **to** program a videogame.
7. My brother **does** not / **doesn't** know how to drive.
8. Where **can** I buy fresh vegetables?
9. I need to do my homework now. I **wasn't** able to finish it last night.
10. This food is too spicy. I **can't** eat it. / This food is very spicy, but I can eat it.
11. May I **borrow** your pen?
12. Can I **park** in this parking lot?

CHAPTER 13: MODALS, PART 2: ADVICE, NECESSITY, REQUESTS, SUGGESTIONS

PRACTICE 1, p. 196

2. should take   5. should call
3. should study   6. should wear
4. should leave

PRACTICE 2, p. 196

2. should   5. should
3. shouldn't   6. should
4. shouldn't   7. shouldn't

PRACTICE 3, p. 196

3. She should study for her tests.
4. She shouldn't stay up late.
5. She shouldn't daydream in class.
6. She shouldn't be absent from class a lot.
7. She should take notes during lectures.
8. She should take her notebooks to school.

PRACTICE 4, p. 197

Sample answers:
2. should talk to the Browns.
3. should see a doctor. / shouldn't dance with a backache.
4. should see a dentist.

5. should be careful with his money. / shouldn't spend too much.
6. should apply for visas now. / shouldn't wait to apply for visas.

PRACTICE 5, p. 198

2. have to leave   8. don't have to leave
3. have to leave   9. doesn't have to leave
4. have to leave   10. don't have to leave
5. has to leave   11. Does … have to
6. has to leave   12. do … have to
7. don't have to leave

PRACTICE 6, p. 198

3. has to   6. has to
4. doesn't have to   7. has to
5. doesn't have to

PRACTICE 7, p. 198

2. don't have to   7. doesn't have to
3. has to   8. have to
4. have to   9. has to
5. don't have to   10. doesn't have to
6. have to

PRACTICE 8, p. 199

2. had to   6. had to
3. didn't have to   7. didn't have to
4. had to   8. had to
5. didn't have to

PRACTICE 9, p. 200

2. didn't have to   6. had to
3. didn't have to   7. didn't have to
4. had to   8. had to
5. didn't have to

PRACTICE 10, p. 200

Answers will vary.

PRACTICE 11, p. 201

2. must not   4. must not
3. must   5. must

PRACTICE 12, p. 201

2. must   5. must not
3. must not   6. must
4. must not

PRACTICE 13, p. 201

2. should   6. should
3. must   7. must
4. must   8. must
5. should

PRACTICE 14, p. 202

2. Could   5. Would
3. Can   6. A: Could
4. Can   B: Would

PRACTICE 15, p. 202

3. Could / Would / Can you please clean your bedroom?
4. Could / Would / Can you please give me some money for a movie?
5. May / Could / Can I please sharpen my pencil?
6. May / Could / Can I please borrow your cell phone?
7. Could / Would / Can you please take a picture of us?
8. Could / Would / Can you please turn down the TV?

PRACTICE 16, p. 203

2. Ø	5. Ø	8. Ø
3. Ø	6. Ø	9. to
4. to	7. to	10. Ø

PRACTICE 17, p. 203

2. a	4. c	6. c	8. b
3. b	5. c	7. a	

PRACTICE 18, p. 204

Sample answers:
2. Let's take a break.
3. Let's buy her a gift.
4. Let's eat.
5. Let's go to Mario's Pizzeria tonight.

PRACTICE 19, p. 204

2. c	5. b	8. b
3. c	6. a	9. c
4. a	7. c	10. a

PRACTICE 20, p. 205

2. a, c	5. a, c	8. a, b, d
3. a, b, d	6. b, d	
4. b, d	7. b, c, d	

PRACTICE 21, p. 206

2. Where should we **have** lunch this afternoon?
3. Alex has to **work** tomorrow.
4. I was sick yesterday. I had to **go** to the doctor.
5. You must **wear** a seatbelt when you drive.
6. Today is a holiday. We **don't** have to go to school.
7. What time **do** you have to work tomorrow?
8. **Could / Would / Can** you help me with this homework?
9. Could you please **turn** off the light?
10. The weather is beautiful. **Let's** eat outside.

CHAPTER 14: NOUNS AND MODIFIERS

PRACTICE 1, p. 207

Adjectives: pretty, sad, hot, true, happy
Nouns: pens, boat, store, horse, truth

PRACTICE 2, p. 207

1. delicious, chicken, great, vegetable
2. flower, great, rose, vegetable
3. friendly, grammar, great, math
4. airplane, concert, great, movie

PRACTICE 3, p. 208

2. noun	5. noun	8. adjective
3. noun	6. adjective	9. adjective
4. adjective	7. noun	10. noun

PRACTICE 4, p. 208

2. magazine articles
3. business card
4. dentist appointment
5. spaghetti sauce
6. house key
7. phone chargers
8. milk carton
9. grocery stores
10. shower curtain

PRACTICE 5, p. 209

2. a. messy kitchen
   b. kitchen cabinets
   c. kitchen counter
3. a. city bus
   b. bus schedule
   c. bus route
4. a. airplane noise
   b. small airplane
   c. airplane ticket
5. a. apartment manager
   b. new apartment
   c. apartment building
6. a. phone number
   b. smart phone
   c. phone call
7. a. hospital patient
   b. sick patient
   c. patient information

PRACTICE 6, p. 210

Opinion: delicious, easy, nice, pretty
Size: big, short, small, tiny
Age: modern, new, old, young
Color: green, purple, red, yellow
Nationality: British, Japanese, Spanish, Thai
Material: glass, metal, silk, wood

PRACTICE 7, p. 210

2. b	4. b	6. a	8. a
3. b	5. a	7. b	9. a

PRACTICE 8, p. 211

2. spicy Mexican food
3. kind young man
4. dirty brown shoes
5. fun new videogame
6. interesting old paintings
7. tall glass building
8. little yellow flowers
9. short middle-aged woman
10. Chinese silk dress

PRACTICE 9, p. 211

Check:
2. <u>sound</u>	6. <u>smell</u>	9. <u>felt</u>
5. <u>taste</u>	7. <u>look</u>	10. <u>seems</u>

PRACTICE 10, p. 212

Sample answers:
2. tired	5. terrible	8. awful
3. wonderful	6. bad	
4. great	7. fun	

PRACTICE 11, p. 212

2. clearly	7. early	12. honestly
3. neatly	8. carefully	13. fast
4. correctly	9. quickly	14. easily
5. hard	10. slowly	
6. well	11. late	

PRACTICE 12, p. 213

2. easily	5. fast	8. honestly
3. late	6. hard	9. softly
4. late	7. well	10. quickly

PRACTICE 13, p. 213

2. beautifully, beautiful, beautiful
3. good, well
4. good, good
5. interesting, interesting
6. hard, hard, hard
7. fast, fast

PRACTICE 14, p. 214

2. correctly, correct	8. easily, easy
3. late, late	9. well, good
4. beautiful, beautifully	10. quickly, quick
5. honest, honestly	11. sweet, sweet
6. handsome, handsome	12. careless, carelessly
7. good, good	

PRACTICE 15, p. 214

2. slowly	7. fluent, fluently
3. hard	8. neat
4. hard	9. carefully
5. clear	10. good
6. early	11. well

PRACTICE 16, p. 215

2. c   3. a, b   4. a

PRACTICE 17, p. 215

2. 90%	5. 50%	8. 85%
3. 100%	6. 75%	9. 100%
4. 60%	7. 30%	10. 97%

PRACTICE 18, p. 216

2. are	5. are	8. are
3. is	6. are	9. is
4. is	7. are	10. are

PRACTICE 19, p. 216

2. are	6. are	10. are	14. is
3. is	7. are	11. is	15. are
4. are	8. are	12. is	
5. is	9. is	13. are	

PRACTICE 20, p. 217

2. a	4. b	6. b
3. b	5. b	7. a

PRACTICE 21, p. 217

2. a	4. b	6. b	8. b
3. b	5. a	7. a	

PRACTICE 22, p. 217

2. a	5. a	8. b
3. b	6. b	9. a
4. a	7. a	10. a

PRACTICE 23, p. 218

Check:
2. Every **student** is on time too.
4. Everything in the kitchen sink **is** dirty.
5. Where **do** all of your friends live?
7. Everybody in my family **likes** dessert after dinner.
8. **Does** everyone in your family **like** dessert?
10. **Were** all of the people at the wedding your friends?
11. Everyone **is** friendly.

PRACTICE 24, p. 219

2. someone / somebody ... anyone / anybody
3. something / anything
4. someone / somebody / anyone / anybody
5. something ... anything
6. someone / somebody ... anyone / anybody
7. anything / something
8. anyone / anybody / someone / somebody

PRACTICE 25, p. 219

1. a, c, d, e	3. a, c
2. a, b, c, d, e, f	4. b, f

PRACTICE 26, p. 220

2. anyone / anybody / someone / somebody
3. something
4. someone / somebody
5. anything / something
6. anyone / anybody / someone / somebody
7. something / anything
8. someone / somebody
9. Someone / Somebody
10. someone / somebody / something

PRACTICE 27, p. 220

2. I can't find my **car** keys.
3. Chris drives a **small black** car.
4. We watched an **interesting Italian** film last weekend.
5. Those flowers look **beautiful**.
6. Sara always drives **carefully**.
7. The weather is **clear** today.
8. I finished almost all of **my / the** homework this afternoon.
9. All of my **friends** are here today.
10. Everyone in my class **is** very nice.
11. Every **computer** in this store is expensive.
12. You dropped **something**. I think it was a pen.

CHAPTER 15: MAKING COMPARISONS

PRACTICE 1, p. 221
2. wider than
3. cheaper than
4. darker than
5. smarter than
6. older than
7. happier than
8. more important than
9. more difficult than
10. more expensive than
11. easier than
12. funnier than
13. better than
14. farther / further than
15. fatter than
16. hotter than
17. thinner than
18. worse than
19. prettier than
20. more famous than

PRACTICE 2, p. 222
2. funnier than
3. more interesting than
4. smarter than
5. wider than
6. larger than
7. darker than
8. better than
9. worse than
10. more confusing than
11. farther … than
12. easier than
13. younger than
14. more expensive than

PRACTICE 3, p. 222
Sample answers:
2. Life in the city is more expensive than life in the country.
3. Life in the country is more relaxing than life in the city.
4. Life is the city is busier than life in the country.
5. Life in the suburbs is more convenient than life in the country.
6. Life in the country is more beautiful than life in the suburbs.
7. Life in the country is cheaper than life in the city.
8. Life in the city is nicer than life in the country.
9. Life in the suburbs is safer than life in the city.
10. Life in the country is better than life in the city.

PRACTICE 4, p. 223
2. 101 B is more boring than 101 A.
3. 101 B is harder than 101 A.
4. 101 A is easier than 101 B.
5. 101 A is more popular than 101 B.
6. 101 B is more difficult than 101 A.
7. 101 A is more enjoyable than 101 B.
8. 101 A is more fun than 101 B.

PRACTICE 5, p. 224
2. lazier than, the laziest
3. cleaner than, the cleanest
4. older than, the oldest
5. younger than, the youngest
6. newer than, the newest
7. more beautiful than, the most beautiful
8. more exciting than, the most exciting
9. nicer than, the nicest
10. quieter than, the quietest
11. worse than, the worst
12. fatter than, the fattest
13. thinner than, the thinnest
14. hotter than, the hottest
15. better than, the best
16. cheaper than, the cheapest
17. farther than, the farthest
18. funnier than, the funniest

PRACTICE 6, p. 224
2. The most beautiful city in the world is … .
3. The most interesting show on TV is … .
4. The most boring sport to watch is … .
5. The easiest language to learn is … .
6. The most talented movie star is … .
7. The most relaxing place to go for vacation is … .
8. The best place to live is … .

PRACTICE 7, p. 225
2. … is the most convenient.
3. … is the most relaxing.
4. … is the busiest.
5. … is the nicest
6. … is the most interesting.
7. … is the most popular.
8. … is the quietest.
9. … is the cheapest.
10. … is the most useful.

PRACTICE 8, p. 226
Sample answers:
2. Rex is more active than Fluffy.
   Rex is the most active.
3. Fluffy is younger than Rex.
   Fluffy is the youngest.
4. Rex is heavier than Polly.
   Rex is the heaviest.
5. Polly is more colorful than Fluffy.
   Polly is the most colorful.
6. Rex is bigger than Polly.
   Rex is the biggest.
7. Polly is older than Fluffy.
   Polly is the oldest.
8. Polly is smaller than Rex.
   Polly is the smallest.
9. Polly is lighter than Rex.
   Polly is the lightest.

PRACTICE 9, p. 227
2. the fastest cars
3. the happiest families
4. the funniest children
5. the best managers
6. the tallest women
7. the oldest men
8. the most interesting professors
9. the scariest animals
10. the easiest languages

PRACTICE 10, p. 227
2. … is one of the most dangerous activities.
3. … is one of the most expensive activities.
4. … is one of the safest activities.
5. … is one of the most difficult activities.
6. … is one of the most interesting activities.
7. … is one of the healthiest activities.
8. … is one of the best activities for children.

PRACTICE 11, p. 228

2. ... is one of the biggest cities
3. ... is one of the hardest languages
4. ... is one of the most interesting places
5. ... is one of the prettiest places
6. ... is one of the most expensive cities
7. ... is one of the most important people

PRACTICE 12, p. 228

2. bigger than
3. the hottest places
4. the coldest places
5. longer than
6. larger than
7. the largest
8. scarier than
9. the scariest
10. the most dangerous animals
11. the most expensive cities
12. more expensive than
13. the longest
14. The smallest

PRACTICE 13, p. 229

2. clearly, more clearly, the most clearly
3. slowly, more slowly, the most slowly
4. beautifully, more beautifully, the most beautifully
5. neatly, more neatly, the most neatly
6. carefully, more carefully, the most carefully
7. fluently, more fluently, the most fluently
8. well, better, the best
9. hard, harder, the hardest
10. early, earlier, the earliest
11. late, later, the latest
12. fast, faster, the fastest

PRACTICE 14, p. 230

2. more carefully than
3. the most quickly
4. the hardest
5. later than
6. the earliest
7. better than
8. more quickly than
9. more slowly than
10. the most fluently
11. faster than
12. the fastest

PRACTICE 15, p. 230

1. b. more dangerously than
   c. the most dangerously
2. a. more clearly than
   b. clearer than
   c. the most clearly
3. a. harder than
   b. harder than
   c. the hardest
4. a. better than
   b. the best
   c. better than
5. a. faster than
   b. faster than
   c. the fastest
6. a. neater than
   b. more neatly than
   c. the neatest

PRACTICE 16, p. 231

2. as
3. Ø
4. Ø
5. from
6. to
7. Ø
8. Ø

PRACTICE 17, p. 231

3. similar
4. different
5. different from
6. similar to
7. different
8. different from
9. the same as
10. the same

PRACTICE 18, p. 232

2. a. Trains and buses are similar.
   b. Trains are similar to buses.
3. a. Your grammar book is the same as my grammar book.
   b. Your grammar book and my grammar book are the same.
4. a. Cats and dogs are different.
   b. Cats are different from dogs.

PRACTICE 19, p. 232

2. alike
3. alike
4. alike
5. like
6. alike
7. like
8. like
9. alike
10. like
11. alike
12. like

PRACTICE 20, p. 233

Sample answers:
2. White chocolate and dark chocolate are alike. They are sweet.
3. Magazines are like newspapers. They have articles.
4. Scissors and knives are alike. They are sharp.
5. Malaysia and Thailand are alike. They are countries in Asia.
6. Ice cream cones are like milkshakes. They are desserts.
7. Chemistry and physics are alike. They are science subjects.

PRACTICE 21, p. 233

1. a, e
2. b, d
3. b

PRACTICE 22, p. 234

Check: 2, 3, 5

PRACTICE 23, p. 234

Sample answers:
2. cold
3. hard / difficult
4. hard / difficult
5. short
6. cheap / inexpensive
7. comfortable
8. dark
9. heavy
10. new / modern

PRACTICE 24, p. 235

2. can
3. do
4. don't
5. doesn't
6. wasn't
7. will
8. does
9. didn't
10. don't
11. is
12. can't
13. won't
14. are
15. was
16. did
17. aren't

PRACTICE 25, p. 235

Sample answers:

2. cats don't
3. dogs can't
4. flowers do
5. the weather in the mountains isn't
6. loose shoes are
7. lemons aren't
8. it is today
9. you won't
10. my roommate did

PRACTICE 26, p. 236

2. b	5. d	8. c	11. a
3. c	6. b	9. b	12. d
4. a	7. c	10. a	

PRACTICE 27, p. 237

2. The weather today is **worse** than it was yesterday.
3. This class is **easier** than our math class.
4. Do you feel **better** today?
5. Chicago is one of the biggest **cities** in the United States.
6. What is **the** coldest month of the year?
7. You type more **quickly** than I do.
8. Jackson works **harder** than his brother.
9. Make sure all your passwords are not **the** same. They need to be **different**.
10. Frozen yogurt is similar **to** ice cream.
11. William and his twin brother look **alike**.
12. Helen can't speak Chinese, but her parents **can**.

Credits

(T-Top, B-Bottom, C-Center, R-Right, and L-Left)

Page 2L: Chekart/Shutterstock; **2R**: Tartila/Shutterstock; **4T**: Nadezhda Shoshina/Shutterstock; **4B**: Murina Natalia/ Shutterstock; **5**: Faenkova Elena/Shutterstock; **8T**: Seafowl/Shutterstock; **8C**: ArdeaA/Shutterstock; **8B**: Nesibe seyman/ Shutterstock; **9**: Robuart/Shutterstock; **13** (1): Rolffimages/123RF; **13** (2): Volosovich Igor/Shutterstock; **13** (3): Arvind Singh Negi/Red Reef Design Studio. Pearson India Education Services Pvt. Ltd; **13** (4): Arvind Singh Negi/Red Reef Design Studio. Pearson India Education Services Pvt. Ltd; **13** (5): Dragance137/Shutterstock; **13** (6): Debanjan Basak/ Pearson India Education Services Pvt. Ltd; **13** (7): Rangsan paidaen/Shutterstock; **13** (8): Arvind Singh Negi/Red Reef Design Studio. Pearson India Education Services Pvt. Ltd; **14** (1): Fedorov Oleksiy/Shutterstock; **14** (2): Ekler/ Shutterstock; **14** (3): Pagina/Shutterstock; **14** (4): Kang1993/Shutterstock; **14** (5L): Zzveillust/Shutterstock; **14** (5R): Zzveillust/Shutterstock; **17**: Tynyuk/Shutterstock; **21**: Neyro2008/123RF; **22**: Studio_G/Shutterstock; **23T**: Shri Vishishta Chintamani Technologies Private Limited/Pearson India Education Services Pvt. Ltd; **23C**: Suns07butterfly/Shutterstock; **23B**: Pradip Kumar Bhowal/Pearson India Education Services Pvt. Ltd; **24**: Rvector/Shutterstock; **25**: Neyro2008/123RF; **30**: Artisticco LLC/123RF; **36**: Ildar Galeev/Shutterstock; **40L**: GoodStudio/Shutterstock; **40C**: Rastudio/123RF; **40R**: Maxim Maksutov/Shutterstock; **45**: Artisticco/Shutterstock; **45R**: Artisticco LLC/123RF; **52**: Matrioshka/Shutterstock; **53**: Pretty Vectors/Shutterstock; **61**: CkyBe/Shutterstock; **62**: Mohd Suhail/Pearson India Education Services Pvt. Ltd; **64** (1): John T Takai/Shutterstock; **64** (2): Oxinoxi/Shutterstock; **64** (3): Rafael Torres Castaño/123RF; **65** (4): Standard Studio/Shutterstock; **65** (5): Supernick299/Shutterstock; **65** (6): Supanut piyakanont/Shutterstock; **65** (7): GraphEGO/Shutterstock; **65** (8): Powerful Design/Shutterstock; **65** (9): James Weston/123RF; **65** (10): DeiMosz/ Shutterstock; **65** (11): Arc Tina/Shutterstock; **65** (12): Standard Studio/Shutterstock; **66**: Andrew Angelov/Shutterstock; **72**: KanKhem/Shutterstock; **73**: Curiosity/Shutterstock; **88**: Bus109/Shutterstock; **89L**: Nina Sitkevich/123RF; **89C**: Nina Sitkevich/123RF; **89R**: Nina Sitkevich/123RF; **90T**: Oleh Tokarev/123RF; **90B**: Utsav Academy and Art Studio/ Pearson India Education Services Pvt. Ltd; **91**: Arvind Singh Negi/Red Reef Design Studio/Pearson India Education Services Pvt. Ltd; **92**: GoodStudio/Shutterstock; **95T**: ArtDesign Illustration/Shutterstock; **95B**: Uiliaaa/Shutterstock; **96**: BigMouse/Shutterstock; **97**: Alexeyzet/123RF; **98**: Amit John/Pearson India Education Services Pvt. Ltd; **99**: Kumer Oksana/Shutterstock; **105**: Iconic Bestiary/Shutterstock; **106T**: Elvetica/Shutterstock; **105B**: Tomacco/Shutterstock; **109**: Milkymilka/123RF; **110B**: Naddya/123RF; **117** (1): Margarita Levina/Shutterstock; **117** (2): Artisticco/Shutterstock; **117** (3): Vasilyeva Larisa/Shutterstock; **117** (4): ProStockStudio/Shutterstock; **117** (5): Iconic Bestiary/Shutterstock; **118T**: Jongcreative/Shutterstock; **118B**: Iconic Bestiary/Shutterstock; **124T**: Javi ruiz/Shutterstock; **124B**: Artisticco LLC/123RF; **127**: Pavel Fiadkevich/Shutterstock; **130TL**: Bessyana/Shutterstock; **130TR**: Blueringmedia/123RF; **130B**: Tatyana Okhitina/Shutterstock; **131**: 3DMAVR/Shutterstock; **134**: Ioulia Bolchakova/123RF; **142**: Tynyuk/ Shutterstock; **143**: Arvind Singh Negi/Red Reef Design Studio. Pearson India Education Services Pvt. Ltd; **145**: Evgenii Naumov/123RF; **146**: Artbesouro/Shutterstock; **147**: BesticonPark/Shutterstock; **150**: Lemberg Vector studio/Shutterstock; **155**: Louis D. Wiyono/Shutterstock; **157**: Vitya_M/Shutterstock; **160**: Samuelch50/Shutterstock; **161**: David Roland/ Shutterstock; **163**: Iconic Bestiary/Shutterstock; **173**: Costazzurra/Shutterstock; **175**: SunshineVector/Shutterstock; **179**: Pratyaksa/123RF; **184**: Andrei Krauchuk/123RF; **185** (1): Artisticco LLC/123RF; **185** (2): Rastudio/123RF; **185** (3): Rastudio/123RF; **185** (4): Illustratorovich/123RF; **185** (5): Kwok Design/Shutterstock; **185** (6): Kram78/Shutterstock; **186T**: Amit John. Pearson India Education Services Pvt. Ltd; **186B**: NBerthuz/123RF; **187**: Artisticco LLC/123RF; **189** (gear stick): Sashkin/Shutterstock; **189** (sewing machine): Renu Sharma. Pearson India Education Services Pvt. Ltd; **189** (knit): Danish Zaidi. Pearson India Education Services Pvt. Ltd; **189** (chopsticks): Victoruler/Shutterstock; **189** (drone): Liubov Kotliar/123RF; **189** (mountain climbing): Johavel/Shutterstock; **189** (math): Seamartini Graphics/ Shutterstock; **189** (ski): Robuart/Shutterstock; **189** (cabin): Memo Angeles/Shutterstock; **196**: Vladimir Yudin/123RF; **198**: Irina Strelnikova/123RF; **201**: Sahua d/Shutterstock; **205**: Unitone Vector/Shutterstock; **207**: Mohd Suhail. Pearson India Education Services Pvt. Ltd.; **222L**: Amanita Silvicora/Shutterstock; **222C**: Denis Cristo/Shutterstock; **222R**: Valeri Hadeev/Shutterstock; **225L**: Artisticco LLC/123RF; **225C**: Unitone Vector/Shutterstock; **225R**: Artisticco LLC/123RF; **226L**: Vectorshowstudio/123RF; **226C**: WinWin artlab/Shutterstock; **226R**: KittyVector/Shutterstock; **227**: GoodStudio/ Shutterstock; **230**: Anastasia Mazeina/Shutterstock.